THE
LAST ESSAYS OF ELIA

THE
PIRATES OF ASIA

THE
LAST ESSAYS OF ELIA

BY

CHARLES LAMB

EDITED WITH AN INTRODUCTION

BY

EDMUND BLUNDEN

AND NOTES BY

FREDERICK PAGE

OXFORD UNIVERSITY PRESS
LONDON: HUMPHREY MILFORD

OXFORD UNIVERSITY PRESS
AMEN HOUSE, E.C. 4
LONDON EDINBURGH GLASGOW
LEIPZIG NEW YORK TORONTO
MELBOURNE CAPETOWN BOMBAY
CALCUTTA MADRAS SHANGHAI
HUMPHREY MILFORD
PUBLISHER TO THE
UNIVERSITY

First published 1929
Reprinted 1932

Printed in Great Britain

NOTE

The text used is that of *The Works of Charles
and Mary Lamb* edited by Mr. Thomas Hutchin-
son for the Oxford University Press. Every
annotator of Lamb must necessarily be indebted
to Mr. E. V. Lucas; and the labours of Messrs.
Hallward and Hill have often assisted me in
tracing quotations.

F. P.

NOTE

The frontispiece is a fac-simile of a page
of a MS. prescribed by Mr. Thomas Hughes
... from the Oxford University Press. The
... of Lamb from the sketch published
... in 1875, ... et et the Islands of the ...
Buildings will have often appeared in the
... of ...

CONTENTS

CONTENTS

INTRODUCTION

THE original notion of 'Elia' as a signature for essay-writing and, more than that, as a character under which the writer might express a part of his nature with affectionate humour, and fond delay—a peaceful dramatization such as Addison had played in *The Spectator* and Johnson in *The Rambler*, but more subtle—need not now involve us in arguments. It may be mere coincidence that the name was an anagram of A Lie. Lamb may have written his youthful 'Chas.' in haste so that it was read 'Elia'. On his own testimony, we know that 'the name fairly devolved to him' from an old clerk with whom he was acquainted, in early times at the South-Sea House; the first Essay was a dream of old South-Sea House personalities, and the signature 'Elia' below it was peculiarly fitting and kindly.

By 'the first Essay' we mean the first that Lamb contributed to the *London Magazine*, when that periodical became the property and great literary hope of two remarkable publishers, John Taylor and James Hessey. There has never been anything quite equal to it under the best part of their management and hospitable union of contributors. It was in the position, which so often calls forth courageous fineness whether in art or action or athletics, of being a youthful and not yet celebrated competitor of established and flourishing performers. It needed enthusiasm and quality and such ideas as could be kept up and enriched until the reading public would be unwilling to miss 'this month's instalment'. These essentials were for some time brilliantly provided by the writers who dined with Taylor and Hessey in the parlour of their bookshop, and especially by Lamb. The year 1820, in which the new *London* began, found Lamb

at the age of forty-five eager for some sound journal in
which he could 'expatiate and confer' at his ease,
instead of scattering his wit and wisdom through the
quickly vanishing columns of newspapers with political
limitations. Ten years earlier, he had shown what he
could do in the wonderful essays printed in Leigh
Hunt's *Reflector*, a quarterly allowing him all the space
he wanted; and now the *London* gave him both space
and a continuing opportunity. Throughout 1821 and
1822, surrounded with the friends both social and literary of Taylor and Hessey, 'Elia' bloomed richly in the
London Magazine.

But with all their admirable points the publishers
gradually revealed a weakness which meant the decline
of their magazine. They could not, or would not, venture to risk the expense of appointing an editor proper.
Their exemplary endeavour to support the genius of the
day—such as the poetry of Keats—resulted in a low
state of the firm's finances, and in a growing anxiety
and makeshift habit in the department of the *London*.
The dinners of the circle became less frequent and less
attended. Lamb, who had the instinct of knowing the
tendency of a literary movement as a doctor knows the
condition of a patient, felt that the inspiration which
had called up 'Elia' was going. He collected 'Elia:
Essays which have appeared under that signature in the
London Magazine' at the end of 1822, and, the inimitable
and exquisite volume being published, he marked his
sense of the change by signing his 'Rejoicings on the
New Year's Coming of Age', in the magazine for
January, 1823, 'Elia's Ghost'. At the same time, with
artistic ceremony, he printed a kind of funeral sermon,
'A Character of the Late Elia: By a Friend,' to whom
he gave the name 'Phil-Elia'.

From this time until the close of his life (1834), Lamb was once more without a regular and wholly congenial medium for his prose writings. He did his best for the *London* until the autumn of 1825, when it passed into other hands, having lost its individual freshness. He was now 'the Author of *Elia* rather than 'Elia'; yet we find him still from time to time using the name which had made him famous with the genuine reading world, as in the *New Monthly Magazine*, a brilliant and well-equipped review. Having for two or three years companioned some of his friends in writing for the *New Monthly*, Lamb turned aside to assist less opulent undertakings and to prepare one or two little books for publication. It was his special pleasure, now that he was growing old, to prompt and promote the valuable labours of others. Above all, he had at heart the career of a young publisher—'bookseller', Lamb preferred to say—named Edward Moxon, who married Lamb's adopted daughter. He sent him on his way towards an enviable reputation for the production of English classics in a form worthy of their substance, giving him among other things the selection of his more recent prose entitled *The Last Essays of Elia*.

Lamb in his sub-title called this volume 'A Sequel', perhaps with a wistful recollection that sequels are generally disappointments. He had been drastic enough in excluding candidates for his table of contents, yet the *Last Essays* made up a volume almost of its predecessor's quantity. In quality and variety, it rivalled that masterly book; but the character of 'Elia' is naturally not so ubiquitous and pervasive in it. Charles Lamb appears without his disguise more often. However, 'Elia' opens both of these collections of essays; in the first, he is discovered in the eighteenth century, lingering with old realities in the dream-like passages of the South-Sea House; in the second, he lives over anew the intense experience of childhood in the deserted mansion of Blakesmoor in Hertfordshire. 'Their importance is from the past.'

With the *Last Essays* by themselves in our hands, we may quickly discover what it is in Charles Lamb that has made his memory so perfect and his spiritual presence so delightful to a century of humanity. We instantly comprehend that we are in contact with a genius for appreciation, a lover of existence remote alike from empty-minded and profitless distaste, and from weak monotonous indiscriminate bliss. In 'The Old Margate Hoy', we see Lamb the man of imagination, capable of entering into all the grand and wild and terrible meanings of 'the sea'. But his complete honesty of self-estimate does not fail. We see him 'on the naked beach', wishing himself back in Cheapside, or shifting his gaze from the 'horrid fissures of dusty innutritious rocks' to the more communicative faces of the gentry hanging about the boats. 'I like a smuggler. He is the only honest thief. He robs nothing but the revenue—an abstraction I never greatly cared about.' In 'Captain Jackson', we have an example of Lamb's delight in the oddities of this vale of tears, and of that noble admiration for the heroism of mortality which Lamb veils in humorous comment. Would not most people dismiss the poor Captain with his perpetual 'self-delusion' as a tedious prevaricator? One hears the chatter, 'Trying to tell us those were silver spoons', 'That girl a pianist? Well—' And then, one hears the voice of a Shakespearean reader of human nature, declaring the true virtue and praise of Captain Jackson's 'stretchers'.

Those who know Lamb well through his works and correspondence have often echoed the 'Saint Charles' of Thackeray. He would have thought the expression far from apt. His reverence for certain illustrious beings whose lives were saintly would have been offended. Yet, in all matters which are referred to in the term 'morality', Lamb's life is a pattern, and his writings are altogether the truthful reflection of his life. The episodes and natures which he has honoured in the *Last Essays* reveal something of his own invincible innocence, which is made all the brighter by some hints of the dark difficulties encountered by Lamb. There is no preaching in him (he left that to Coleridge), but the effect of his confessions and allusions is that of excellent doctrine. He is the last man to commend discomfort and want to those who have probably experienced little else, but he would not gladly exchange the battle of life for a silly Arcadian vacancy. The pleasures, for him, exist in harmony with the hardships. So, in 'Old China', he puts the philosophical sentiment into the mouth of Bridget Elia: 'I see no harm in people making much of themselves, in that sense of the word,' i.e. when they are bold in their poverty, and fight for a brief luxury. 'It may give them a hint how to make much of others. But now—what I mean by the word—we never do make much of ourselves. None but the poor can do it. I do not mean the veriest poor of all, but persons as we were, just above poverty.' So the subject proceeds, with the mingled intention of leaving a serious truth under the current of pretty sketches of intimate happiness, until, with his faculty for knowing when enough has been hinted (for Lamb invariably respects the reader's intelligent sympathies), the worshipper of Old China takes his leave: 'and now do just look at that merry

little Chinese waiter holding an umbrella, big enough
for a bed-tester, over the head of that pretty insipid
half-Madonna-ish chit of a lady in that very blue
summer-house.'

It has been supposed by some judges, among whom
was Robert Southey, that Lamb wanted 'religious
feeling'. He did not often publish anything direct on
the question of God and Man. In that reticence, two
main sources are concerned. For Lamb, religion was
the most private and inviolable of all emotions, the
most subtle and venerable of topics, a mystery indeed.
Then, although he had read, with his wonderful gift for
extensive yet minute reading, a great mass of theology
and the creeds of sects, and had decided for himself that
he must follow other paths of approach to eternal
Wisdom, it was his rule to avoid the danger of causing
pain and distress to those who cherished forms of faith
unlike his own. Their faith, if it were active, outshone
the possible error. No delicacy could surpass that
which his verses on discovering, in some 'Lives of the
Saints', a painted flower containing a little picture of
St. Anne, embody in their earnest simplicity:

O lift with reverent hand that tarnish'd flower . . .

If we desire from Lamb something more mystical and
glorious, we find it in the *Last Essays*. Modern religion
has shown itself in no sweeter, no braver parable than
'The Child Angel', conceived at a time when humanity
still was commonly viewed under the image of
'poor sinful worms' and as altogether born in sin. With
shyness, joking gently, Lamb comes to his theme of
a union between earth and heaven, of the beauty (here
emerges the characteristic direction of Lamb's sympathy) implicit in the adaptation of 'bright intelligences'

towards imperfect understanding, 'so that Humility and Aspiration went on even-paced.' This last Essay enchants us not less by the ethereal style than the ethereal story. The music and cadence of these sentences are winged as the visionary lyrics of Shelley, but with a lingering sighing undersong: 'And it could not taste of death, by reason of its adoption into immortal palaces: but it was to know weakness, and reliance, and the shadow of human imbecility; and it went with a lame gait; but in its goings it exceeded all mortal children in grace and swiftness.'

We must be modest for a modest man. Those words also are Lamb's. Whoever writes any estimate of him or his writings, although the injunction is ever in his conscience, will be aware that he is composing a considerable vote of thanks. No eulogy could be too great, although it might not be on the properest foundations. Lamb himself disapproved of the epithet 'gentle' as a definition of him, since it had ceased to convey what it did once when the falcon was 'gentle'. It had sunk usually into a meaning verging upon ineffectiveness. Lamb was conscious of power. His intellect, though 'cheerfulness would break in' and humour and modesty withheld him from deliberate philosophical expansion, was decisive. In the *Last Essays* we meet with one splendid display of his truth-finding insight—that paper evidencing the 'Barrenness of the Imaginative Faculty in the Productions of Modern Art'. What is that muddle which is commonly called Imagination ? It is the fantastic cat's-cradle of some fiction-writer, who sees China as a series of opium-dungeons and a society of murderous magicians with drooping whiskers, and poisonous reptiles in their fans; or London as a stage of unknown fingers pressing unseen triggers and being duly gripped

by unbeatable crime-waiters; or the 1950's as a period
when we shall all be, by the blessings of 'Science',

> Washing our hands with invisible soap
> In imperceptible water.

What *is* Imagination?

It is in the critical writings of Lamb and his friends
that the answer is contained, and though he is hereabouts
in competition with Wordsworth, Coleridge, Hazlitt, and
Hunt he perhaps gives the answer most perfectly and
persuasively. He proves that it is not in the ingenious
provision of curious details that the imagination shows,
but in the recognition of some single and unique signs
of the spirit; not in the satisfaction of the outward eye
or even the plain intelligence, but in the creation of
wonder or passion from our deeper associations. The
'Bacchus and Ariadne', interpreted by him, in its
Einstein-like chronologism, becomes a key to the
intellectual secrets of great art; equally John Martin,
with all the bewildering contrivances of his strange
panoramas, is made a permanent index to minor percep-
tions, despite the great popularity of his pictures at the
time of Lamb's discriminative essay. With Lamb in our
minds, we should know what we are looking for in art
or letters.

This best illuminator of difficult principles was one
of the most learned of men, and deserves our attentive
following both in the matter of his range of information
and in his dexterous delicacy of introducing it. In the
Last Essays (to explore his reading no farther), we
become aware that he is a master of his Bible, of his
classical mythology, of writers on heraldry, of medieval
geographers, of Elizabethan drama and Caroline poetry,
of general biography, of the standard novelists, of the
commentators. With a serious or sly quotation, he pays

his respects to, and desires the reader's affectionate remembrance of, poetry so diverse as the 'Night Thoughts' of Young and the 'Lines written above Tintern Abbey' of Wordsworth. It might be hard nowadays even to acquire copies of some of Lamb's favourite authors; Sir Thomas Browne we have always with us, but not Tom Brown 'of facetious memory'; we may own a tolerably representative Swift, but are scarcely likely to pick up 'the old "Athenian Oracle"' of Swift' days, where Lamb found means of 'wonder and delight'. Nor should the man be heavily blameworthy whose taste did not concur with Lamb's; who did not dote on the poems of Cowley, or Bishop Andrewes' Sermons (concerning which, consult Mr. T. S. Eliot). But these 'asides' do not trouble the main case. Lamb sets the example of eager independence and loving minuteness in the mental life. He is 'rich in the simple worship' of sympathy. Little or nothing can happen to him without awakening a music of humanities, partly derived from his old and new authors. He *lived* where the multitude only see the calendar and clock; and one of his secrets is the right use of the bookstall, and that profitable investment, desultory reading.

When it comes to writing, Lamb is not the first man who would be put forward as a model. The influence of his essays has been immense; but particular imitations have not been very successful. (A clever pen, Laman Blanchard, produced a series of 'Popular Fallacies' in continuation of those in the *Last Essays*.) The trouble is this: it is the 'affected array of antique modes and phrases' in 'Elia' which catches the eye, and seems to be Lamb's mystery. 'Hath', 'oftentimes', 'peradventure', 'my Lord Shaftesbury'—those are the presumed elements of Elian style. Who presumes so, is mistaken.

Those touches are necessary finishes to a character-study, not the essence of Lamb's writing. We may, and we should, emulate that. It is correctness, distinctness, and readiness of expression. The modern (or ancient) notion that by hurling words out in a violent hurry we create atmosphere and impression is unsound. Bombardment is exciting, but transient. If we examine Lamb, or Dickens, or Hardy—famous creators of atmosphere—we find an 'almost feminine partiality' for precise tint and tone, in choice of word, in sequence of sentence, in variation of passages. Take a phrase like 'the hollowness of a day's pleasuring'; attempt to substitute, for 'hollowness', 'emptiness', 'vacancy', 'meaninglessness', 'tastelessness', 'disappointment'; and feel what a world of metaphor and emphatic sound is lost. Or reword a sentence. Lamb: 'I had no repugnance then— why should I now have ?—to those little, lawless, azure-tinctured grotesques, that under the notion of men and women, float about, uncircumscribed by any element, in that world before perspective—a china tea-cup.' Non-Lamb: 'As I did not object to the eccentric blue miniature figures, which are supposed to be men and women (they do not belong to any world we know), on china tea-cups, when I first saw them, I admit that I have no objection to them now.' Impressionist: 'Quaint gentry, these tea-cup men and women. Rather good, *I* think. I always have thought. China's *different*, somehow. Hanging these blue birds out in the void. Older than television . . .'

But our sermon must come to an end, and the conclusion of all notices of Charles Lamb must be that no one has read him without deeper and finer feelings for life. Sometimes he shows us the possibilities of intellectual sport, as in his 'Rejoicings upon the New Year's

Coming of Age', where with tradition, wit, and poetry
he transforms the almanack into a carnival or a play.
We do not usually see in the day of the month such
radiant life and cordiality. Elsewhere, Lamb instructs
us in an even greater art of life, that of human observation and response, smilingly, as in the account of the
Poor Relation; gravely and commandingly, as in the
reflection on society in the twelfth 'Popular Fallacy':
'The children of the very poor have no young times.
It makes the very heart to bleed to overhear the casual
street-talk between a poor woman and her little girl. . . .
It is not of toys, of nursery books, of summer holidays
(fitting that age); of the promised sight, or play; of
praised sufficiency at school. It is of mangling and
clear-starching, of the price of coals, or of potatoes.
The questions of the child, that should be the very outpourings of curiosity in idleness, are marked with forecast and melancholy providence. It has come to be
a woman, before it was a child. It has learned to go to
market; it chaffers, it haggles, it envies, it murmurs; it
is knowing, acute, sharpened; it never prattles. Had
we not reason to say, that the home of the very poor is
no home?' So spoke the childless man, neither a revo-
lutionary nor a sentimentalist, whose undying charm is
that he was so 'much of the boy-man. . . . The impressions of infancy had burnt into him.' He supremely
combined innocence and experience.

EDMUND BLUNDEN.

THE LAST ESSAYS OF ELIA

PREFACE

BY A FRIEND OF THE LATE ELIA

[Printed in *The London Magazine*, vol. vii, no. xxxvii, p. 19 (Jan., 1823). Collected, with some omissions, in *The Last Essays of Elia*, 1833. Text of 1833.]

[1]THIS poor gentleman, who for some months past had been in a declining way, hath at length paid his final tribute to nature.

To say truth, it is time he were gone. The humour of the thing, if there were ever much in it, was pretty well exhausted ; and a two years' and a half existence has been a tolerable duration for a phantom.

I am now at liberty to confess, that much which I have heard objected to my late friend's writings was well-founded. Crude they are, I grant you—a sort of unlicked, incondite things—villainously pranked in an affected array of antique modes and phrases. They had not been *his*, if they had been other than such ; and better it is, that a writer should be natural in a self-pleasing quaintness, than to affect a naturalness (so called) that should be strange to him. Egotistical they have been pronounced by some who did not know, that what he tells us, as of himself, was often true only (historically) of another ; as in [2]a former Essay (to save many instances)—where under the *first person* (his favourite figure) he shadows forth the forlorn estate of a country-boy placed at a London school, far from his friends and connections—in direct opposition to his own early history. If it be egotism to imply and twine with his own identity the griefs and affections of another—making himself many, or reducing many unto

---

[1] *For the text of this Preface as printed in the* L. M., *Jan.*, 1823, *see Editor's Notes.*   [2] A former] his fourth 1822.

B

himself—then is the skilful novelist, who all along brings in
his hero, or heroine, speaking of themselves, the greatest
egotist of all ; who yet has never, therefore, been accused
of that narrowness. And how shall the intenser dramatist
escape being faulty, who doubtless, under cover of passion
uttered by another, oftentimes gives blameless vent to his
most inward feelings and expresses his own story modestly?

My late friend was in many respects a singular character.
Those who did not like him, hated him ; and some, who
once liked him, afterwards became his bitterest haters. The
truth is, he gave himself too little concern what he uttered,
and in whose presence. He observed neither time nor place,
and would e'en out with what came uppermost. With the
severe religionist he would pass for a free-thinker ; while
the other faction set him down for a bigot, or persuaded
themselves that he belied his sentiments. Few understood
him ; and I am not certain that at all times he quite understood himself. He too much affected that dangerous figure
—irony. He sowed doubtful speeches, and reaped plain,
unequivocal hatred.—He would interrupt the gravest discussion with some light jest ; and yet, perhaps, not quite
irrelevant in ears that could understand it. Your long
and much talkers hated him. The informal habit of his
mind, joined to an inveterate impediment of speech,
forbade him to be an orator ; and he seemed determined
that no one else should play that part when he was present.
He was *petit* and ordinary in his person and appearance.
I have seen him sometimes in what is called good company,
but where he has been a stranger, sit silent, and be suspected for an odd fellow ; till some unlucky occasion provoking it, he would stutter out some senseless pun (not
altogether senseless perhaps, if rightly taken), which has
stamped his character for the evening. It was hit or miss
with him ; but nine times out of ten, he contrived by this
device to send away a whole company his enemies. His
conceptions rose kindlier than his utterance, and his
happiest *impromptus* had the appearance of effort. He has
been accused of trying to be witty, when in truth he was
but struggling to give his poor thoughts articulation. He
chose his companions for some individuality of character
which they manifested.—Hence, not many persons of

science, and few professed *literati*, were of his councils.
They were, for the most part, persons of an uncertain
fortune ; and, as to such people commonly nothing is
more obnoxious than a gentleman of settled (though
moderate) income, he passed with most of them for a great
miser. To my knowledge this was a mistake. His *intimados*, to confess a truth, were in the world's eye a ragged
regiment. He found them floating on the surface of society ;
and the colour, or something else, in the weed pleased him.
The burrs stuck to him—but they were good and loving
burrs for all that. He never greatly cared for the society
of what are called good people. If any of these were
scandalised (and offences were sure to arise), he could not
help it. When he has been remonstrated with for not
making more concessions to the feelings of good people,
he would retort by asking, what one point did these good
people ever concede to him ? He was temperate in his
meals and diversions, but always kept a little on this side
of abstemiousness. Only in the use of the Indian weed
he might be thought a little excessive. He took it, he
would say, as a solvent of speech. Marry—as the friendly
vapour ascended, how his prattle would curl up sometimes
with it ! the ligaments, which tongue-tied him, were
loosened, and the stammerer proceeded a statist !

I do not know whether I ought to bemoan or rejoice that
my old friend is departed. His jests were beginning to
grow obsolete, and his stories to be found out. He felt
the approaches of age ; and while he pretended to cling
to life, you saw how slender were the ties left to bind him.
Discoursing with him latterly on this subject, he expressed
himself with a pettishness, which I thought unworthy of
him. In our walks about his suburban retreat (as he called
it) at Shacklewell, some children belonging to a school of
industry had met us, and bowed and curtseyed, as he
thought, in an especial manner to *him*. ' They take me
for a visiting governor,' he muttered earnestly. He had
a horror, which he carried to a foible, of looking like
anything important and parochial. He thought that he
approached nearer to that stamp daily. He had a general
aversion from being treated like a grave or respectable
character, and kept a wary eye upon the advances of age

that should so entitle him. He herded always, while it was possible, with people younger than himself. He did not conform to the march of time, but was dragged along in the procession. His manners lagged behind his years. He was too much of the boy-man. The *toga virilis* never sate gracefully on his shoulders. The impressions of infancy had burnt into him, and he resented the impertinence of manhood. These were weaknesses ; but such as they were, they are a key to explicate some of his writings.

BLAKESMOOR IN H——SHIRE

[Printed in *The London Magazine*, vol. x, no. lvii, p. 225 (Sept., 1824). Collected in *The Last Essays of Elia*, 1833. Text of 1833.]

I DO not know a pleasure more affecting than to range at will over the deserted apartments of some fine old family mansion. The traces of extinct grandeur admit of a better passion than envy : and contemplations on the great and good, whom we fancy in succession to have been its inhabitants, weave for us illusions, incompatible with the bustle of modern occupancy, and vanities of foolish present aristocracy. The same difference of feeling, I think, attends us between entering an empty and a crowded church. In the latter it is chance but some present human frailty—an act of inattention on the part of some of the auditory—or a trait of affectation, or worse, vain-glory, on that of the preacher—puts us by our best thoughts, disharmonising the place and the occasion. But would'st thou know the beauty of holiness ?—go alone on some week-day, borrowing the keys of good Master Sexton, traverse the cool aisles of some country church : think of the piety that has kneeled there—the congregations, old and young, that have found consolation there—the meek pastor—the docile parishioner. With no disturbing emotions, no cross conflicting comparisons, drink in the tranquillity of the place, till thou thyself become as fixed and motionless as the marble effigies that kneel and weep around thee.

Journeying northward lately, I could not resist going some few miles out of my road to look upon the remains of an old great house with which I had been impressed in this way in infancy. I was apprised that the owner of it had lately pulled it down; still I had a vague notion that it could not all have perished, that so much solidity with magnificence could not have been crushed all at once into the mere dust and rubbish which I found it.

The work of ruin had proceeded with a swift hand indeed, and the demolition of a few weeks had reduced it to—an antiquity.

I was astonished at the indistinction of everything. Where had stood the great gates? What bounded the court-yard? Whereabout did the out-houses commence? a few bricks only lay as representatives of that which was so stately and so spacious.

Death does not shrink up his human victim at this rate. The burnt ashes of a man weigh more in their proportion.

Had I seen these brick-and-mortar knaves at their process of destruction, at the plucking of every panel I should have felt the varlets at my heart. I should have cried out to them to spare a plank at least out of the cheerful store-room, in whose hot window-seat I used to sit and read Cowley, with the grass-plat before, and the hum and flappings of that one solitary wasp that ever haunted it about me—it is in mine ears now, as oft as summer returns; or a pannel of the yellow room.

Why, every plank and pannel of that house for me had magic in it. The tapestried bed-rooms—tapestry so much better than painting—not adorning merely, but peopling the wainscots—at which childhood ever and anon would steal a look, shifting its coverlid (replaced as quickly) to exercise its tender courage in a momentary eye-encounter with those stern bright visages, staring reciprocally—all Ovid on the walls, in colours vivider than his descriptions. Actæon in mid sprout, with the unappeasable prudery of Diana; and the still more provoking, and almost culinary coolness of Dan Phœbus, eel-fashion, deliberately divesting of Marsyas.

Then, that haunted room—in which old Mrs. Battle died—whereinto I have crept, but always in the day-time, with a passion of fear; and a sneaking curiosity, terror-tainted, to hold communication with the past.—*How shall they build it up again?*

It was an old deserted place, yet not so long deserted but that traces of the splendour of past inmates were everywhere apparent. Its furniture was still standing—even to the tarnished gilt leather battledores, and crumbling feathers of shuttlecocks in the nursery, which told that children had once played there. But I was a lonely child, and had the range of every apartment, knew every nook and corner, wondered and worshipped everywhere.

The solitude of childhood is not so much the mother of thought, as it is the feeder of love, and silence, and admiration. So strange a passion for the place possessed me in those years, that, though there lay—I shame to say how few roods distant from the mansion—half hid by trees, what I judged some romantic lake, such was the spell which bound me to the house, and such my carefulness not to pass its strict and proper precincts, that the idle waters lay unexplored for me ; and not till late in life, curiosity prevailing over elder devotion, I found, to my astonishment, a pretty brawling brook had been the Lacus Incognitus of my infancy. Variegated views, extensive prospects—and those at no great distance from the house— I was told of such—what were they to me, being out of the boundaries of my Eden ?—So far from a wish to roam, I would have drawn, methought, still closer the fences of my chosen prison ; and have been hemmed in by a yet securer cincture of those excluding garden walls. I could have exclaimed with that garden-loving poet—

> Bind me, ye woodbines, in your 'twines,
> Curl me about, ye gadding vines ;
> And oh so close your circles lace,
> That I may never leave this place ;
> But, lest your fetters prove too weak,
> Ere I your silken bondage break,
> Do you, O brambles, chain me too,
> And, courteous briars, nail me ᵃthrough !

I was here as in a lonely temple. Snug firesides—the low-built roof—parlours ten feet by ten—frugal boards, and all the homeliness of home—these were the condition of my birth—the wholesome soil which I was planted in. Yet, without impeachment to their tenderest lessons, I am not sorry to have had glances of something beyond ;

ᵃ Marvell, on Appleton House, to the Lord Fairfax [1824 *only*].

and to have taken, if but a peep, in childhood, at the contrasting accidents of a great fortune.

To have the feeling of gentility, it is not necessary to have been born gentle. The pride of ancestry may be had on cheaper terms than to be obliged to an importunate race of ancestors ; and the coatless antiquary in his un-emblazoned cell, revolving the long line of a Mowbray's or De Clifford's pedigree, at those sounding names may warm himself into as gay a vanity as those who do inherit them. The claims of birth are ideal merely, and what herald shall go about to strip me of an idea ? Is it trenchant to their swords ? can it be hacked off as a spur can ? or torn away like a tarnished garter ?

What, else, were the families of the great to us ? what pleasure should we take in their tedious genealogies, or their capitulatory brass monuments ? What to us the uninterrupted current of their bloods, if our own did not answer within us to a cognate and correspondent eleva-tion ?

Or wherefore, else, O tattered and diminished 'Scutcheon that hung upon the time-worn walls of thy princely stairs, BLAKESMOOR ! have I in childhood so oft stood poring upon thy mystic characters—thy emblematic supporters, with their prophetic ' Resurgam '—till, every dreg of peasantry purging off, I received into myself Very Gentility ? Thou wert first in my morning eyes ; and of nights, hast detained my steps from bedwards, till it was but a step from gazing at thee to dreaming on thee.

This is the only true gentry by adoption ; the veritable change of blood, and, not, as empirics have fabled, by transfusion.

Who it was by dying that had earned the splendid trophy, I know not, I inquired not ; but its fading rags, and colours cobweb-stained, told that its subject was of two centuries back.

And what if my ancestor at that date was some Damœtas —feeding flocks, not his own, upon the hills of Lincoln— did I in less earnest vindicate to myself the family trappings of this once proud Ægon ?—repaying by a backward triumph the insults he might possibly have heaped in his life-time upon my poor pastoral progenitor.

If it were presumption so to speculate, the present owners of the mansion had least reason to complain. They had long forsaken the old house of their fathers for a newer trifle ; and I was left to appropriate to myself what images I could pick up, to raise my fancy, or to soothe my vanity.

I was the true descendant of those old W——s ; and not the present family of that name, who had fled the old waste places.

Mine was that gallery of good old family portraits, which as I have gone over, giving them in fancy my own family name, one—and then another—would seem to smile, reaching forward from the canvas, to recognise the new relationship ; while the rest looked grave, as it seemed, at the vacancy in their dwelling, and thoughts of fled posterity.

That Beauty with the cool blue pastoral drapery, and a lamb—that hung next the great bay window—with the bright yellow H——shire hair, and eye of watchet blue —so like my Alice !—I am persuaded she was a true Elia, —Mildred Elia, I take [1]it.

Mine too, BLAKESMOOR, was thy noble Marble Hall, with its mosaic pavements, and its Twelve Cæsars—stately busts in marble—ranged round : of whose countenances, young reader of faces as I was, the frowning beauty of Nero, I remember, had most of my wonder ; but the mild Galba had my love. There they stood in the coldness of death, yet freshness of immortality.

Mine too, thy lofty Justice Hall, with its one chair of authority, high-backed and wickered, once the terror of luckless poacher, or self-forgetful maiden—so common since, that bats have roosted in it.

Mine too—whose else ?—thy costly fruit-garden, with its sun-baked southern wall ; the ampler pleasure-garden, rising backwards from the house in triple terraces, with flower-pots now of palest lead, save that a speck here and there, saved from the elements, bespake their pristine state

---

[1] it.] it. From her, and from my passion for her—for I first learned love from a picture—Bridget took·the hint of those pretty whimsical lines, which thou mayst see, if haply thou hast never seen them, Reader, in the margin. But my Mildred grew not old, like the imaginary Helen. [*The poem* HELEN *is appended as a footnote.*] 1824.

to have been gilt and glittering; the verdant quarters
backwarder still; and, stretching still beyond, in old for-
mality, thy firry wilderness, the haunt of [1]the squirrel,
and the day-long murmuring woodpigeon, with that
antique image in the centre, God or Goddess I wist not;
but child of Athens or old Rome paid never a sincerer
worship to Pan or to Sylvanus in their groves, than I to
that fragmental mystery.

Was it for this, that I kissed my childish hands too
fervently in your idol worship, walks and windings of
BLAKESMOOR! for this, or what sin of mine, has the
plough passed over your pleasant places? I sometimes
think that as men, when they die, do not die all, so of
their extinguished habitations there may be a hope—a germ
to be revivified.

POOR RELATIONS

[Printed in *The London Magazine*, vol. vii, no. xxix, p. 533 (May,
1823). Collected in *The Last Essays of Elia*, 1833. Text of 1833.]

A POOR Relation—is the most irrelevant thing in nature,—
a piece of impertinent correspondency,—an odious approximation,—a haunting conscience,—a preposterous shadow,
lengthening in the noontide of your prosperity,—an unwelcome remembrancer,—a perpetually recurring mortification,—a drain on your purse,—a more intolerable dun upon
your pride,—a drawback upon success,—a rebuke to your
rising,—a stain in your blood,—a blot on your scutcheon,—
a rent in your garment,—a death's head at your banquet,—
Agathocles' pot,—a Mordecai in your gate,—a Lazarus at
your door,—a lion in your path,—a frog in your chamber,
—a fly in your ointment,—a mote in your eye,—a triumph
to your enemy—an apology to your friends,—the one thing
not needful,—the hail in harvest,—the ounce of sour in a
pound of [2]sweet.

He is known by his knock. Your heart telleth you
'That is Mr. ——'. A rap, between familiarity and respect;
that demands, and, at the same time, seems to despair
of, entertainment. He entereth smiling, and—embarrassed.
He holdeth out his hand to you to shake, and—draweth

[1] the] *omit* 1824.   [2] sweet.] sweet,—the bore *par excellence.* 1823.

it back again. He casually looketh in about dinner time
—when the table is full. He offereth to go away, seeing
you have company—but is induced to stay. He filleth
a chair, and your visitor's two children are accommodated
at a side table. He never cometh upon open days, when
your wife says with some complacency, ' My dear, perhaps
Mr. —— will drop in to-day.' He remembereth birthdays—and professeth he is fortunate to have stumbled
upon one. He declareth against fish, the turbot being
small—yet suffereth himself to be importuned into a
slice against his first resolution. He sticketh by the port
—yet will be prevailed upon to empty the remainder glass
of claret, if a stranger press it upon him. He is a puzzle
to the servants, who are fearful of being too obsequious,
or not civil enough, to him. The guests think ' they have
seen him before '. Every one speculateth upon his condition ; and the most part take him to be—a tide-waiter.
He calleth you by your Christian name, to imply that his
other is the same with your own. He is too familiar by
half, yet you wish he had less diffidence. With half the
familiarity he might pass for a casual dependent ; with
more boldness he would be in no danger of being taken
for what he is. He is too humble for a friend, yet taketh
on him more state than befits a client. He is a worse guest
than a country tenant, inasmuch as he bringeth up no
rent—yet 'tis odds, from his garb and demeanour, that
your guests take him for one. He is asked to make one
at the whist table ; refuseth on the score of poverty, and
—resents being left out. When the company break up,
he proffereth to go for a coach—and lets the servant
go. He recollects your grandfather ; and will thrust in
some mean, and quite unimportant anecdote of—the
family. He knew it when it was not quite so flourishing
as ' he is blest in seeing it now '. He reviveth past situations, to institute what he calleth—favourable comparisons.
With a reflecting sort of congratulation, he will inquire
the price of your furniture ; and insults you with a special
commendation of your window-curtains. He is of opinion
that the urn is the more elegant shape, but, after all, there
was something more comfortable about the old tea-kettle
—which you must remember. He dare say you must find

a great convenience in having a carriage of your own, and
appealeth to your lady if it is not so. Inquireth if you
have had your arms done on vellum yet ; and did not know
till lately, that such-and-such had been the crest of the
family. His memory is unseasonable ; his compliments
perverse ; his talk a trouble ; his stay pertinacious ; and
when he goeth away, you dismiss his chair into a corner,
as precipitately as possible, and feel fairly rid of two
nuisances.

There is a worse evil under the sun, and that is—a female
Poor Relation. You may do something with the other ;
you may pass him off tolerably well ; but your indigent
she-relative is hopeless. ' He is an old humourist,' you
may say, 'and affects to go threadbare. His circumstances
are better than folks would take them to be. You are fond
of having a Character at your table, and truly he is one.'
But in the indications of female poverty there can be no
disguise. No woman dresses below herself from caprice.
The truth must out without shuffling. ' She is plainly
related to the L—s ; or what does she at their house ? '
She is, in all probability, your wife's cousin. Nine times
out of ten, at least, this is the case. Her garb is something
between a gentlewoman and a beggar, yet the former
evidently predominates. She is most provokingly humble
and ostentatiously sensible to her inferiority. He may
require to be repressed sometimes—*aliquando sufflaminandus
erat*—but there is no raising her. You send her soup at
dinner, and she begs to be helped—after the gentlemen.
Mr. —— requests the honour of taking wine with her ; she
hesitates between Port and Madeira, and chooses the former
—because he does. She calls the servant *Sir ;* and insists
on not troubling him to hold her plate. The housekeeper
patronizes her. The children's governess takes upon her
to correct her, when she has mistaken the piano for a
harpsichord.

Richard Amlet, Esq., in the play, is a notable instance
of the disadvantages, to which this chimerical notion of
affinity constituting a claim to acquaintance, may subject
the spirit of a gentleman. A little foolish blood is all that
is betwixt him and a lady of great estate. His stars are
perpetually crossed by the malignant maternity of an old

woman, who persists in calling him ' her son Dick '. But
she has wherewithal in the end to recompense his indignities,
and float him again upon the brilliant surface, under which
it had been her seeming business and pleasure all along to
sink him.   All men, besides, are not of Dick's temperament.
I knew an Amlet in real life, who, wanting Dick's buoyancy,
sank indeed.   Poor W—— was of my own standing at
Christ's, a fine classic, and a youth of promise.   If he had
a blemish, it was too much pride ; but its quality was
inoffensive ; it was not of that sort which hardens the
heart, and serves to keep inferiors at a distance ; it only
sought to ward off derogation from itself.   It was the
principle of self-respect carried as far as it could go, without
infringing upon that respect, which he would have every
one else equally maintain for himself.   He would have you
to think alike with him on this topic.   Many a quarrel
have I had with him, when we were rather older boys,
and our tallness made us more obnoxious to observation
in the blue clothes, because I would not [1]thread the alleys
and blind ways of the town with him to elude notice,
when we have been out together on a holiday in the streets
of this sneering and prying metropolis.   W—— went, sore
with these notions, to Oxford, where the dignity and sweetness of a scholar's life, meeting with the alloy of a humble
introduction, wrought in him a passionate devotion to
the place, with a profound aversion from the society.
The servitor's gown (worse than his school array) clung
to him with Nessian venom.   He thought himself ridiculous
in a garb, under which Latimer must have walked erect ;
and in which Hooker, in his young days, possibly flaunted
in a vein of no discommendable vanity.   In the depth of
college shades, or in his lonely chamber, the poor student
shrunk from observation.   He found shelter among books,
which insult not ; and studies, that ask no questions
of a youth's finances.   He was lord of his library, and
seldom cared for looking out beyond his domains.   The
healing influence of studious pursuits was upon him, to
soothe and to abstract.   He was almost a healthy man ;
when the waywardness of his fate broke out against him
with a second and worse malignity.   The father of W——

[1] thread] thrid 1823.

had hitherto exercised the humble profession of house-painter at N——, near Oxford. A supposed interest with some of the heads of the colleges had now induced him to take up his abode in that city, with the hope of being employed upon some public works which were talked of. From that moment I read in the countenance of the young man, the determination which at length tore him from academical pursuits for ever. To a person unacquainted with our Universities, the distance between the gownsmen and the townsmen, as they are called—the trading part of the latter especially—is carried to an excess that would appear harsh and incredible. The temperament of W——'s father was diametrically the reverse of his own. Old W—— was a little, busy, cringing tradesman, who, with his son upon his arm, would stand bowing and scraping, cap in hand, to anything that wore the semblance of a gown—insensible to the winks and opener remonstrances of the young man, to whose chamber-fellow, or equal in standing, perhaps, he was thus obsequiously and gratuitously ducking. Such a state of things could not last. W—— must change the air of Oxford or be suffocated. He chose the former ; and let the sturdy moralist, who strains the point of the filial duties as high as they can bear, censure the dereliction ; he cannot estimate the struggle. I stood with W——, the last afternoon I ever saw him, under the eaves of his paternal dwelling. It was in the fine lane leading from the High-street to the back of ***** college, where W—— kept his rooms. He seemed thoughtful, and more reconciled. I ventured to rally him—finding him in a better mood—upon a representation of the Artist Evangelist, which the old man, whose affairs were beginning to flourish, had caused to be set up in a splendid sort of frame over his really handsome shop, either as a token of prosperity, or badge of gratitude to his saint. W—— looked up at the Luke, and, like Satan, ' knew his mounted sign—and fled.' A letter on his father's table the next morning, announced that he had accepted a commission in a regiment about to embark for Portugal. He was among the first who perished before the walls of St. Sebastian.

I do not know how, upon a subject which I began with treating half seriously, I should have fallen upon a recital so eminently painful ; but this theme of poor relationship is replete with so much matter for tragic as well as comic associations, that it is difficult to keep the account distinct without blending. The earliest impressions which I received on this matter, are certainly not attended with anything painful, or very humiliating, in the recalling. At my father's table (no very splendid one) was to be found, every Saturday, the mysterious figure of an aged gentleman, clothed in neat black, of a sad yet comely appearance. His deportment was of the essence of gravity ; his words few or none ; and I was not to make a noise in his presence. I had little inclination to have done so—for my cue was to admire in silence. A particular elbow chair was appropriated to him, which was in no case to be violated. A peculiar sort of sweet pudding, which appeared on no other occasion, distinguished the days of his coming. I used to think him a prodigiously rich man. All I could make out of him was, that he and my father had been schoolfellows a world ago at Lincoln, and that he came from the Mint. The Mint I knew to be a place where all the money was coined—and I thought he was the owner of all that money. Awful ideas of the Tower twined themselves about his presence. He seemed above human infirmities and passions. A sort of melancholy grandeur invested him. From some inexplicable doom I fancied him obliged to go about in an eternal suit of mourning ; a captive—a stately being, let out of the Tower on Saturdays. Often have I wondered at the temerity of my father, who, in spite of an habitual general respect which we all in common manifested towards him, would venture now and then to stand up against him in some argument, touching their youthful days. The houses of the ancient city of Lincoln are divided (as most of my readers know) between the dwellers on the hill, and in the valley. This marked distinction formed an obvious division between the boys who lived above (however brought together in a common school) and the boys whose paternal residence was on the plain ; a sufficient cause of hostility in the code of these young Grotiuses. My father had been a leading Mountaineer ; and would still maintain the general superiority, in skill and hardihood, of the *Above Boys* (his own faction) over the *Below Boys*

(so were they called), of which party his contemporary had
been a chieftain. Many and hot were the skirmishes on
this topic—the only one upon which the old gentleman
was ever brought out—and bad blood bred ; even sometimes almost to the recommencement (so I expected) of
actual hostilities. But my father, who scorned to insist
upon advantages, generally contrived to turn the conversation upon some adroit by-commendation of the old Minster ;
in the general preference of which, before all other cathedrals
in the island, the dweller on the hill, and the plain-born,
could meet on a conciliating level, and lay down their less
important differences. Once only I saw the old gentleman
really ruffled, and I remember with anguish the thought
that came over me : ' Perhaps he will never come here
again.' He had been pressed to take another plate of
the viand, which I have already mentioned as the indispensable concomitant of his visits. He had refused,
with a resistance amounting to rigour—when my aunt, an
old Lincolnian, but who had something of this, in common
with my cousin Bridget, that she would sometimes press
civility out of season—uttered the following memorable
application—' Do take another slice, Mr. Billet, for you
do not get pudding every day.' The old gentleman said
nothing at the time—but he took occasion in the course
of the evening, when some argument had intervened
between them, to utter with an emphasis which chilled
the company, and which chills me now as I write it—
' Woman, you are superannuated.' John Billet did not
survive long, after the digesting of this affront ; but he
survived long enough to assure me that peace was actually
restored ! and, if I remember aright, another pudding was
discreetly substituted in the place of that which had
occasioned the offence. He died at the Mint (Anno 1781)
where he had long held, what he accounted, a comfortable
independence ; and with five pounds, fourteen shillings,
and a penny, which were found in his escrutoire after his
decease, left the world, blessing God that he had enough
to bury him, and that he had never been obliged to any
man for a sixpence. This was—a Poor Relation.

STAGE ILLUSION

[Printed under the title, *Imperfect Dramatic Illusion* in *The London Magazine, New Series*, vol. ii, no. viii, p. 599 (Aug., 1825). Collected in *The Last Essays of Elia*, 1833. Text of 1833.]

A PLAY is said to be well or ill acted in proportion to the scenical illusion produced. Whether such illusion can in any case be perfect, is not the question. The nearest approach to it, we are told, is, when the actor appears wholly unconscious of the presence of spectators. In tragedy—in all which is to affect the feelings—this undivided attention to his stage business, seems indispensable. Yet it is, in fact, dispensed with every day by our cleverest tragedians ; and while these references to an audience, in the shape of rant or sentiment, are not too frequent or palpable, a sufficient quantity of illusion for the purposes of dramatic interest may be said to be produced in spite of them. But, tragedy apart, it may be inquired whether, in certain characters in comedy, especially those which are a little extravagant, or which involve some notion repugnant to the moral sense, it is not a proof of the highest skill in the comedian when, without absolutely appealing to an audience, he keeps up a tacit understanding with them ; and makes them, unconsciously to themselves, a party in the scene. The utmost nicety is required in the mode of doing this ; but we speak only of the great artists in the profession.

The most mortifying infirmity in human nature, to feel in ourselves, or to contemplate in another, is, perhaps, cowardice. To see a coward *done to the life* upon a stage would produce anything but mirth. Yet we most of us remember Jack Bannister's cowards. Could any thing be more agreeable, more pleasant ? We loved the rogues. How was this effected but by the exquisite art of the actor in a perpetual sub-insinuation to us, the spectators, even in the extremity of the shaking fit, that he was not half such a coward as we took him for ? We saw all the common symptoms of the malady upon him ; the quivering lip, the cowering knees, the teeth chattering ; and could have sworn ' that man was frightened '. But we forgot all the while—or kept it almost a secret to ourselves—that he

never once lost his self-possession ; that he let out by
a thousand droll looks and gestures—meant at *us*, and not
at all supposed to be visible to his fellows in the scene, that
his confidence in his own resources had never once deserted
him.   Was this a genuine picture of a coward ?   or not
rather a likeness, which the clever artist contrived to palm
upon us instead of an original ; while we secretly connived
at the delusion for the purpose of greater pleasure, than
a more genuine counterfeiting of the imbecility, helpless-
ness, and utter self-desertion, which we know to be concomitants of cowardice in real life, could have given us ?

Why are misers so hateful in the world, and so endurable
on the stage, but because the skilful actor, by a sort of
sub-reference, rather than direct appeal to us, disarms the
character of a great deal of its odiousness, by seeming to
engage *our* compassion for the insecure tenure by which
he holds his money bags and parchments ?   By this subtle
vent half of the hatefulness of the character—the self-
closeness with which in real life it coils itself up from
the sympathies of men—evaporates.   The miser becomes
sympathetic ; *i.e.* is no genuine miser.   Here again a diverting likeness is substituted for a very disagreeable reality.

Spleen, irritability—the pitiable infirmities of old men,
which produce only pain to behold in the realities, counterfeited upon a stage, divert not altogether for the comic
appendages to them, but in part from an inner conviction
that they are *being acted* before us ;   that a likeness only
is going on, and not the thing itself.   They please by being
done under the life, or beside it ;   not *to the life*.   When
Gatty acts an old man, is he angry indeed ?   or only a
pleasant counterfeit, just enough of a likeness to recognise,
without pressing upon us the uneasy sense of reality ?

Comedians, paradoxical as it may seem, may be too
natural.   It was the case with a late actor.   Nothing could
be more earnest or true than the manner of Mr. Emery ;
this told excellently in his Tyke, and characters of a tragic
cast.   But when he carried the same rigid exclusiveness
of attention to the stage business, and wilful blindness and
oblivion of everything before the curtain into his comedy,
it produced a harsh and dissonant effect.   He was out of
keeping with the rest of the *Personæ Dramatis*.   There was

as little link between him and them as betwixt himself and
the audience. He was a third estate, dry, repulsive, and
unsocial to all. Individually considered, his execution was
masterly. But comedy is not this unbending thing ; for
this reason, that the same degree of credibility is not
required of it as to serious scenes. The degrees of credibility demanded to the two things may be illustrated by
the different sort of truth which we expect when a man
tells us a mournful or a merry story. If we suspect the
former of falsehood in any one tittle, we reject it altogether.
Our tears refuse to flow at a suspected imposition. But
the teller of a mirthful tale has latitude allowed him. We
are content with less than absolute truth. 'Tis the same
with dramatic illusion. We confess we love in comedy to
see an audience naturalised behind the scenes, taken in
into the interest of the drama, welcomed as by-standers
however. There is something ungracious in a comic actor
holding himself aloof from all participation or concern with
those who are come to be diverted by him. Macbeth must
see the dagger, and no ear but his own be told of it ; but
an old fool in farce may think he *sees something*, and by
conscious words and looks express it, as plainly as he can
speak, to pit, box, and gallery. When an impertinent in
tragedy, an Osric, for instance, breaks in upon the serious
passions of the scene, we approve of the contempt with
which he is treated. But when the pleasant impertinent
of comedy, in a piece purely meant to give delight, and
raise mirth out of whimsical perplexities, worries the
studious man with taking up his leisure, or making his house
his home, the same sort of contempt expressed (however
natural) would destroy the balance of delight in the spectators. To make the intrusion comic, the actor who plays
the annoyed man must a little desert nature ; he must, in
short, be thinking of the audience, and express only so
much dissatisfaction and peevishness as is consistent with
the pleasure of comedy. In other words, his perplexity
must seem half put on. If he repel the intruder with the
sober set face of a man in earnest, and more especially if
he deliver his expostulations in a tone which in the world
must necessarily provoke a duel ; his real-life manner will
destroy the whimsical and purely dramatic existence of the

other character (which to render it comic demands an antagonist comicality on the part of the character opposed to it), and convert what was meant for mirth, rather than belief, into a downright piece of impertinence indeed, which would raise no diversion in us, but rather stir pain, to see inflicted in earnest upon any [1]unworthy person. A very judicious actor (in most of his parts) seems to have fallen into an error of this sort in his playing with Mr. Wrench in the farce of Free and Easy.

Many instances would be tedious ; these may suffice to show that comic acting at least does not always demand from the performer that strict abstraction from all reference to an audience, which is exacted of it ; but that in some cases a sort of compromise may take place, and all the purposes of dramatic delight be attained by a judicious understanding, not too openly announced, between the ladies and gentlemen—on both sides of the curtain.

TO THE SHADE OF ELLISTON

[Printed along with the following essay, under the title, *Reminiscences of Elliston*, in *The Englishman's Magazine*, Aug., 1831, p. 554. Collected in *The Last Essays of Elia*, 1833. Text of 1833.]

JOYOUSEST of once embodied spirits, whither at length hast thou flown ? to what genial region are we permitted to conjecture that thou hast flitted ?

Art thou sowing thy WILD OATS yet (the harvest time was still to come with thee) upon casual sands of Avernus ? or art thou enacting ROVER (as we would gladlier think) by wandering Elysian streams ?

This mortal frame, while thou didst play thy brief antics amongst us, was in truth any thing but a prison to thee, as the vain Platonist dreams of this *body* to be no better than a county gaol, forsooth, or some house of durance vile, whereof the five senses are the fetters. Thou knewest better than to be in a hurry to cast off those gyves ; and had notice to quit, I fear, before thou wert quite ready to abandon this fleshly tenement. It was thy Pleasure House,

[1] unworthy] worthy 1825 ; unworthy *is probably an error of the printer.*

thy Palace of Dainty Devices ; thy Louvre, or thy White
Hall.

What new mysterious lodgings dost thou tenant now ? or
when may we expect thy aërial house-warming ?

Tartarus we know, and we have read of the Blessed
Shades ; now cannot I intelligibly fancy thee in either.

Is it too much to hazard a conjecture, that (as the school-
men admitted a receptacle apart for Patriarchs and unchrisom Babes) there may exist—not far perchance from
that storehouse of all vanities, which Milton saw in visions
—a LIMBO somewhere for PLAYERS ? and that

> Up thither like aërial vapours fly
> Both all Stage things, and all that in Stage things
> Built their fond hopes of glory, or lasting fame ?
> All the unaccomplish'd works of Authors' hands,
> Abortive, monstrous, or unkindly mix'd,
> Damn'd upon earth, fleet thither—
> Play, Opera, Farce, with all their trumpery—

There, by the neighbouring moon (by some not improperly
supposed thy Regent Planet upon earth) mayst thou not
still be acting thy managerial [1]pranks, great disembodied
Lessee ? but Lessee still, and still a Manager.

In Green Rooms, impervious to mortal eye, the muse
beholds thee wielding posthumous empire.

Thin ghosts of Figurantes (never plump on earth) [2]circle
thee in endlessly, and still their song is *Fye on sinful
Phantasy*.

Magnificent were thy capriccios on this globe of earth,
ROBERT WILLIAM ELLISTON ! for as yet we know not thy
new name in heaven.

It irks me to think, that, stript of thy regalities, thou
shouldst ferry over, a poor forked shade, in crazy Stygian

---

[1] pranks] capriccios 1831.   [2] circle ... *Phantasy*.] admire, while
with uplifted toe retributive you inflict vengeance incorporeal upon the
shadowy rear of obnoxious author, just arrived—

> ————what seem'd his tail,
> The likeness of a kingly kick had on.
> *   *   *   *   *   *
> Yet soon he heals ; for spirits that live throughout
> Vital in every part, not as frail man
> In entrails, head, or heart, liver, or reins,
> Can in their liquid texture mortal wound
> Receive no more, than can the liquid air.
> All heart they live, all head, &c.   1831.

wherry. Methinks I hear the old boatman, paddling by the weedy wharf, with raucid voice, bawling ' SCULLS, SCULLS ' : to which, with waving hand, and majestic action, thou deignest no reply, other than in two curt monosyllables, ' No : OARS.'

But the laws of Pluto's kingdom know small difference between king, and cobbler ; manager, and call-boy ; and, if haply your dates of life were conterminant, you are quietly taking your passage, cheek by cheek (O ignoble levelling of Death) with the shade of some recently departed candle-snuffer.

But mercy ! what strippings, what tearing off of histrionic robes, and private vanities ! what denudations to the bone, before the surly Ferryman will admit you to set a foot within his battered lighter !

Crowns, sceptres ; shield, sword, and truncheon ; thy own coronation robes (for thou hast brought the whole property man's wardrobe with thee, enough to sink a navy) ; the judge's ermine ; the coxcomb's wig ; the snuff-box *à la Foppington*—all must overboard, he positively swears—and that ancient mariner brooks no denial ; for, since the tiresome monodrame of the old Thracian Harper, Charon, it is to be believed, hath shown small taste for theatricals.

Aye, now 'tis done. You are just boat weight ; *pura et puta anima.*

But bless me, how *little* you look !

So shall we all look—kings, and keysars—stript for the last voyage.

But the murky rogue pushes off. Adieu, pleasant, and thrice pleasant shade ! with my parting thanks for many a heavy hour of life lightened by thy harmless extravaganzas, public or domestic.

Rhadamanthus, who tries the lighter causes below, leaving to his two brethren the heavy calendars—honest Rhadamanth, always partial to players, weighing their particoloured existence here upon earth,—making account of the few foibles, that may have shaded thy *real life* as we call it, (though, substantially, scarcely less a vapour than thy idlest vagaries upon the boards of Drury,) as but of so many echoes, natural re-percussions, and results to be

expected from the assumed extravagancies of thy *secondary*
or *mock life*, nightly upon a stage—after a lenient castiga-
tion, with rods lighter than of those Medusean ringlets, but
just enough to ' whip the offending Adam out of thee '—
shall courteously dismiss thee at the right hand gate—the
O. P. side of Hades—that conducts to masques, and merry-
makings, in the Theatre Royal of Proserpine.

PLAUDITO, ET ¹VALETO.

ELLISTONIANA

[Printed in continuation of the essay here preceding, under the title
Reminiscences of Elliston, in *The Englishman's Magazine*, Aug., 1831,
p. 556.   Collected in *The Last Essays of Elia*, 1833.   Text of 1833.]

My acquaintance with the pleasant creature, whose loss
we all deplore, was but slight.

²My first introduction to E., which afterwards ripened
into an acquaintance a little on this side of intimacy, was
over a counter of the Leamington Spa Library, then newly
entered upon by a branch of his family.   E., whom nothing
misbecame—to auspicate, I suppose, the filial concern,
and set it a going with a lustre—was serving in person two
damsels fair, who had come into the shop ostensibly to
inquire for some new publication, but in reality to have
a sight of the illustrious shopman, hoping some conference.
With what an air did he reach down the volume, dispassion-
ately giving his opinion upon the worth of the work in
question, and launching out into a dissertation on its
comparative merits with those of certain publications of
a similar stamp, its rivals !   his enchanted customers fairly
hanging ³on his lips, subdued to their authoritative sentence.
So have I seen a gentleman in comedy *acting* the shopman.
So Lovelace sold his gloves in King Street.   I admired the
histrionic art, by which he contrived to carry clean away
every notion of disgrace, from the occupation he had so
generously submitted to ;   and from that hour I judged

¹ VALETO.]   VALETO. | Thy friend upon earth, | Though thou did'st
connive at his d——n, | Mr. H. 1831.   ² *This paragraph is printed
as a footnote in* 1831.   ³ on] upon 1831.

him, with no after repentance, to be a person, with whom it
would be a felicity to be more acquainted.

[1]To descant upon his merits as a Comedian would be
superfluous. With his blended private and professional
habits alone I have to do ; that harmonious fusion of the
manners of the player into those of every day life, which
brought the stage boards into streets, and dining-parlours,
and kept up the play when the play was ended.—' I like
Wrench,' a friend was saying to him one day, ' because he
is the same natural, easy creature, *on* the stage, that he is
off.' ' My case exactly,' retorted Elliston—with a charming
forgetfulness, that the converse of a proposition does not
always lead to the same conclusion—' I am the same person
off the stage that I am *on*.' The inference, at first sight,
seems identical ; but examine it a little, and it confesses
only, that the one performer was never, and the other
always, *acting*.

And in truth this was the charm of Elliston's private
deportment. You had a spirited performance always going
on before your eyes, with nothing to pay. As where
a monarch takes up his casual abode for a night, the poorest
hovel which he honours by his sleeping in it, becomes *ipso
facto* for that time a palace ; so wherever Elliston walked,
sate, or stood still, there was the theatre. He carried about
with him his pit, [2]boxes, and galleries, and set up his
portable playhouse at corners of streets, and in the market-
places. Upon flintiest pavements he trod the boards still ;
and if his theme chanced to be passionate, the green baize
carpet of tragedy spontaneously rose beneath his feet.
Now this was hearty, and showed a love for his art. So
Apelles *always* painted—in thought. So G. D. *always*
poetises. I hate a lukewarm artist. I have known actors
—and some of them of Elliston's own stamp—who shall
have agreeably been amusing you in the part of a rake or
a coxcomb, through the two or three hours of their dramatic
existence ; but no sooner does the curtain fall with its
leaden clatter, but a spirit of lead seems to seize on all their
faculties. They emerge sour, morose persons, intolerable

---

[1] *In* 1831 *this paragraph begins :* The anecdotes which I have to tell
of him are trivial, save in as much as they may elucidate character.
To descant, *etc.*   [2] boxes] box 1831.

to their families, servants, &c. Another shall have been
expanding your heart with generous deeds and sentiments,
till it even beats with yearnings of universal sympathy ;
you absolutely long to go home, and do some good action.
The play seems tedious, till you can get fairly out of the
house, and realise your laudable intentions. At length the
final bell rings, and this cordial representative of all that is
amiable in human breasts steps forth—a miser. Elliston
was more of a piece. Did he *play* Ranger ? and did Ranger
fill the general bosom of the town with satisfaction ? why
should *he* not be Ranger, and diffuse the same cordial satisfaction among his private circles ? with *his* temperament,
his animal spirits, *his* good-nature, *his* follies perchance,
could he do better than identify himself with his impersona-
tion ? Are we to like a pleasant rake, or coxcomb, on the
stage, and give ourselves airs of aversion for the identical
character presented to us in actual life ? or what would the
performer have gained by divesting himself of the imper-
sonation ? Could the man Elliston have been essentially
different from his part, even if he had avoided to reflect to
us studiously, in private circles, the airy briskness, the
frowardness, and 'scapegoat trickeries of his prototype ?
  ' But there is something not natural in this everlasting
acting ; we want the real man.'
  Are you quite sure that it is not the man himself, whom
you cannot, or will not see, under some adventitious trappings, which, nevertheless, sit not at all inconsistently
upon him ? What if it is the nature of some men to be
highly artificial ? The fault is least reprehensible in *players.*
Cibber was his own Foppington, with almost as much wit
as Vanburgh could add to it.
  ' My conceit of his person ',—it is Ben Jonson speaking
of Lord Bacon,—' was never increased towards him by
his *place* or *honours.* But I have, and do reverence him
for the *greatness,* that was only proper to himself ; in that
he seemed to me ever one of the *greatest* men, that had been
in many ages. In his adversity I ever prayed that heaven
would give him strength ; for *greatness* he could not want.'
  The quality here commended was scarcely less conspicuous
in the subject of these idle reminiscences, than in my Lord
Verulam. Those who have imagined that an unexpected

elevation to the direction of a great London Theatre, affected the consequence of Elliston, or at all changed his nature, knew not the essential *greatness* of the man whom they disparage. It was my fortune to encounter him near St. Dunstan's Church (which, with its punctual giants, is now no more than dust and a shadow), on the morning of his election to that high office. Grasping my hand with a look of significance, he only uttered,—' Have you heard the news ? '—then with another look following up the blow, he subjoined, ' I am the future Manager of Drury Lane Theatre.'—Breathless as he saw me, he stayed not for congratulation or reply, but mutely stalked away, leaving me to chew upon his new-blown dignities at leisure. In fact, nothing could be said to it. Expressive silence alone could muse his praise. This was in his *great* style.

But was he less *great*, (be witness, O ye Powers of Equanimity, that supported in the ruins of Carthage the consular exile, and more recently transmuted for a more illustrious exile, the barren constableship of Elba into an image of Imperial France), when, in melancholy after-years, again, much near the same spot, I met him, when that sceptre had been wrested from his hand, and his dominion was curtailed to the petty managership, and part proprietorship, of the small Olympic, *his Elba ?* He still played nightly upon the boards of Drury, but in parts, alas ! allotted to him, not magnificently distributed by him. Waiving his great loss as nothing, and magnificently sinking the sense of fallen *material* grandeur in the more liberal resentment of depreciations done to his more lofty *intellectual* pretensions, ' Have you heard ' (his customary exordium)—' have you heard,' said he, ' how they treat me ? they put me in *comedy.*' Thought I—but his finger on his lips forbade any verbal interruption—' where could they have put you better ? ' Then, after a pause—' Where I formerly played Romeo, I now play Mercutio,'—and so again he stalked away, neither staying, nor caring for, responses.

O, it was a rich scene,—but Sir A—— C——, the best of story-tellers and surgeons, who mends a lame narrative almost as well as he sets a fracture, alone could do justice to it—that I was witness to, in the tarnished room (that had once been green) of that same little Olympic. There,

after his deposition from Imperial Drury, he substituted
a throne. That Olympic Hill was his 'highest heaven';
himself 'Jove in his chair'. There he sat in state, while
before him, on complaint of prompter, was brought for
judgment—how shall I describe her ?—one of those little
tawdry things that flirt at the tails of choruses—a proba-
tioner for the town, in either of its senses—the pertest little
drab—a dirty fringe and appendage of the lamps' smoke—
who, it seems, on some disapprobation expressed by
a 'highly respectable' audience, had precipitately quitted
her station on the boards, and withdrawn her small talents
in disgust.

'And how dare you,' said her Manager—assuming a cen-
sorial severity which would have crushed the confidence of
a Vestris, and disarmed that beautiful Rebel herself of her
professional caprices—I verily believe, he thought *her*
standing before him—'how dare you, Madam, withdraw
yourself, without a notice, from your theatrical duties ?'
'I was hissed, Sir.' 'And you have the presumption to
decide upon the taste of the town ?' 'I don't know that,
Sir, but I will never stand to be hissed,' was the subjoinder
of young Confidence—when gathering up his features into
one significant mass of wonder, pity, and expostulatory
indignation—in a lesson never to have been lost upon
a creature less forward than she who stood before him—
his words were these : 'They have hissed *me*.'

'Twas the identical argument *a fortiori*, which the son of
Peleus uses to Lycaon trembling under his lance, to persuade
him to take his destiny with a good grace. 'I too am
mortal.' And it is to be believed that in both cases the
rhetoric missed of its application, for want of a proper
understanding with the faculties of the respective recipients.

'Quite an Opera pit,' he said to me, as he was courteously
conducting me over the benches of his Surrey Theatre, the
last retreat, and recess, of his every-day waning grandeur.

Those who knew Elliston, will know the *manner* in which
he pronounced the latter sentence of the few words I am
about to record. One proud day to me he took his roast
mutton with us in the Temple, to which I had superadded
a preliminary haddock. After a rather plentiful partaking
of the meagre banquet, not unrefreshed with the humbler

sort of liquors, I made a sort of apology for the humility of the fare, observing that for my own part I never ate but of one dish at dinner. 'I too never eat but one thing at dinner '—was his reply—then after a pause—'reckoning fish as nothing.' The manner was all. It was as if by one peremptory sentence he had decreed the annihilation of all the savory esculents, which the pleasant and nutritious-food-giving Ocean pours forth upon poor humans from her watery bosom. This was *greatness*, tempered with considerate *tenderness* to the feelings of his scanty but welcoming entertainer.

Great wert thou in thy life, Robert William Elliston! and *not lessened* in thy death, if report speak truly, which says that thou didst direct that thy mortal remains should repose under no inscription but one of pure *Latinity*. Classical was thy bringing up! and beautiful was the feeling on thy last bed, which, connecting the man with the boy, took thee back in thy latest exercise of imagination, to the days when, undreaming of Theatres and Managerships, thou wert a scholar, and an early ripe one, under the roofs builded by the munificent and pious Colet. For thee the Pauline Muses weep. In elegies, that shall silence this crude prose, they shall celebrate thy praise.

DETACHED THOUGHTS ON BOOKS AND READING

[Printed in *The London Magazine*, vol. vi, no. xxxi, p. 33 (July, 1822). Collected in *The Last Essays of Elia*, 1833. Text of 1833.]

To mind the inside of a book is to entertain one's self with the forced product of another man's brain. Now I think a man of quality and breeding may be much amused with the natural sprouts of his own.
Lord Foppington in the Relapse.

AN ingenious acquaintance of my own was so much struck with this bright sally of his Lordship, that he has left off reading altogether, to the great improvement of his originality. At the hazard of losing some credit on this head, I must confess that I dedicate no inconsiderable portion of my time to other people's thoughts. I dream away my life in others' speculations. I love to lose myself

in other men's minds. When I am not walking, I am
reading ; I cannot sit and think. Books think for me.

I have no repugnances. Shaftesbury is not too genteel
for me, nor Jonathan Wild too low. I can read any thing
which I call a *book*. There are things in that shape which
I cannot allow for such.

In this catalogue of *books which are no books—biblia
a-biblia*—I reckon Court Calendars, Directories, Pocket
[1]Books, Draught Boards bound and lettered at the back,
Scientific Treatises, Almanacks, Statutes at Large ; the
works of Hume, Gibbon, Robertson, Beattie, Soame Jenyns,
and, generally, all those volumes which ' no gentleman's
library should be without ' : the Histories of Flavius
Josephus (that learned Jew), and Paley's Moral Philosophy.
With these exceptions, I can read almost any thing. I bless
my stars for a taste so catholic, so unexcluding.

I confess that it moves my spleen to see these *things in
books' clothing* perched upon shelves, like false saints,
usurpers of true shrines, intruders into the sanctuary,
thrusting out the legitimate occupants. To reach down
a well-bound semblance of a volume, and hope it is some
kind-hearted play-book, then, opening what ' seem its
leaves ', to come bolt upon a withering Population Essay.
To expect a Steele, or a Farquhar, and find—Adam Smith.
To view a well-arranged assortment of blockheaded Ency-
clopædias (Anglicanas or Metropolitanas) set out in an
array of Russia, or Morocco, when a tithe of that good
leather would comfortably re-clothe my shivering folios ;
would renovate Paracelsus himself, and enable old Raymund
[2]Lully to look like himself again in the world. I never see
these impostors, but I long to strip them, to warm my
ragged veterans in their spoils.

To be strong-backed and neat-bound is the desideratum
of a volume. Magnificence comes after. This, when it can
be afforded, is not to be lavished upon all kinds of books
indiscriminately. I would not dress a set of Magazines,
for instance, in full suit. The dishabille, or half-binding
(with Russia backs ever) is *our* costume. A Shakespeare,
or a Milton (unless the first editions), it were mere foppery

---

[1] Books] Books (the Literary excepted) 1822.   [2] Lully] Lully—I
have them both, reader—1822.

to trick out in gay apparel. The possession of them confers
no distinction. The exterior of them (the things themselves
being so common), strange to say, raises no sweet emotions,
no tickling sense of property in the owner. Thomson's
Seasons, again, looks best (I maintain it) a little torn, and
dog's-eared. How beautiful to a genuine lover of reading
are the sullied leaves, and worn out appearance, nay, the
very odour (beyond Russia), if we would not forget kind
feelings in fastidiousness, of an old ' Circulating Library '
Tom Jones, or Vicar of Wakefield ! How they speak of
the thousand thumbs, that have turned over their pages
with delight !—of the lone sempstress, whom they may
have cheered (milliner, or harder-working mantua-maker)
after her long day's needle-toil, running far into midnight,
when she has snatched an hour, ill spared from sleep, to
steep her cares, as in some Lethean cup, in spelling out
their enchanting contents ! Who would have them a whit
less soiled ? What better condition could we desire to see
them in ?

In some respects the better a book is, the less it demands
from binding. Fielding, Smollett, Sterne, and all that class
of perpetually self-reproductive volumes—Great Nature's
Stereotypes—we see them individually perish with less
regret, because we know the copies of them to be ' eterne '.
But where a book is at once both good and rare—where the
individual is almost the species, and when *that* perishes,

> We know not where is that Promethean torch
> That can its light relumine—

such a book, for instance, as the Life of the Duke of Newcastle, by his Duchess—no casket is rich enough, no casing
sufficiently durable, to honour and keep safe such a jewel.

Not only rare volumes of this description, which seem
hopeless ever to be reprinted ; but old editions of writers,
such as Sir Philip Sidney, Bishop Taylor, Milton in his
prose-works, Fuller—of whom we *have* reprints, yet the
books themselves, though they go about, and are talked
of here and there, we know, have not endenizened themselves (nor possibly ever will) in the national heart, so as
to become stock books—it is good to possess these in
durable and costly covers. I do not care for a First Folio

of [1]Shakspeare. I rather prefer the common editions of
Rowe and Tonson, without notes, and with *plates*, which,
being so execrably bad, serve as maps, or modest remem-
brancers, to the text ; and without pretending to any
supposable emulation with it, are so much better than the
Shakspeare gallery *engravings*, which *did*. I have a community of feeling with my countrymen about his Plays,
and I like those editions of him best, which have been
oftenest tumbled about and handled.—On the contrary,
I cannot read Beaumont and Fletcher but in Folio. The
Octavo editions are painful to look at. I have no sympathy
with [2]them. If they were as much read as the current
editions of the other poet, I should prefer them in that
shape to the older one. I do not know a more heartless
sight than the reprint of the Anatomy of Melancholy.
What need was there of unearthing the bones of that fantastic old great man, to expose them in a winding-sheet of
the [3]newest fashion to modern censure ? what hapless
stationer could dream of Burton ever becoming popular ?—
The wretched Malone could not do worse, when he bribed the
sexton of Stratford church to let him white-wash the
painted effigy of old Shakspeare, which stood there, in rude
but lively fashion depicted, to the very colour of the cheek,
the eye, the eye-brow, hair, the very dress he used to wear
—the only authentic testimony we had, however imperfect,
of these curious parts and parcels of him. They covered
him over with a coat of white paint. By ——, if I had
been a justice of peace for Warwickshire, I would have
clapt both commentator and sexton fast in the stocks, for
a pair of meddling sacrilegious varlets.

I think I see them at their work—these sapient trouble-
tombs.

Shall I be thought fantastical, if I confess, that the names
of some of our poets sound sweeter, and have a finer relish
to the ear—to mine, at least—than that of Milton or of
Shakspeare ? It may be, that the latter are more staled
and rung upon in common discourse. The sweetest names,

[1] Shakspeare.] Shakspeare. You cannot make a *pet* book of an
author whom everybody reads. 1822.   [2] them.] them, nor with
Mr. Gifford's Ben Jonson. 1822.   [3] newest fashion] latest edition
1822.

and which carry a perfume in the mention, are, Kit Marlowe, Drayton, Drummond of Hawthornden, and Cowley.

Much depends upon *when* and *where* you read a book. In the five or six impatient minutes, before the dinner is quite ready, who would think of taking up the Fairy Queen for a stop-gap, or a volume of Bishop Andrewes' sermons ?

Milton almost requires a solemn service of music to be played before you enter upon him. But he brings his music, to which, who listens, had need bring docile thoughts, and purged ears.

Winter evenings—the world shut out—with less of cere-mony the gentle Shakspeare enters. At such a season, the Tempest, or his own Winter's Tale—

These two poets you cannot avoid reading aloud—to yourself, or (as it chances) to some single person listening. More than one—and it degenerates into an audience.

Books of quick interest, that hurry on for incidents, are for the eye to glide over only. It will not do to read them out. I could never listen to even the better kind of modern novels without extreme irksomeness.

A newspaper, read out, is intolerable. In some of the Bank offices it is the custom (to save so much individual time) for one of the clerks—who is the best scholar—to commence upon the Times, or the Chronicle, and recite its entire contents aloud *pro bono publico*. With every advantage of lungs and elocution, the effect is singularly vapid. In barbers' shops and public-houses a fellow will get up, and spell out a paragraph, which he communicates as some discovery. Another follows with *his* selection. So the entire journal transpires at length by piece-meal. Seldom-readers are slow readers, and, without this expedient no one in the company would probably ever travel through the contents of a whole paper.

Newspapers always excite curiosity. No one ever lays one down without a feeling of disappointment.

What an eternal time that gentleman in black, at Nando's, keeps the paper ! I am sick of hearing the waiter bawling out incessantly, ' the Chronicle is in hand, [1]Sir.'

[1] Sir.'] Sir ' As in these little Diurnals I generally skip the Foreign News—the Debates—and the Politics—I find the *Morning Herald* by

Coming in to an inn at night—having ordered your supper—what can be more delightful than to find lying in the window-seat, left there time out of mind by the carelessness of some former guest—two or three numbers of the old Town and Country Magazine, with its amusing *tête-à-tête* pictures—' The Royal Lover and Lady G—— ; ' ' The Melting Platonic and the Old Beau,'—and such like antiquated scandal ?   Would you exchange it—at that time, and in that place—for a better book ?

Poor Tobin, who latterly fell blind, did not regret it so much for the weightier kinds of reading—the Paradise Lost, or Comus, he could have *read* to him—but he missed the pleasure of skimming over with his own eye a magazine, or a light pamphlet.

I should not care to be caught in the serious avenues of some cathedral alone, and reading *Candide*.

I do not remember a more whimsical surprise than having been once detected—by a familiar damsel—reclined at my ease upon the grass, on Primrose Hill (her Cythera), reading —*Pamela*.   There was nothing in the book to make a man seriously ashamed at the exposure ; but as she seated herself down by me, and seemed determined to read in company, I could have wished it had been—any other book. We read on very sociably for a few pages ; and, not finding the author much to her taste, she got up, and—went away. Gentle casuist, I leave it to thee to conjecture, whether the blush (for there was one between us) was the property of the nymph or the swain in this dilemma.   From me you shall never get the secret.

I am not much a friend to out-of-doors reading. I cannot settle my spirits to it. I knew a Unitarian minister, who was generally to be seen upon Snow-hill (as yet Skinner's-street *was not*), between the hours of ten and eleven in the morning, studying a volume of Lardner. I own this to have been a strain of abstraction beyond my reach. I used to admire how he sidled along, keeping clear of secular contacts.   An illiterate encounter with a porter's knot, or a bread basket, would have quickly put to flight all the

far the most entertaining of them.   It is an agreeable miscellany, rather than a newspaper.   1822.

theology I am master of, and have left me worse than indifferent to the five points.[1]

There is a class of street-readers, whom I can never contemplate without affection—the poor gentry, who, not having wherewithal to buy or hire a book, filch a little learning at the open stalls—the owner, with his hard eye, casting envious looks at them all the while, and thinking when they will have done. Venturing tenderly, page after page, expecting every moment when he shall interpose his interdict, and yet unable to deny themselves the gratification, they ' snatch a fearful joy '. Martin B——, in this way, by daily fragments, got through two volumes of Clarissa, when the stall-keeper damped his laudable ambition, by asking him (it was in his younger days) whether he meant to purchase the work. M. declares that under no circumstances of his life did he ever peruse a book with half the satisfaction which he took in those uneasy snatches. A quaint poetess of our day has moralised upon this subject in two very touching but homely stanzas

[2] I saw a boy with eager eye
Open a book upon a stall,
And read, as he'd devour it all ;
Which when the stall-man did espy,
Soon to the boy I heard him call,
' You, Sir, you never buy a book,
Therefore in one you shall not look.'
The boy pass'd slowly on and with a sigh
He wish'd he never had been taught to read,
Then of the old churl's books he should have had no need.

Of sufferings the poor have many,
Which never can the rich annoy :
I soon perceiv'd another boy,
Who look'd as if he'd not had any
Food, for that day at least—enjoy
The sight of cold meat in a tavern larder.
This boy's case, then thought I, is surely harder,
Thus hungry, longing, thus without a penny,
Beholding choice of dainty-dressed meat :
No wonder if he wish he ne'er had learn'd to eat.

[1] For a paragraph in the L. M., here omitted, see Editor's Notes   [2] In the L.M. these lines are headed THE TWO BOYS.   [3] In the L. M., below these lines come the words : (To be continued.)

THE OLD MARGATE HOY ✓

[Printed in *The London Magazine*, vol. viii, no. xliii, p. 21 (July, 1823). Collected in *The Last Essays of Elia*, 1833. Text of 1833.]

I AM fond of passing my vacations (I believe I have said so before) at one or other of the Universities. Next to these my choice would fix me at some woody spot, such as the neighbourhood of Henley affords in abundance, upon the banks of my beloved Thames. But somehow or other my cousin contrives to wheedle me once in three or four seasons to a watering place. Old attachments cling to me in spite of experience. We have been dull at Worthing one summer, duller at Brighton another, dullest at East-bourn a third, and are at this moment doing dreary penance at—Hastings !—and all because we were happy many years ago for a brief week at—Margate. That was our first sea-side experiment, and many circumstances combined to make it the most agreeable holyday of my life. We had neither of us seen the sea, and we had never been from home so long together in company.

Can I forget thee, thou old Margate Hoy, with thy weather-beaten, sun-burnt captain, and his rough accom-modations—ill exchanged for the foppery and fresh-water niceness of the modern steam-packet ? To the winds and waves thou committedst thy goodly freightage, and didst ask no aid of magic fumes, and spells, and boiling cauldrons. With the gales of heaven thou wentest swimmingly ; or, when it was their pleasure, stoodest still with sailor-like patience. Thy course was natural, not forced, as in a hot-bed ; nor didst thou go poisoning the breath of ocean with sulphureous smoke—a great sea-chimæra, chimneying and furnacing the deep ; or liker to that [1]fire-god parching up Scamander.

Can I forget thy honest, yet slender crew, with their coy reluctant responses (yet to the suppression of anything like contempt) to the raw questions, which we of the great city would be ever and anon putting to them, as to the uses of this or that strange naval implement ? 'Specially can I forget thee, thou happy medium, thou shade of refuge

[1] fire-] sea- 1823.

between us and them, conciliating interpreter of their skill
to our simplicity, comfortable ambassador between sea
and land!—whose sailor-trowsers did not more convincingly
assure thee to be an adopted denizen of the former, than
thy white cap, and whiter apron over them, with thy neat-
fingered practice in thy culinary vocation, bespoke thee to
have been of inland nurture heretofore—a master cook of
Eastcheap? How busily didst thou ply thy multifarious
occupation, cook, mariner, attendant, chamberlain; here,
there, like another Ariel, flaming at once about all parts of
the deck, yet with kindlier ministrations—not to assist the
tempest, but, as if touched with a kindred sense of our
infirmities, to soothe the qualms which that untried motion
might haply raise in our crude land-fancies. And when
the o'er-washing billows drove us below deck (for it was
far gone in October, and we had stiff and blowing weather,
how did thy officious ministerings, still catering for our
comfort, with cards, and cordials, and thy more cordial
conversation, alleviate the closeness and the confinement
of thy else (truth to say) not very savoury, nor very inviting,
little cabin!

With these additaments to boot, we had on board a fellow-
passenger, whose discourse in verity might have beguiled
a longer voyage than we meditated, and have made mirth
and wonder abound as far [1]as the Azores. He was a dark,
Spanish complexioned young man, remarkably handsome,
with an officer-like assurance, and an insuppressible volu-
bility of assertion. He was, in fact, the greatest liar I had
met with then, or since. He was none of your hesitating,
half story-tellers (a most painful description of mortals)
who go on sounding your belief, and only giving you as
much as they can see you can swallow at a time—the
nibbling pickpockets of your patience—but one who committed downright, day-light depredations upon his neighbour's faith. He did not stand shivering upon the brink,
but was a hearty thorough-paced liar, and plunged at once
into the depths of your credulity. I partly believe, he
made pretty sure of his company. Not many rich, not
many wise, or learned, composed at that time the common
stowage of a Margate packet. We were, I am afraid, a set

[1] as the] as from Thames to the 1823.

D 2

of as [1]unseasoned Londoners (let our enemies give it a worse
name) as [2]Aldermanbury, or Watling-street, at that time
of day could have supplied.   There might be an exception
or two among us, but I scorn to make any invidious distinctions among such a jolly, companionable ship's company, as those were whom I sailed with.   Something too
must be conceded to the *Genius Loci*.   Had the confident
fellow told us half the legends on land, which he favoured
us with on the other element, I flatter myself the good
sense of most of us would have revolted.   But we were in
a new world, with everything unfamiliar about us, and the
time and place disposed us to the reception of any prodigious
marvel whatsoever.   Time has obliterated from my memory
much of his wild fablings ; and the rest would appear but
dull, as written, and to be read on shore.   He had been
Aid-de-camp (among other rare accidents and fortunes) to
a Persian prince, and at one blow had stricken off the head
of the King of Carimania on horseback.   He, of course,
married the Prince's daughter.   I forget what unlucky
turn in the politics of that court, combining with the loss
of his consort, was the reason of his quitting Persia ; but
with the rapidity of a magician he transported himself,
along with his hearers, back to England, where we still
found him in the confidence of great ladies.   There was
some story of a Princess—Elizabeth, if I remember—having
intrusted to his care an extraordinary casket of jewels, upon
some extraordinary occasion—but as I am not certain of
the name or circumstance at this distance of time, I must
leave it to the royal daughters of England to settle the
honour among themselves in private.   I cannot call to
mind half his pleasant wonders ; but I perfectly remember,
that in the course of his travels he had seen a phœnix ; and
he obligingly undeceived us of the vulgar error, that there is
but one of that species at a time, assuring us that they were
not uncommon in some parts of Upper Egypt.   Hitherto
he had found the most implicit listeners.   His dreaming
fancies had transported us beyond the ' ignorant present '.
But when (still hardying more and more in his triumphs
over our simplicity) he went on to affirm that he had

[1] unseasoned] unfledged 1823.   [2] Aldermanbury, or Watling-street]
Thames or Tooley-street 1823.

actually sailed through the legs of the Colossus at Rhodes, it really became necessary to make a stand. And here I must do justice to the good sense and intrepidity of one of our party, a youth, that had hitherto been one of his most deferential auditors, who, from his recent reading, made bold to assure the gentleman, that there must be some mistake, as ' the Colossus in question had been destroyed long since ' : to whose opinion, delivered with all modesty, our hero was obliging enough to concede thus much, that ' the figure was indeed a little damaged '. This was the only opposition he met with, and it did not at all seem to stagger him, for he proceeded with his fables, which the same youth appeared to swallow with still more complacency than ever,—confirmed, as it were, by the extreme candour of that concession. With these prodigies he wheedled us on till we came in sight of the Reculvers, which one of our own company (having been the voyage before) immediately recognising, and pointing out to us, was considered by us as no ordinary seaman.

All this time sat upon the edge of the deck quite a different character. It was a lad, apparently very poor, very infirm, and very patient. His eye was ever on the sea, with a smile : and, if he caught now and then some snatches of these wild legends, it was by accident, and they seemed not to concern him. The waves to him whispered more pleasant stories. He was as one, being with us, but not of us. He heard the bell of dinner ring without stirring ; and when some of us pulled out our private stores—our cold meat and our salads —he produced none, and seemed to want none. Only a solitary biscuit he had laid in ; provision for the one or two days and nights, to which these vessels then were oftentimes obliged to prolong their voyage. Upon a nearer acquaintance with him, which he seemed neither to court nor decline, we learned that he was going to Margate, with the hope of being admitted into the Infirmary there for sea-bathing. His disease was a scrofula, which appeared to have eaten all over him. He expressed great hopes of a cure ; and when we asked him, whether he had any friends where he was going, he replied, ' he *had* no friends.'

These pleasant, and some mournful passages, with the first sight of the sea, co-operating with youth, and a sense

of holydays, and out-of-door adventure, to me that had
been pent up in populous cities for many months before,—
have left upon my mind the fragrance as of summer days
gone by, bequeathing nothing but their remembrance for
cold and wintry hours to chew upon.

Will it be thought a digression (it may spare some unwelcome comparisons), if I endeavour to account for the
dissatisfaction which I have heard so many persons confess
to have felt (as I did myself feel in part on this occasion),
at the sight of the sea for the first time ? I think the reason
usually given—referring to the incapacity of actual objects
for satisfying our preconceptions of them—scarcely goes
deep enough into the question. Let the same person see
a lion, an elephant, a mountain, for the first time in his
life, and he shall perhaps feel himself a little mortified.
The things do not fill up that space, which the idea of them
seemed to take up in his mind. But they have still a correspondency to his first notion, and in time grow up to it,
so as to produce a very similar impression : enlarging
themselves (if I may say so) upon familiarity. But the sea
remains a disappointment.—Is it not, that in *the latter* we
had expected to behold (absurdly, I grant, but, I am afraid,
by the law of imagination unavoidably) not a definite object,
as those wild beasts, or that mountain compassable by the
eye, but *all the sea at once*, THE COMMENSURATE ANTAGONIST
OF THE EARTH ! I do not say we tell ourselves so much,
but the craving of the mind is to be satisfied with nothing
less. I will suppose the case of a young person of fifteen
(as I then was) knowing nothing of the sea, but from
description. He comes to it for the first time—all that he
has been reading of it all his life, and *that* the most enthusi-
astic part of life,—all he has gathered from narratives of
wandering seamen ; what he has gained from true voyages,
and what he cherishes as credulously from romance and
poetry ; crowding their images, and exacting strange
tributes from expectation.—He thinks of the great deep,
and of those who go down into it ; of its thousand isles,
and of the vast continents it washes ; of its receiving the
mighty Plata, or Orellana, into its bosom, without disturbance, or sense of augmentation ; of Biscay swells, and
the mariner

For many a day, and many a dreadful night,
Incessant labouring round the stormy Cape ;

of fatal rocks, and the ' still-vexed Bermoothes ' ; of great
whirlpools, and the water-spout ; of sunken ships, and
sumless treasures swallowed up in the unrestoring depths:
of fishes and quaint monsters, to which all that is terrible
on earth—

Be but as buggs to frighten babes withal,
Compared with the creatures in the sea's entral ;

of naked savages, and Juan Fernandez ; of pearls, and
shells ; of coral beds, and of enchanted isles ; of mermaids'
grots—

I do not assert that in sober earnest he expects to be shown
all these wonders at once, but he is under the tyranny of
a mighty faculty, which haunts him with confused hints
and shadows of all these ; and when the actual object
opens first upon him, seen (in tame weather too most likely)
from our unromantic coasts—a speck, a slip of sea-water as
it shows to him—what can it prove but a very unsatisfying
and even diminutive entertainment ?   Or if he has come
to it from the mouth of a river, was it much more than the
river widening ? and, even out of sight of land, what had
he but a flat watery horizon about him, nothing comparable
to the vast o'er-curtaining sky, his familiar object, seen
daily without dread or amazement ?—Who, in similar
circumstances, has not been tempted to exclaim with
Charoba, in the poem of Gebir,—

Is this the mighty ocean ?—is this *all ?*

I love town, or country ; but this detestable Cinque
Port is neither.   I hate these scrubbed shoots, thrusting out
their starved foliage from between the horrid fissures of
dusty innutritious rocks ; which the amateur calls ' verdure
to the edge of the sea '.   I require woods, and they show
me stunted coppices.   I cry out for the water-brooks, and
pant for fresh streams, and inland murmurs.   I cannot
stand all day on the naked beach, watching the capricious
hues of the sea, shifting like the colours of a dying mullet.
I am tired of looking out at the windows of this island-
prison.   I would fain retire into the interior of my cage.
While I gaze upon the sea, I want to be on it, over it, across

it. It binds me in with chains, as of iron. My thoughts are abroad. I should not so feel in Staffordshire. There is no home for me here. There is no sense of home at Hastings. It is a place of fugitive resort, an heterogeneous assemblage of sea-mews and stock-brokers, Amphitrites of the town, and misses that coquet with the Ocean. If it were what it was in its primitive shape, and what it ought to have remained, a fair honest fishing town, and no more, it were something—with a few straggling fishermen's huts scattered about, artless as its cliffs, and with their materials filched from them, it were something. I could abide to dwell with Meschek ; to assort with fisher-swains, and smugglers. There are, or I dream there are, many of this latter occupation here. Their faces become the place. I like a smuggler. He is the only honest thief. He robs nothing but the revenue,—an abstraction I never greatly cared about. I could go out with them in their mackarel boats, or about their less ostensible business, with some satisfaction. I can even tolerate those poor victims to monotony, who from day to day pace along the beach, in endless progress and recurrence, to watch their illicit countrymen—townsfolk or brethren perchance—whistling to the sheathing and unsheathing of their cutlasses (their only solace), who under the mild name of preventive service, keep up a legitimated civil warfare in the deplorable absence of a foreign one, to show their detestation of run hollands, and zeal for old England. But it is the visitants from town, that come here to *say* that they have been here, with no more relish of the sea than a pond perch, or a dace might be supposed to have, that are my aversion. I feel like a foolish dace in these regions, and have as little toleration for myself here, as for them. What can they want here ? if they had a true relish of the ocean, why have they brought all this land luggage with them ? or why pitch their civilised tents in the desert ? What mean these scanty book-rooms—marine libraries as they entitle them— if the sea were, as they would have us believe, a book ' to read strange matter in ' ? what are their foolish concert-rooms, if they come, as they would fain be thought to do, to listen to the music of the waves ? All is false and hollow pretension. They come, because it is the fashion, and to spoil the nature of the place. They are mostly, as I have said, stockbrokers; but I have watched the better sort of them—now and then, an honest citizen (of the old stamp), in the simplicity of his heart, shall bring down his wife and daughters, to taste the sea breezes. I always know the date of their arrival. It is easy to see it in their countenance. A day or two they go wandering on the shingles, picking up cockle-shells, and thinking them great things; but, in a poor week, imagination slackens: they begin to discover that cockles produce no pearls, and then—O then!—if I could interpret for the pretty creatures (I know they have not the courage to confess it themselves) how gladly would they exchange their sea-side rambles for a Sunday walk on the green-sward of their accustomed Twickenham meadows!

I would ask of one of these sea-charmed emigrants, who think they truly love the sea, with its wild usages, what would their feelings be, if some of the unsophisticated aborigines of this place, encouraged by their courteous questionings here, should venture, on the faith of such assured sympathy between them, to return the visit, and come up to see—London. I must imagine them with their fishing tackle on their back, as we carry our town necessaries. What a sensation would it cause in Lothbury? What vehement laughter would it not excite among

> The daughters of Cheapside, and wives of Lombard-street.

I am sure that no town-bred, or inland-born subjects, can feel their true and natural nourishment at these sea-places. Nature, where she does not mean us for mariners and vagabonds, bids us stay at home. The salt foam seems to nourish a spleen. I am not half so good-natured as by the milder waters of my natural river. I would exchange these sea-gulls for swans, and scud a swallow for ever about the banks of Thamesis.

THE CONVALESCENT ✓

[Printed in *The London Magazine*, *New Series*, vol. ii, no. vii, p. 376 (July, 1825). Collected in *The Last Essays of Elia*, 1833. Text of 1833.]

A PRETTY severe fit of indisposition which, under the name of a nervous fever, has made a prisoner of me for some weeks past, and is but slowly leaving me, has reduced me to an incapacity of reflecting upon any topic foreign to itself. Expect no healthy conclusions from me this month, reader ; I can offer you only sick men's dreams.

And truly the whole state of sickness is such ; for what else is it but a magnificent dream for a man to lie a-bed, and draw day-light curtains about him ; and, shutting out the sun, to induce a total oblivion of all the works which are going on under it ? To become insensible to all the operations of life, except the beatings of one feeble pulse ?

If there be a regal solitude, it is a sick bed. How the patient lords it there ! what caprices he acts without controul ! how king-like he sways his pillow—tumbling, and tossing, and shifting, and lowering, and thumping, and flatting, and moulding it, to the ever varying requisitions of his throbbing temples.

He changes *sides* oftener than a politician. Now he lies full length, then half-length, obliquely, transversely, head and feet quite across the bed ; and none accuses him of tergiversation. Within the four curtains he is absolute. They are his Mare Clausum.

How sickness enlarges the dimensions of a man's self to himself ! he is his own exclusive object. Supreme selfishness is inculcated upon him as his only duty. 'Tis the Two Tables of the Law to him. He has nothing to think of but how to get well. What passes out of doors, or within them, so he hear not the jarring of them, affects him not.

A little while ago he was greatly concerned in the event of a law-suit, which was to be the making or the marring of his dearest friend. He was to be seen trudging about upon this man's errand to fifty quarters of the town at once, jogging this witness, refreshing that solicitor. The cause was to come on yesterday. He is absolutely as indifferent to the decision, as if it were a question to be tried at Pekin. Peradventure from some whispering, going on about the house, not intended for his hearing, he picks up enough to make him understand, that things went cross-grained in the Court yesterday, and his friend is ruined. But the word 'friend', and the word 'ruin', disturb him no more than so much jargon. He is not to think of anything but how to get better.

What a world of foreign cares are merged in that absorbing consideration !

He has put on the strong armour of sickness, he is wrapped in the callous hide of suffering; he keeps his sympathy, like some curious vintage, under trusty lock and key, for his own use only.

He lies pitying himself, honing and moaning to himself; he yearneth over himself; his bowels are even melted within him, to think what he suffers; he is not ashamed to weep over himself.

He is for ever plotting how to do some good to himself; studying little stratagems and artificial alleviations.

He makes the most of himself; dividing himself, by an allowable fiction, into as many distinct individuals, as he hath sore and sorrowing members. Sometimes he meditates—as of a thing apart from him—upon his poor aching head, and that dull pain which, dozing or waking, lay in it all the past night like a log, or palpable substance of pain, not to be removed without opening the very scull, as it seemed, to take it thence. Or he pities his long, clammy, attenuated fingers. He compassionates himself all over; and his bed is a very discipline of humanity, and tender heart.

He is his own sympathiser; and instinctively feels that none can so well perform that office for him. He cares for few spectators to his tragedy. Only that punctual face of the old nurse pleases him, that announces his broths, and his cordials. He likes it because it is so unmoved, and because he can pour forth his feverish ejaculations before it as unreservedly as to his bed-post.

To the world's business he is dead. He understands

not what the callings and occupations of mortals are ; only
he has a glimmering conceit of some such thing, when the
doctor makes his daily call : and even in the lines of that
busy face he reads no multiplicity of patients, but solely
conceives of himself as *the sick man.* To what other uneasy
couch the good man is hastening, when he slips out of his
chamber, folding up his thin douceur so carefully for fear
of rustling—is no speculation which he can at present
entertain. He thinks only of the regular return of the
same phenomenon at the same hour to-morrow.

Household rumours touch him not. Some faint murmur,
indicative of life going on within the house, soothes him,
while he knows not distinctly what it is. He is not to know
any thing, not to think of any thing. Servants gliding up
or down the distant staircase, treading as upon velvet,
gently keep his ear awake, so long as he troubles not himself further than with some feeble guess at their errands.

Exacter knowledge would be a burthen to him : he can
just endure the pressure of conjecture. He opens his eye
faintly at the dull stroke of the muffled knocker, and
closes it again without asking ' who was it ? ' He is
flattered by a general notion that inquiries are making
after him, but he cares not to know the name of the inquirer.
In the general stillness, and awful hush of the house, he
lies in state, and feels his sovereignty.

To be sick is to enjoy monarchal prerogatives. Compare
the silent tread, and quiet ministry, almost by the eye
only, with which he is served—with the careless demeanour,
the unceremonious goings in and out (slapping of doors,
or [1]leaving them open) of the very same attendants, when
he is getting a little better—and you will confess, that from
the bed of sickness (throne let me rather call it) to the
elbow chair of convalescence, is a fall from dignity, amounting to a deposition.

How convalescence shrinks a man back to his pristine
stature ! where is now the space, which he occupied so
lately, in his own, in the family's eye ? The scene of his
regalities, his sick room, which was his presence chamber,
where he lay and acted his despotic fancies—how is it
reduced to a common bed-room ! The trimness of the very

[1] leaving] leaving of 1825.

bed has something petty and unmeaning about it. It is
made every day. How unlike to that wavy, many-fur-
rowed, oceanic surface, which it presented so short a time
since, when to *make* it was a service not to be thought of
at oftener than three or four day revolutions, when the
patient was with pain and grief to be lifted for a little while
out of it, to submit to the encroachments of unwelcome
neatness, and decencies which his shaken frame deprecated;
then to be lifted into it again, for another three or four
days' respite, to flounder it out of shape again, while every
fresh furrow was a historical record of some shifting posture,
some uneasy turning, some seeking for a little ease; and the
shrunken skin scarce told a truer story than the crumpled
coverlid.

Hushed are those mysterious sighs—those groans—so
much more awful, while we knew not from what caverns
of vast hidden suffering they proceeded. The Lernean
pangs are quenched. The riddle of sickness is solved; and
Philoctetes is become an ordinary personage.

Perhaps some relic of the sick man's dream of greatness
survives in the still lingering visitations of the medical
attendant. But how is he too changed with every thing
else! Can this be he—this man of news—of chat—of
anecdote—of every thing but physic—can this be he, who
so lately came between the patient and his cruel enemy,
as on some solemn embassy from Nature, erecting herself
into a high mediating party?—Pshaw! 'tis some old
woman.

Farewell with him all that made sickness pompous—the
spell that hushed the household—the desart-like stillness,
felt throughout its inmost chambers—the mute attendance
—the inquiry by looks—the still softer delicacies of self-
attention—the sole and single eye of distemper alonely
fixed upon itself—world-thoughts excluded—the man a
world unto himself—his own theatre—

What a speck is he dwindled into!

In this flat swamp of convalescence, left by the ebb of
sickness, yet far enough from the terra firma of established health, your note, dear Editor, reached me, requesting
—an article. In Articulo Mortis, thought I; but it is

something hard—and the quibble, wretched as it was,
relieved me. The summons, unseasonable as it appeared,
seemed to link me on again to the petty businesses of life,
which I had lost sight of ; a gentle call to activity, however
trivial ; a wholesome weaning from that preposterous
dream of self-absorption—the puffy state of sickness—in
which I confess to have lain so long, insensible to the
magazines, and monarchies, of the world alike; to its laws,
and to its literature. The hypochondriac flatus is subsiding ; the acres, which in imagination I had spread
over—for the sick man swells in the sole contemplation
of his single sufferings, till he becomes a Tityus to himself—
are wasting to a span ; and for the giant of self-importance,
which I was so lately, you have me once again in my
natural pretensions—the lean and meagre figure of your
insignificant [1]Essayist.

SANITY OF TRUE GENIUS

[Printed under the title *Popular Fallacies : * xvi.—*That great Wit is
allied to Madness*, in *The New Monthly Magazine*, May, 1826, p. 159.
Collected in *The Last Essays of Elia*, 1833. Text of 1833.]

[2]So far from the position holding true, that great wit
(or genius, in our modern way of speaking), has a necessary
alliance with insanity, the greatest wits, on the contrary,
will ever be found to be the sanest writers. It is impossible
for the mind to conceive of a mad Shakspeare. The
greatness of wit, by which the poetic talent is here chiefly
to be understood, manifests itself in the admirable balance
of all the faculties. Madness is the disproportionate
straining or excess of any one of them. 'So strong a wit',
says Cowley, speaking of a poetical friend,

> '——did Nature to him frame,
> As all things but his judgment overcame,
> His judgment like the heavenly moon did show,
> Tempering that mighty sea below.'

The ground of the [3]mistake is, that men, finding in the

---

[1] Essayist] contributor 1825.　　[2] So far . . . will ever] So far
from this being true, the greatest wits will ever 1826.　　[3] mistake]
fallacy 1826.

raptures of the higher poetry a condition of exaltation, to
which they have no parallel in their own experience, besides
the spurious resemblance of it in dreams and fevers, impute
a state of dreaminess and fever to the poet. But the true
poet dreams being awake. He is not possessed by his
subject, but has dominion over it. In the groves of Eden
he walks familiar as in his native paths. He ascends the
empyrean heaven, and is not intoxicated. He treads the
burning marl without dismay; he wins his flight without
self-loss through realms of chaos 'and old night'. Or if,
abandoning himself to that severer chaos of a 'human
mind untuned', he is content awhile to be mad with Lear,
or to hate mankind (a sort of madness) with Timon, neither
is that madness, nor this misanthropy, so unchecked, but
that,—never letting the reins of reason wholly go, while
most he seems to do so,—he has his better genius still
whispering at his ear, with the good servant Kent suggest-
ing saner counsels, or with the honest steward Flavius
recommending kindlier resolutions. Where he seems most
to recede from humanity, he will be found the truest to it.
From beyond the scope of Nature if he summon possible
existences, he subjugates them to the law of her consistency.
He is beautifully loyal to that sovereign directress, even
when he appears most to betray and desert her. His
ideal tribes submit to policy ; his very monsters are tamed
to his hand, even as that wild sea-brood, shepherded by
Proteus. He tames, and he clothes them with attributes
of flesh and blood, till they wonder at themselves, like
Indian Islanders forced to submit to European vesture.
Caliban, the Witches, are as true to the laws of their own
nature (ours with a difference), as Othello, Hamlet, and
Macbeth. Herein the great and the little wits are differenced ; that if the latter wander ever so little from nature
or actual existence, they lose themselves, and their readers.
Their phantoms are lawless ; their visions nightmares.
They do not create, which implies shaping and consistency.
Their imaginations are not active—for to be active is to
call something into act and form—but passive, as men in
sick dreams. For the super-natural, or something superadded to what we know of nature, they give you the plainly
non-natural. And if this were all, and that these mental

hallucinations were discoverable only in the treatment of
subjects out of nature, or transcending it, the judgment
might with some plea be pardoned if it ran riot, and a
little wantonized : but even in the describing of real and
every day life, that which is before their eyes, one of these
lesser wits shall more deviate from nature—show more of
that inconsequence, which has a natural alliance with
frenzy,—than a great genius in his 'maddest fits', as
Withers somewhere calls them. We appeal to any one
that is acquainted with the common run of Lane's novels,—
as they existed some twenty or thirty years back,—those
scanty intellectual viands of the whole female reading
public, till a happier genius arose, and expelled for ever
the innutritious phantoms,—whether he has not found his
brain more 'betossed', his memory more puzzled, his
sense of when and where more confounded, among the
improbable events, the incoherent incidents, the inconsistent characters, or no-characters, of some third-rate
love intrigue—where the persons shall be a Lord Glendamour
and a Miss Rivers, and the scene only alternate between
Bath and Bond-street—a more bewildering dreaminess
induced upon him, than he has felt wandering over all
the fairy grounds of Spenser. In the productions we refer
to, nothing but names and places is familiar ; the persons
are neither of this world nor of any other conceivable one ;
an endless string of activities without purpose, of purposes
destitute of motive :—we meet phantoms in our known
walks ; *fantasques* only christened. In the poet we have
names which announce fiction ; and we have absolutely no
place at all, for the things and persons of the Fairy Queen
prate not of their 'whereabout'. But in their inner nature,
and the law of their speech and actions, we are at home
and upon acquainted ground. The one turns life into
a dream ; the other to the wildest dreams gives the
sobrieties of every day occurrences. By what subtile art
of tracing the mental processes it is effected, we are not
philosophers enough to explain, but in that wonderful
episode of the cave of Mammon, in which the Money God
appears first in the lowest form of a miser, is then a worker
of metals, and becomes the god of all the treasures of the
world ; and has a daughter, Ambition, before whom all

the world kneels for favours—with the Hesperian fruit, the waters of Tantalus, with Pilate washing his hands vainly, but not impertinently, in the same stream—that we should be at one moment in the cave of an old hoarder of treasures, at the next at the forge of the Cyclops, in a palace and yet in hell, all at once, with the shifting mutations of the most rambling dream, and our judgment yet all the time awake, and neither able nor willing to detect the fallacy,—is a proof of that hidden sanity which still guides the poet in his widest seeming-aberrations.

It is not enough to say that the whole episode is a copy of the mind's conceptions in sleep ; it is, in some sort— but what a copy ! Let the most romantic of us, that has been entertained all night with the spectacle of some wild and magnificent vision, recombine it in the morning, and try it by his waking judgment. That which appeared so shifting, and yet so coherent, while that faculty was passive, when it comes under cool examination, shall appear so reasonless and so unlinked, that we are ashamed to have been so deluded ; and to have taken, though but in sleep, a monster for a god. But the transitions in this episode are every whit as violent as in the most extra-vagant dream, and yet the waking judgment ratifies them.

CAPTAIN JACKSON ✓

[Printed in *The London Magazine*, vol. x, no. lix, p. 481 (Nov., 1824). Collected in *The Last Essays of Elia*, 1833. Text of 1833.]

AMONG the deaths in our obituary for this month, I observe with concern ' At his cottage on the Bath road, Captain Jackson '. The name and attribution are common enough ; but a feeling like reproach persuades me, that this could have been no other in fact than my dear old friend, who some five-and-twenty years ago rented a tene-ment, which he was pleased to dignify with the appellation here used, about a mile from Westbourn Green. Alack, how good men, and the good turns they do us, slide out of memory, and are recalled but by the surprise of

some such sad memento as that which now lies before
[1]us !

He whom I mean was a retired half-pay officer, with a
wife and two grown-up daughters, whom he maintained
with the port and notions of gentlewomen upon that
slender professional allowance. Comely girls they were
too.

And was I in danger of forgetting this man ?—his cheerful suppers—the noble tone of hospitality, when first you
set your foot in *the cottage*—the anxious ministerings about
you, where little or nothing (God knows) was to be minis-
tered.—Althea's horn in a poor platter—the power of
self-enchantment, by which, in his magnificent wishes to
entertain you, he multiplied his means to bounties.

You saw with your bodily eyes indeed what seemed
a bare scrag—cold savings from the foregone meal—
remnant hardly sufficient to send a mendicant from the
door contented. But in the copious will—the revelling
imagination of your host—the 'mind, the mind, Master
Shallow', whole beeves were spread before you—hecatombs
—no end appeared to the profusion.

It was the widow's cruse—the loaves and fishes ; carving
could not lessen nor helping diminish it—the stamina were
left—the elemental bone still flourished, divested of its
accidents.

'Let us live while we can,' methinks I hear the open-
handed creature exclaim ; 'while we have, let us not want,'
'here is plenty left ;' 'want for nothing'—with many
more such hospitable sayings, the spurs of appetite, and
old concomitants of smoking boards, and feast-oppressed
chargers.   Then sliding a slender ratio of Single Gloucester
upon his wife's plate, or the daughter's, he would convey
the remanent rind into his own, with a merry quirk of
'the nearer the bone', &c., and declaring that he universally preferred the outside.   For we had our table distinctions, you are to know, and some of us in a manner sate
above the salt.   None but his guest or guests dreamed of
tasting flesh luxuries at night, the fragments were *verè
hospitibus sacra*.   But of one thing or another there was

---

[1] us] me 1824.

always enough, and leavings : only he would sometimes finish the remainder crust, to show that he wished no savings.

Wine he had none ; nor, except on very rare occasions, spirits ; but the sensation of wine was there. Some thin kind of ale I remember—'British beverage,' he would say ! 'Push about, my boys ; ' 'Drink to your sweethearts, girls.' At every meagre draught a toast must ensue, or a song. All the forms of good liquor were there, with none of the effects wanting. Shut your eyes, and you would swear a capacious bowl of punch was foaming in the centre, with beams of generous Port or Madeira radiating to it from each of the table corners. You got flustered, without knowing whence ; tipsy upon words ; and reeled under the potency of his unperforming Bacchanalian encouragements.

We had our songs—'Why, Soldiers, Why'—and the 'British Grenadiers'—in which last we were all obliged to bear chorus. Both the daughters sang. Their proficiency was a nightly theme—the masters he had given them—the 'no-expence' which he spared to accomplish them in a science 'so necessary to young women'. But then—they could not sing 'without the instrument'.

Sacred, and by me, never-to-be violated, Secrets of Poverty ! Should I disclose your honest aims at grandeur, your makeshift efforts of magnificence ? Sleep, sleep, with all thy broken keys, if one of the bunch be extant ; thrummed by a thousand ancestral thumbs ; dear, cracked spinnet of dearer Louisa ! Without mention of mine, be dumb, thou thin accompanier of her thinner warble ! A veil be spread over the dear delighted face of the well-deluded father, who now haply listening to cherubic notes, scarce feels sincerer pleasure than when she awakened thy time-shaken chords responsive to the twitterings of that slender image of a voice.

We were not without our literary talk either. It did not extend far, but as far as it went, it was good. It was bottomed well ; had good grounds to go upon. In *the cottage* was a room, which tradition authenticated to have been the same in which Glover, in his occasional retirements, had penned the greater part of his Leonidas. This

E 2

circumstance was nightly quoted, though none of the present inmates, that I could discover, appeared ever to have met with the poem in question. But that was no matter. Glover had written there, and the anecdote was pressed into the account of the family importance. It diffused a learned air through the apartment, the little side casement of which (the poet's study window), opening upon a superb view as far as to the pretty spire of Harrow, over domains and patrimonial acres, not a rood nor square yard whereof our host could call his own, yet gave occasion to an immoderate expansion of—vanity shall I call it ?—in his bosom, as he showed them in a glowing summer evening. It was all his, he took it all in, and communicated rich portions of it to his guests. It was a part of his largess, his hospitality ; it was going over his grounds ; he was lord for the time of showing them, and you the implicit lookers-up to his magnificence.

He was a juggler, who threw mists before your eyes— you had no time to detect his fallacies. He would say ' hand me the *silver* sugar tongs ' ; and, before you could discover it was a single spoon, and that *plated*, he would disturb and captivate your imagination by a misnomer of ' the urn ' for a tea kettle ; or by calling a homely bench a sofa. Rich men direct you to their furniture, poor ones divert you from it ; he neither did one nor the other, but by simply assuming that everything was handsome about him, you were positively at a demur what you did, or did not see, at *the cottage*. With nothing to live on, he seemed to live on everything. He had a stock of wealth in his mind ; not that which is properly termed *Content*, for in truth he was not to be *contained* at all, but overflowed all bounds by the force of a magnificent self-delusion.

Enthusiasm is catching ; and even his wife, a sober native of North Britain, who generally saw things more as they were, was not proof against the continual collision of his credulity. Her daughters were rational and discreet young women ; in the main, perhaps, not insensible to their true circumstances. I have seen them assume a thoughtful air at times. But such was the preponderating opulence of his fancy, that I am persuaded, not for any half hour together, did they ever look their own prospects fairly in the face. There was no resisting the vortex of his temperament. His riotous imagination conjured up handsome settlements before their eyes, which kept them up in the eye of the world too, and seem at last to have realised themselves ; for they both have married since, I am told, more than respectably.

It is long since, and my memory waxes dim on some subjects, or I should wish to convey some notion of the manner in which the pleasant creature described the circumstances of his own wedding-day. I faintly remember something of a chaise and four, in which he made his entry into Glasgow on that morning to fetch the bride home, or carry her thither, I forget which. It so completely made out the stanza of the old ballad—

> When we came down through Glasgow town,
> We were a comely sight to see ;
> My love was clad in black velvet,
> And I myself in cramasie.

I suppose it was the only occasion upon which his own actual splendour at all corresponded with the world's notions on that subject. In homely cart, or travelling caravan, by whatever humble vehicle they chanced to be transported in less prosperous days, the ride through Glasgow came back upon his fancy, not as a humiliating contrast, but as a fair occasion for reverting to that one day's state. It seemed an ' equipage etern ' from which no power of fate or fortune, once mounted, had power thereafter to dislodge him.

There is some merit in putting a handsome face upon indigent circumstances. To bully and swagger away the sense of them before strangers, may be not always discommendable. Tibbs, and Bobadil, even when detected, have more of our admiration than contempt. But for a man to put the cheat upon himself ; to play the Bobadil at home ; and, steeped in poverty up to the lips, to fancy himself all the while chin-deep in riches, is a strain of constitutional philosophy, and a mastery over fortune, which was reserved for my old friend Captain Jackson.

THE SUPERANNUATED MAN

[Printed in two parts in *The London Magazine, New Series*, vol. ii, no. v, p. 67 (May, 1825). Collected in *The Last Essays of Elia*, 1833. Text of 1833.]

> Sera tamen respexit
> Libertas.   VIRGIL.

> A Clerk I was in London gay.
>   O'KEEFE.

IF peradventure, Reader, it has been thy lot to waste the golden years of thy life—thy shining youth—in the irksome confinement of an office ; to have thy prison days prolonged through middle age down to decrepitude and silver hairs, without hope of release or respite ; to have lived to forget that there are such things as holidays, or to remember them but as the prerogatives of childhood ; then, and then only, will you be able to appreciate my deliverance.

It is now six and thirty years since I took my seat at the desk in Mincing-lane. Melancholy was the transition at fourteen from the abundant play-time, and the frequently-intervening vacations of school days, to the eight, nine, and sometimes ten hours' a-day attendance at a counting-house. But time partially reconciles us to anything. I gradually became content—doggedly contented, as wild animals in cages.

It is true I had my Sundays to myself ; but Sundays, admirable as the institution of them is for purposes of worship, are for that very reason the very worst adapted for days of unbending and [1]recreation. In particular, there is a gloom for me attendant upon a city Sunday, a weight in the air. I miss the cheerful cries of London, the music, and the ballad-singers—the buzz and stirring murmur of the streets. Those eternal bells depress me. The closed shops repel me. Prints, pictures, all the glittering and endless succession of knacks and gewgaws, and ostentatiously displayed wares of tradesmen, which make a week-day saunter through the less busy parts of the metropolis so delightful—are shut out. No book-stalls deliciously to idle over—No busy faces to recreate the

[1] *For a footnote here in the* L. M. *see Editor's Notes.*

THE SUPERANNUATED MAN

55

idle man who contemplates them ever passing by—the very face of business a charm by contrast to his temporary relaxation from it. Nothing to be seen but unhappy countenances—or half-happy at best—of emancipated 'prentices and little tradesfolks, with here and there a servant maid that has got leave to go out, who, slaving all the week, with the habit has lost almost the capacity of enjoying a free hour ; and livelily expressing the hollowness of a day's pleasuring. The very strollers in the fields on that day look anything but comfortable.

But besides Sundays I had a day at Easter, and a day at Christmas, with a full week in the summer to go and air myself in my native fields of Hertfordshire. This last was a great indulgence ; and the prospect of its recurrence, I believe, alone kept me up through the year, and made my durance tolerable. But when the week came round, did the glittering phantom of the distance keep touch with me ? or rather was it not a series of seven uneasy days, spent in restless pursuit of pleasure, and a wearisome anxiety to find out how to make the most of them ? Where was the quiet, where the promised rest ? Before I had a taste of it, it was vanished. I was at the desk again, counting upon the fifty-one tedious weeks that must intervene before such another snatch would come. Still the prospect of its coming threw something of an illumination upon the darker side of my captivity. Without it, as I have said, I could scarcely have sustained my thraldom.

Independently of the rigours of attendance, I have ever been haunted with a sense (perhaps a mere caprice) of incapacity for business. This, during my latter years, had increased to such a degree, that it was visible in all the lines of my countenance. My health and my good spirits flagged. I had perpetually a dread of some crisis, to which I should be found unequal. Besides my daylight servitude, I served over again all night in my sleep, and would awake with terrors of imaginary false entries, errors in my accounts, and the like. I was fifty years of age, and no prospect of emancipation presented itself. I had grown to my desk, as it were ; and the wood had entered into my soul.

My fellows in the office would sometimes rally me upon

the trouble legible in my countenance ; but I did not know that it had raised the suspicions of any of my employers, when, on the 5th of last month, a day ever to be remembered by me, L——, the junior partner in the firm, calling me on one side, directly taxed me with my bad looks, and frankly inquired the cause of them. So taxed, I honestly made confession of my infirmity, and added that I was afraid I should eventually be obliged to resign his service. He spoke some words of course to hearten me, and there the matter rested. A whole week I remained labouring under the impression that I had acted imprudently in my disclosure ; that I had foolishly given a handle against myself, and had been anticipating my own dismissal. A week passed in this manner, the most anxious one, I verily believe, in my whole life, when on the evening of the 12th of April, just as I was about quitting my desk to go home (it might be about eight o'clock) I received an awful summons to attend the presence of the whole assembled firm in the formidable back parlour. I thought, now my time is surely come, I have done for myself, I am going to be told that they have no longer occasion for me. L——, I could see, smiled at the terror I was in, which was a little relief to me,—when to my utter astonishment B——, the eldest partner, began a formal harangue to me on the length of my services, my very meritorious conduct during the whole of the time (the deuce, thought I, how did he find out that ? I protest I never had the confidence to think as much). He went on to descant on the expediency of retiring at a certain time of life (how my heart panted !) and asking me a few questions as to the amount of my own property, of which I have a little, ended with a proposal, to which his three partners nodded a grave assent, that I should accept from the house, which I had served so well, a pension for life to the amount of two-thirds of my accustomed salary—a magnificent offer ! I do not know what I answered between surprise and gratitude, but it was understood that I accepted their proposal, and I was told that I was free from that hour to leave their service. I stammered out a bow, and at just ten minutes after eight I went home—for ever. This noble benefit—gratitude forbids me to conceal their names

—I owe to the kindness of the most munificent firm in the world—the house of Boldero, Merryweather, Bosanquet and Lacy.

Esto perpetua !

For the first day or two I felt stunned, overwhelmed. I could only apprehend my felicity ; I was too confused to taste it sincerely. I wandered about, thinking I was happy, and knowing that I was not. I was in the condition of a prisoner in the old Bastile, suddenly let loose after a forty years' confinement. I could scarce trust myself with myself. It was like passing out of Time into Eternity—for it is a sort of Eternity for a man to have his Time all to himself. It seemed to me that I had more time on my hands than I could ever manage. From a poor man, poor in Time, I was suddenly lifted up into a vast revenue ; I could see no end of my possessions ; I wanted some steward, or judicious bailiff, to manage my estates in Time for me. And here let me caution persons grown old in active business, not lightly, nor without weighing their own resources, to forego their customary employment all at once, for there may be danger in it. I feel it by myself, but I know that my resources are sufficient ; and now that those first giddy raptures have subsided, I have a quiet home-feeling of the blessedness of my condition. I am in no hurry. Having all holidays, I am as though I had none. If Time hung heavy upon me, I could walk it away ; but I do *not* walk all day long, as I used to do in those old transient holidays, thirty miles a day, to make the most of them. If Time were troublesome, I could read it away, but I do *not* read in that violent measure, with which, having no Time my own but candle-light Time, I used to weary out my head and eyesight in by-gone winters. I walk, read or scribble (as now) just when the fit seizes me. I no longer hunt after pleasure ; I let it come to me. I am like the man

> ————That's born, and has his years come to him,
> In some green desart.

'Years,' you will say ! 'what is this superannuated simpleton calculating upon ? He has already told us, he is past fifty.'

I have indeed lived nominally fifty years, but deduct
out of them the hours which I have lived to other people,
and not to myself, and you will find me still a young fellow.
For *that* is the only true Time, which a man can properly
call his own, that which he has all to himself ; the rest,
though in some sense he may be said to live it, is other
people's time, not his. The remnant of my poor days,
long or short, is at least multiplied for me three-fold. My
ten next years, if I stretch so far, will be as long as any
preceding thirty. 'Tis a fair rule-of-three sum.

Among the strange fantasies which beset me at the
commencement of my freedom, and of which all traces
are not yet gone, one was, that a vast tract of time had
intervened since I quitted the Counting House. I could
not conceive of it as an affair of yesterday. The partners,
and the clerks, with whom I had for so many years, and
for so many hours in each day of the year, been closely
associated—being suddenly removed from them—they
seemed as dead to me. There is a fine passage, which
may serve to illustrate this fancy, in a Tragedy by Sir
Robert Howard, speaking of a friend's death :

> ————'Twas but just now he went away ;
> I have not since had time to shed a tear ;
> And yet the distance does the same appear
> As if he had been a thousand years from me.
> Time takes no measure in Eternity.

To dissipate this awkward feeling, I have been fain to
go among them once or twice since ; to visit my old desk-
fellows—my co-brethren of the quill—that I had left
below in the state militant. Not all the kindness with
which they received me could quite restore to me that
pleasant familiarity, which I had heretofore enjoyed among
them. We cracked some of our old jokes, but methought
they went off but faintly. My old desk ; the peg where
I hung my hat, were appropriated to another. I knew
it must be, but I could not take it kindly. D——l take
me, if I did not feel some remorse—beast, if I had not,—at
quitting my old compeers, the faithful partners of my toils
for six and thirty years, that smoothed for me with their
jokes [1]and conundrums the ruggedness of my professional

[1] and] and their 1825.

road. Had it been so rugged then after all ? or was
I a coward simply ? Well, it is too late to repent ; and
I also know, that these suggestions are a common fallacy
of the mind on such occasions. But my heart smote me.
I had violently broken the bands betwixt us. It was at
least not courteous. I shall be some time before I get
quite reconciled to the separation. Farewell, old cronies,
yet not for long, for again and again I will come among
ye, if I shall have your leave. Farewell Ch——, dry, sar-
castic, and friendly ! Do——, mild, slow to move, and
gentlemanly ! Pl——, officious to do, and to volunteer,
good services !—and thou, thou dreary pile, fit mansion
for a Gresham or a Whittington of old, stately House of
Merchants ; with thy labyrinthine passages, and light-
excluding, pent-up offices, where candles for one half the
year supplied the place of the sun's light ; unhealthy
contributor to my weal, stern fosterer of my living, farewell ! In thee remain, and not in the obscure collection
of some wandering bookseller, my ' works ! ' There let
them rest, as I do from my labours, piled on thy massy
shelves, more MSS. in folio than ever Aquinas left, and
full as useful ! My mantle I bequeath among ye.

[1]A fortnight has passed since the date of my first communication. At that period I was approaching to tranquillity, but had not reached it. I boasted of a calm
indeed, but it was comparative only. Something of the
first flutter was left ; an unsettling sense of novelty ;
the dazzle to weak eyes of unaccustomed light. I missed
my old chains, forsooth, as if they had been some necessary
part of my apparel. I was a poor Carthusian, from strict
cellular discipline suddenly by some revolution returned
upon the world. I am now as if I had never been other
than my own master. It is natural to me to go where
I please, to do what I please. I find myself at eleven
o'clock in the day in Bond-street, and it seems to me that
I have been sauntering there at that very hour for years
past. I digress into Soho, to explore a book-stall. Methinks I have been thirty years a collector. There is
nothing strange nor new in it. I find myself before a fine

---

[1] *Here, in the* L. M., *begins the second part, which is headed* No. II,
with the motto, A clerk I was in London gay.—O'KEEFE, *below.*

picture in a morning. Was it ever otherwise ? What is
become of Fish-street Hill ? Where is Fenchurch-street ?
Stones of old Mincing-lane, which I have worn with my
daily pilgrimage for six and thirty years, to the foot-
steps of what toil-worn clerk are your everlasting flints
now vocal ? I indent the gayer flags of Pall Mall. It is
Change time, and I am strangely among the Elgin marbles.
It was no hyperbole when I ventured to compare the
change in my condition to a passing into another world.
Time stands still in a manner to me. I have lost all distinction of season. I do not know the day of the week,
or of the month. Each day used to be individually felt
by me in its reference to the foreign post days ; in its
distance from, or propinquity to, the next Sunday. I had
my Wednesday feelings, my Saturday nights' sensations.
The genius of each day was upon me distinctly during
the whole of it, affecting my appetite, spirits, &c. The
phantom of the next day, with the dreary five to follow,
sate as a load upon my poor Sabbath recreations. What
charm has washed that Ethiop white ? What is gone of
Black Monday ? All days are the same. Sunday itself
—that unfortunate failure of a holyday as it too often
proved, what with my sense of its fugitiveness, and over-
care to get the greatest quantity of pleasure out of it—is
melted down into a week day. I can spare to go to church
now, without grudging the huge cantle which it used to
seem to cut out of the holyday. I have Time for everything. I can visit a sick friend. I can interrupt the man
of much occupation when he is busiest. I can insult over
him with an invitation to take a day's pleasure with me
to Windsor this fine May-morning. It is Lucretian pleasure
to behold the poor drudges, whom I have left behind in
the world, carking and caring ; like horses in a mill,
drudging on in the same eternal round—and what is it all
[1]for ? A man can never have too much Time to himself,
nor too little to do. Had I a little son, I would christen
him NOTHING-TO-DO ; he should do nothing. Man, I
verily believe, is out of his element as long as he is operative.
I am altogether for the life contemplative. Will no kindly

[1] *For a passage in the* L. M., *here omitted, see Editor's Notes.*

earthquake come and swallow up those accursed cotton
mills ?   Take me that lumber of a desk there, and bowl
it down
                    As low as to the fiends.

I am no longer [1]* * * * * *, clerk to the Firm of &c.
I am Retired Leisure. I am to be met with in trim gardens.
I am already come to be known by my vacant face and
careless gesture, perambulating at no fixed pace, nor with
any settled purpose. I walk about ; not to and from.
They tell me, a certain *cum dignitate* air, that has been
buried so long with my other good parts, has begun to
shoot forth in my person. I grow into gentility percepti-
bly. When I take up a newspaper, it is to read the state
of the opera. *Opus operatum est.* I have done all that
I came into this world to do. I have worked task work,
and have the rest of the day to [2]myself.

THE GENTEEL STYLE IN WRITING

[Printed under the title, *Popular Fallacies :* xiv.—*That my Lord
Shaftesbury and Sir William Temple are models of the Genteel Style in
Writing,* in *The New Monthly Magazine,* March, 1826, p. 259.   Collected
in *The Last Essay of Elia,* 1833.   Text of 1833.]

[3]It is an ordinary criticism, that my Lord Shaftesbury,
and Sir William Temple, are models of the genteel style
in writing. We should prefer saying—of the lordly, [4]and
the gentlemanly. Nothing can be more unlike than the
inflated finical rhapsodies of Shaftesbury, and the plain
natural chit-chat of Temple. The man of rank is dis-
cernible in both writers ; but in the one it is only insinuated
gracefully, in the other it stands out offensively. The
peer seems to have written with his coronet on, and his
Earl's mantle before him ; the commoner in his elbow chair
and undress.—What can be more pleasant than the way
in which the retired statesman peeps out in the essays,
penned by the latter in his delightful retreat at Shene ?
They scent of Nimeguen, and the Hague. Scarce an

[1] * * * * * *] J—s D—n 1825.   [2] myself.] myself. | J. D. | Beau-
fort-terrace, Regent-street ; | Late of Ironmonger's-court, Fenchurch-
street. 1825.   [3] It is . . . in writing. *omit* 1826.   [4] and] and of 1826.

authority is quoted under an ambassador. Don Francisco
de Melo, a 'Portugal Envoy in England', tells him it
was frequent in his country for men, spent with age or
other decays, so as they could not hope for above a year or
two of life, to ship themselves away in a Brazil fleet, and
after their arrival there to go on a great length, sometimes
of twenty or thirty years, or more, by the force of that
vigour they recovered with that remove. 'Whether such
an effect (Temple beautifully adds) might grow from the
air, or the fruits of that climate, or by approaching nearer
the sun, which is the fountain of light and heat, when their
natural heat was so far decayed : or whether the piecing
out of an old man's life were worth the pains ; I cannot
tell : perhaps the play is not worth the candle.'—Monsieur
Pompone, 'French Ambassador in his (Sir William's) time
at the Hague,' certifies him, that in his life he had never
heard of any man in France that arrived at a hundred
years of age ; a limitation of life which the old gentleman
imputes to the excellence of their climate, giving them
such a liveliness of temper and humour, as disposes them to
more pleasures of all kinds than in other countries ; and
moralises upon the matter very sensibly. The 'late
Robert Earl of Leicester' furnishes him with a story of
a Countess of Desmond, married out of England in Edward
the Fourth's time, and who lived far in King James's reign.
The 'same noble person' gives him an account, how such
a year, in the same reign, there went about the country
a set of morrice-dancers, composed of ten men who danced,
a Maid Marian, and a tabor and pipe ; and how these twelve,
one with another, made up twelve hundred years. 'It was
not so much (says Temple) that so many in one small
county (Herefordshire) should live to that age, as that
they should be in vigour and in humour to travel and to
dance.' Monsieur Zulichem, one of his 'colleagues at the
Hague', informs him of a cure for the gout ; which is
confirmed by another 'Envoy', Monsieur Serinchamps
in that town, who had tried it.—Old Prince Maurice of
Nassau recommends to him the use of hammocks in that
complaint ; having been allured to sleep, while suffering
under it himself, by the 'constant motion or swinging of
those airy beds'. Count Egmont, and the Rainegrave

who ' was killed last summer before Maestricht ', impart to him their experiences.

But the rank of the writer is never more innocently disclosed, than where he takes for granted the compliments paid by foreigners to his fruit-trees. For the taste and perfection of what we esteem the best, he can truly say, that the French, who have eaten his peaches and grapes at Shene in no very ill year, have generally concluded that the last are as good as any they have eaten in France on this side Fontainebleau ; and the first as good as any they have eat in Gascony. Italians have agreed his white figs to be as good as any of that sort in Italy, which is the earlier kind of white fig there ; for in the later kind and the blue, we cannot come near the warm climates, no more than in the Frontignac or Muscat grape. His orange-trees, too, are as large as any he saw when he was young in France, except those of Fontainebleau, or what he has seen since in the Low Countries ; except some very old ones of the Prince of Orange's. Of grapes he had the honour of bringing over four sorts into England, which he enumerates, and supposes that they are all by this time pretty common among some gardeners in his neighbourhood, as well as several persons of quality ; for he ever thought all things of this kind ' the commoner they are made the better '. The garden pedantry with which he asserts that 'tis to little purpose to plant any of the best fruits, as peaches or grapes, hardly, he doubts, beyond Northamptonshire at the furthest northwards ; and praises the ' Bishop of Munster at Cosevelt ', for attempting nothing beyond cherries in that cold climate ; is equally pleasant and in character. ' I may perhaps ' (he thus ends his sweet Garden Essay with a passage worthy of Cowley) ' be allowed to know something of this trade, since I have so long allowed myself to be good for nothing else, which few men will do, or enjoy their gardens, without often looking abroad to see how other matters play, what motions in the state, and what invitations they may hope for into other scenes. For my own part, as the country life, and this part of it more particularly, were the inclination of my youth itself, so they are the pleasure of my age ; and I can truly say that, among many great employments that have fallen to my share, I have never asked or sought for any of them, but have often endeavoured to escape from them, into the ease and freedom of a private scene, where a man may go his own way and his own pace, in the common paths and circles of life. The measure of choosing well is whether a man likes what he has chosen, which I thank God has befallen on me; and though among the follies of my life, building and planting have not been the least, and have cost me more than I have the confidence to own; yet they have been fully recompensed by the sweetness and satisfaction of this retreat, where, since my resolution taken of never entering again into any public employments, I have passed five years without ever once going to town, though I am almost in sight of it, and have a house there always ready to receive me. Nor has this been any sort of affectation, as some have thought it, but a mere want of desire or humour to make so small a remove; for when I am in this corner, I can truly say with Horace, *Me quoties reficit, &c.*

> ' Me, when the cold Digentian stream revives,
> What does my friend believe I think or ask ?
> Let me yet less possess, so I may live,
> Whate'er of life remains, unto myself.
> May I have books enough; and one year's store,
> Not to depend upon each doubtful hour:
> This is enough of mighty Jove to pray,
> Who, as he pleases, gives and takes away.'

The writings of Temple are, in general, after this easy copy. On one occasion, indeed, his wit, which was mostly subordinate to nature and tenderness, has seduced him into a string of felicitous antitheses; which, it is obvious to remark, have been a model to Addison and succeeding essayists. ' Who would not be covetous, and with reason,' he says, ' if health could be purchased with gold ? Who not ambitious, if it were at the command of power, or restored by honour ? but, alas ! a white staff will not help gouty feet to walk better than a common cane ; nor a blue riband bind up a wound so well as a fillet. The glitter of gold, or of diamonds, will but hurt sore eyes instead of curing them ; and an aching head will be no more eased by wearing a crown, than a common night-cap.' In a far better style, and more accordant with his own humour of

plainness, are the concluding sentences of his 'Discourse
upon Poetry'. Temple took a part in the controversy
about the ancient and the modern learning; and, with
that partiality so natural and so graceful in an old man,
whose state engagements had left him little leisure to look
into modern productions, while his retirement gave him
occasion to look back upon the classic studies of his youth
—decided in favour of the latter. ' Certain it is,' he says,
' that, whether the fierceness of the Gothic humours,
or noise of their perpetual wars, frighted it away, or that
the unequal mixture of the modern languages would not
bear it—the great heights and excellency both of poetry
and music fell with the Roman learning and empire, and
have never since recovered the admiration and applauses
that before attended them.   Yet, such as they are amongst
us, they must be confessed to be the softest and sweetest,
the most general and most innocent amusements of common time and life.   They still find room in the courts of
princes, and the cottages of shepherds.   They serve to
revive and animate the dead calm of poor and idle lives,
and to allay or divert the violent passions and perturbations
of the greatest and the busiest men.   And both these
effects are of equal use to human life ; for the mind of man
is like the sea, which is neither agreeable to the beholder
nor the voyager, in a calm or in a storm, but is so to both
when a little agitated by gentle gales ; and so the mind,
when moved by soft and easy passions or affections.   I
know very well that many who pretend to be wise by the
forms of being grave, are apt to despise both poetry and
music, as toys and trifles too light for the use or entertainment of serious men.   But whoever find themselves wholly
insensible to their charms, would, I think, do well to keep
their own counsel, for fear of reproaching their own temper,
and bringing the goodness of their natures, if not of their
understandings, into question.   While this world lasts
I doubt not but the pleasure and request of these two
entertainments will do so too ; and happy those that content themselves with these, or any other so easy and so
innocent, and do not trouble the world or other men,
because they cannot be quiet themselves, though nobody
hurts them.'   ' When all is done (he concludes), human

life is at the greatest and the best but like a froward child,
that must be played with, and humoured a little, to keep
it quiet, till it falls asleep, and then the care is over.'

BARBARA S——

[Printed in *The London Magazine, New Series,* vol. i, no. iv, p. 511
(April, 1825).   Collected in *The Last Essays of Elia,* 1833.   Text of 1833.]

ON the noon of the 14th of November, 1743 or 4, I forget
which it was, just as the clock had struck one, Barbara
S——, with her accustomed punctuality, ascended the long
rambling staircase, with awkward interposed landing-
places, which led to the office, or rather a sort of box with
a desk in it, whereat sat the then Treasurer of (what few of
our readers may remember) the Old Bath Theatre.   All
over the island it was the custom, and remains so I believe
to this day, for the players to receive their weekly stipend
on the Saturday.   It was not much that Barbara had to
claim.

This little maid had just entered her eleventh year ; but
her important station at the theatre, as it seemed to her,
with the benefits which she felt to accrue from her pious
application of her small earnings, had given an air of
womanhood to her steps and to her behaviour.   You would
have taken her to have been at least five years older.

Till latterly she had merely been employed in choruses,
or where children were wanted to fill up the scene.   But
the manager, observing a diligence and adroitness in her
above her age, had for some few months past intrusted
to her the performance of whole parts.   You may guess
the self-consequence of the promoted Barbara.   She had
already drawn tears in young Arthur ; had rallied Richard
with infantine petulance in the Duke of York ; and in her
turn had rebuked that petulance when she was Prince of
Wales.   She would have done the elder child in Morton's
pathetic after-piece to the life ; but as yet the ' Children
in the Wood ' was not.

Long after this little girl was grown an aged woman,
I have seen some of these small parts, each making two
or three pages at most, copied out in the rudest hand of

the then prompter, who doubtless transcribed a little more carefully and fairly for the grown-up tragedy ladies of the establishment. But such as they were, blotted and scrawled, as for a child's use, she kept them all ; and in the zenith of her after reputation it was a delightful sight to behold them bound up in costliest Morocco, each single —each small part making a *book*—with fine clasps, gilt-splashed, &c. She had conscientiously kept them as they had been delivered to her ; not a blot had been effaced or tampered with. They were precious to her for their affecting remembrancings. They were her principia, her rudiments ; the elementary atoms ; the little steps by which she pressed forward to perfection. 'What ', she would say, ' could Indian rubber, or a pumice stone, have done for these darlings ? '

I am in no hurry to begin my story—indeed I have little or none to tell—so I will just mention an observation of hers connected with that interesting time.

Not long before she died I had been discoursing with her on the quantity of real present emotion which a great tragic performer experiences during acting. I ventured to think, that though in the first instance such players must have possessed the feelings which they so powerfully called up in others, yet by frequent repetition those feelings must become deadened in great measure, and the performer trust to the memory of past emotion, rather than express a present one. She indignantly repelled the notion, that with a truly great tragedian the operation, by which such effects were produced upon an audience, could ever degrade itself into what was purely mechanical. With much delicacy, avoiding to instance in her *self*-experience, she told me, that so long ago as when she used to play the part of the Little Son to Mrs. Porter's Isabella (I think it was), when that impressive actress has been bending over her in some heart-rending colloquy, she has felt real hot tears come trickling from her, which (to use her powerful expression) have perfectly scalded her back.

I am not quite so sure that it was Mrs. Porter ; but it was some great actress of that day. The name is indifferent ; but the fact of the scalding tears I most distinctly re-member.

I was always fond of the society of players, and am not
sure that an impediment in my speech (which certainly
kept me out of the pulpit) even more than certain personal
disqualifications, which are often got over in that profession,
did not prevent me at one time of life from adopting it.
I have had the honour (I must ever call it) once to have
been admitted to the tea-table of Miss Kelly. I have
played at serious whist with Mr. Liston. I have chatted
with ever good-humoured Mrs. Charles Kemble. I have
conversed as friend to friend with her accomplished husband. I have been indulged with a classical conference
with Macready ; and with a sight of the Player-picture
gallery, at Mr. Matthews's, when the kind owner, to re-
munerate me for my love of the old actors (whom he loves
so much) went over it with me, supplying to his capital
collection, what alone the artist could not give them—
voice ; and their living motion. Old tones, half-faded,
of Dodd, and Parsons, and Baddeley, have lived again for
me at his bidding. Only Edwin he could not restore to me.
I have supped with——— ; but I am growing a coxcomb.

As I was about to say—at the desk of the then treasurer
of the old Bath theatre—not Diamond's —presented herself
the little Barbara S———.

The parents of Barbara had been in reputable circumstances. The father had practised, I believe, as an
apothecary in the town. But his practice from causes
which I feel my own infirmity too sensibly that way to
arraign—or perhaps from that pure infelicity which ac-
companies some people in their walk through life, and which
it is impossible to lay at the door of imprudence—was now
reduced to nothing. They were in fact in the very teeth
of starvation, when the manager, who knew and respected
them in better days, took the little Barbara into his company.

At the period I commenced with, her slender earnings were
the sole support of the family, including two younger sisters.
I must throw a veil over some mortifying circumstances.
Enough to say, that her Saturday's pittance was the only
chance of a Sunday's (generally their only) meal of meat.

One thing I will only mention, that in some child's part,
where in her theatrical character she was to sup off a roast

fowl (O joy to Barbara !) some comic actor, who was for
the night caterer for [1]this dainty—in the misguided humour
of his part, threw over the dish such a quantity of salt
(O grief and pain of heart to Barbara !) that when he
crammed a portion of it into her mouth, she was obliged
sputteringly to reject it ; and what with shame of her ill-
acted part, and pain of real appetite at missing such a
dainty, her little heart sobbed almost to breaking, till a
flood of tears, which the well-fed spectators were totally
unable to comprehend, mercifully relieved her.

This was the little starved, meritorious maid, who stood
before old Ravenscroft, the treasurer, for her Saturday's
payment.

Ravenscroft was a man, I have heard many old theatrical
people besides herself say, of all men least calculated for
a treasurer. He had no head for accounts, paid away at
random, kept scarce any books, and summing up at the
week's end, if he found himself a pound or so deficient,
blest himself that it was no worse.

Now Barbara's weekly stipend was a bare half guinea.—
By mistake he popped into her hand a—whole one.

Barbara tripped away.

She was entirely unconscious at first of the mistake :
God knows, Ravenscroft would never have discovered it.

But when she had got down to the first of those uncouth
landing-places, she became sensible of an unusual weight
of metal pressing her little hand.

Now mark the dilemma.

She was by nature a good child. From her parents and
those about her she had imbibed no contrary influence.
But then they had taught her nothing. Poor men's smoky
cabins are not always porticoes of moral philosophy. This
little maid had no instinct to evil, but then she might be
said to have no fixed principle. She had heard honesty
commended, but never dreamed of its application to herself. She thought of it as something which concerned
grown-up people—men and women. She had never known
temptation, or thought of preparing resistance against it.

Her first impulse was to go back to the old treasurer,
and explain to him his blunder. He was already so con-

---

[1] this] this stage 1825.

fused with age, besides a natural want of punctuality,
that she would have had some difficulty in making him
understand it. She saw *that* in an instant. And then
it was such a bit of money! and then the image of a
larger allowance of butcher's meat on their table next day
came across her, till her little eyes glistened, and her
mouth moistened. But then Mr. Ravenscroft had always
been so good-natured, had stood her friend behind the scenes,
and even recommended her promotion to some of her little
parts. But again the old man was reputed to be worth
a world of money. He was supposed to have fifty pounds
a year clear of the theatre. And then came staring upon
her the figure of her little stockingless and shoeless sisters.
And when she looked at her own neat white cotton stockings,
which her situation at the theatre had made it indispensable
for her mother to provide for her, with hard straining and
pinching from the family stock, and thought how glad
she should be to cover their poor feet with the same—
and how then they could accompany her to rehearsals,
which they had hitherto been precluded from doing,
by reason of their unfashionable attire—in these thoughts
she reached the second landing-place—the second, I mean
from the top—for there was still another left to traverse.

Now virtue support Barbara!

And that never-failing friend did step in—for at that
moment a strength not her own, I have heard her say,
was revealed to her—a reason above reasoning—and
without her own agency, as it seemed (for she never felt
her feet to move), she found herself transported back to
the individual desk she had just quitted, and her hand in
the old hand of Ravenscroft, who in silence took back the
refunded treasure, and who had been sitting (good man)
insensible to the lapse of minutes, which to her were
anxious ages; and from that moment a deep peace fell
upon her heart, and she knew the quality of honesty.

A year or two's unrepining application to her profession
brightened up the feet, and the prospects, of her little sisters,
set the whole family upon their legs again, and released her
from the difficulty of discussing moral dogmas upon a
landing-place.

I have heard her say, that it was a surprise, not much

short of mortification to her, to see the coolness with which
the old man pocketed the difference, which had caused
her such mortal throes.

This anecdote of herself I had in the year 1800, from the
mouth of the late Mrs. Crawford,[a] then sixty-seven years
of age (she died soon after) ; and to her struggles upon this
childish occasion I have sometimes ventured to think her
indebted for that power of rending the heart in the representation of conflicting emotions, for which in after years
she was considered as little inferior (if at all so in the
part of Lady Randolph) even to Mrs. Siddons.

THE TOMBS IN THE ABBEY

IN A LETTER TO R—— S——, ESQ.

[Printed, as portion of the *Letter of Elia to Robert Southey*, in *The
London Magazine*, vol. viii, no. xlvi, p. 405 (Oct., 1823). Collected
under above title in *The Last Essays of Elia*, 1833. Text of 1833.]

[1]THOUGH in some points of doctrine, and perhaps of
discipline, I am diffident of lending a perfect assent to that
church which you have so worthily *historified*, yet may
the ill time never come to me, when with a chilled heart,
or a portion of irreverent sentiment, I shall enter her
beautiful and time-hallowed Edifices. Judge then of my
mortification when, after attending the choral anthems
of last Wednesday at Westminster, and being desirous of
renewing my acquaintance, after lapsed years, with the
tombs and antiquities there, I found myself excluded ;
turned out like a dog, or some profane person, into the
common street, with feelings not very congenial to the place,
or to the solemn service which I had been listening to. It
was a jar after that music.

You had your education at Westminster ; and doubtless
among those dim aisles and cloisters, you must have gathered

—————
[a] The maiden name of this lady was Street, which she changed, by
successive marriages, for those of Dancer, Barry, and Crawford. She
was Mrs. Crawford, and a third time a widow, when I knew her.

—————
[1] *This paragraph was re-written in* 1833.

much of that devotional feeling in those young years, on which your purest mind feeds still—and may it feed ! The antiquarian spirit, strong in you, and gracefully blending ever with the religious, may have been sown in you among those wrecks of splendid mortality. You owe it to the place of your education ; you owe it to your learned fondness for the architecture of your ancestors ; you owe it to the venerableness of your ecclesiastical establishment, which is daily lessened and called in question through these practices—to speak aloud your sense of them ; never to desist raising your voice against them, till they be totally done away with and abolished ; till the doors of Westminster Abbey be no longer closed against the decent, though low-in-purse, enthusiast, or blameless devotee, who must commit an injury against his family economy, if he would be indulged with a bare admission within its walls. You owe it to the decencies, which you wish to see maintained in its impressive services, that our Cathedral be no longer an object of inspection to the poor at those times only, in which they must rob from their attendance on the worship every minute which they can bestow upon the fabric. In vain the public prints have taken up this subject, in vain such poor nameless writers as myself express their indignation. A word from you, Sir—a hint in your Journal—would be sufficient to fling open the doors of the Beautiful Temple again, as we can remember them when we were boys. At that time of life, what would the imaginative faculty (such as it is) in both of us, have suffered, if the entrance to so much reflection had been obstructed by the demand of so much silver !—If we had scraped it up to gain an occasional admission (as we certainly should have done) would the sight of those old tombs have been as impressive to us (while we had been weighing anxiously prudence against sentiment) as when the gates stood open, as those of the adjacent Park ; when we could walk in at any time, as the mood brought us, for a shorter or longer time, as that lasted ? Is the being shown over a place the same as silently for ourselves detecting the genius of it ? In no part of our beloved Abbey now can a person find entrance (out of service time) under the sum of *two shillings*. The rich and the great will smile

at the anti-climax, presumed to lie in these two short
words. But you can tell them, Sir, how much quiet
worth, how much capacity for enlarged feeling, how
much taste and genius, may coexist, especially in youth,
with a purse incompetent to this demand.—A respected
friend of ours, during his late visit to the metropolis,
presented himself for admission to Saint Paul's. At the
same time a decently clothed man, with as decent a wife,
and child, were bargaining for the same indulgence. The
price was only two-pence each person. The poor but
decent man hesitated, desirous to go in; but there were
three of them, and he turned away reluctantly. Perhaps
he wished to have seen the tomb of Nelson. Perhaps the
Interior of the Cathedral was his object. But in the state
of his finances, even sixpence might reasonably seem too
much. Tell the Aristocracy of the country (no man can
do it more impressively); instruct them of what value
these insignificant pieces of money, these minims to their
sight, may be to their humbler brethren. Shame these
Sellers out of the [1]Temple. Stifle not the suggestions of
your better nature with the [2]pretext, that an indiscriminate
admission would expose the Tombs to violation. Remember
your boy-days. Did you ever see, or hear, of a mob in the
Abbey, while it was free to all? [3]Do the rabble come there,
or trouble their heads about such speculations? It is
all that you can do to drive them into your churches;
they do not voluntarily offer themselves. They have,
alas! no passion for antiquities; for tomb of king or
prelate, sage or poet. If they had, they would be no longer
the rabble.

For forty years that I have known the Fabric, the only
well-attested charge of violation adduced, has been—
a ridiculous dismemberment committed upon the effigy of
that amiable spy, Major André. And is it for this—the
wanton mischief of some schoolboy, fired perhaps with

[1] Temple.] Temple. Show the poor, that you can sometimes think
of them in some other light than as mutineers and mal-contents. Con-
ciliate them by such kind methods to their superiors, civil and ecclesiastical. Stop the mouths of the railers; and suffer your old friends,
upon the old terms, again to honour and admire you. 1823.   [2] pre-
text] stale evasion 1823.   [3] Do] Did 1823.

raw notions of Transatlantic Freedom—or the remote
possibility of such a mischief occurring again, so easily
to be prevented by stationing a constable within the
walls, if the vergers are incompetent to the duty—is it
upon such wretched pretences, that the people of England
are made to pay a new Peter's Pence, so long abrogated ;
or must content themselves with contemplating the ragged
Exterior of their Cathedral ?   The mischief was done about
the time that you were a scholar there.   Do you know
any thing about the unfortunate [1]relic ?—

AMICUS REDIVIVUS

[Printed in *The London Magazine*, vol. viii, no. xlviii, p. 613 (Dec.,
1823).   Collected in *The Last Essays of Elia*, 1823.   Text of 1833.]

Where were ye, Nymphs, when the remorseless deep
Clos'd o'er the head of your loved Lycidas ?

I DO not know when I have experienced a stranger
sensation, than on seeing my old friend G. D., who had
been paying me a morning visit a few Sundays back,
at my cottage [2]at Islington, upon taking leave, instead of
turning down the right hand path by which he had entered
—with staff in hand, and at noon day, deliberately march
right forwards into the midst of the stream that runs by
us, and totally disappear.

A spectacle like this at dusk would have been appalling
enough ; but, in the broad open daylight, to witness such
an unreserved motion towards self-destruction in a valued
friend, took from me all power of speculation.

How I found my feet, I know not.   Consciousness was
quite gone.   Some spirit, not my own, whirled me to the
spot.   I remember nothing but the silvery apparition of
a good white head emerging ; nigh which a staff (the
hand unseen that wielded it) pointed upwards, as feeling
for the skies.   In a moment (if time was in that time)
he was on my shoulders, and I—freighted with a load more
precious than his who bore Anchises.

And here I cannot but do justice to the officious zeal of
sundry passers by, who, albeit arriving a little too late to

[1] *For the conclusion of 1823 see p.* 302 *above.*   [2] at] near 1823.

participate in the honours of the rescue, in philanthropic
shoals came thronging to communicate their advice as to
the recovery ; prescribing variously the application, or
non-application, of salt, &c., to the person of the patient.
Life meantime was ebbing fast away, amidst the stifle
of conflicting judgments, when one, more sagacious than
the rest, by a bright thought, proposed sending for the
Doctor. Trite as the counsel was, and impossible, as one
should think, to be missed on,—shall I confess ?—in this
emergency, it was to me as if an Angel had spoken. Great
previous exertions—and mine had not been inconsiderable
—are commonly followed by a debility of purpose. This
was a moment of irresolution.

MONOCULUS—for so, in default of catching his true name,
I choose to designate the medical gentleman who now
appeared—is a grave, middle-aged person, who, without
having studied at the college, or truckled to the pedantry
of a diploma, hath employed a great portion of his valuable
time in experimental processes upon the bodies of unfortunate fellow-creatures, in whom the vital spark, to
mere vulgar thinking, would seem extinct, and lost for ever.
He omitteth no occasion of obtruding his services, from a
case of common surfeit-suffocation to the ignobler obstruc-
tions, sometimes induced by a too wilful application of
the plant *Cannabis* outwardly. But though he declineth
not altogether these drier extinctions, his occupation tendeth
for the most part to water-practice ; for the convenience
of which, he hath judiciously fixed his quarters near the
grand repository of the stream mentioned,[a] where, day and
night, from his little watch-tower, at the Middleton's-
Head, he listeneth to detect the wrecks of drowned mortality—partly, as he saith, to be upon the spot—and partly,
because the liquids which he useth to prescribe to himself
and his patients, on these distressing occasions, are
ordinarily more conveniently to be found at these common
hostelries, than in the shops and phials of the apothecaries.
His ear hath arrived to such finesse by practice, that it

[a] The topography of my cottage, and its relation to the river, will
explain this ; as I have been at some cost to have the whole engraved
(in time, I hope, for our next number) as well for the satisfaction of
the reader, as to commemorate so signal a deliverance [1823 *only*].

is reported, he can distinguish a plunge at [1]a half furlong distance ; and can tell, if it be casual or deliberate. He weareth a medal, suspended over a suit, originally of a sad brown, but which, by time, and frequency of nightly divings, has been dinged into a true professional sable. He passeth by the name of Doctor, and is remarkable for wanting his left eye. His remedy—after a sufficient application of warm blankets, friction, &c., is a simple tumbler, or more, of the purest Cognac, with water, made as hot as the convalescent can bear it. Where he findeth, as in the case of my friend, a squeamish subject, he condescendeth to be the taster ; and showeth, by his own example, the innocuous nature of the prescription. Nothing can be more kind or encouraging than this procedure. It addeth confidence to the patient, to see his medical adviser go hand in hand with himself in the remedy. When the doctor swalloweth his own draught, what peevish invalid can refuse to pledge him in the potion ? In fine, MONOCULUS is a humane, sensible man, who, for a slender pittance, scarce enough to sustain life, is content to wear it out in the endeavour to save the lives of others—his pretensions so moderate, that with difficulty I could press a crown upon him, for the price of restoring the existence of such an invaluable creature to society as G. D.

It was pleasant to observe the effect of the subsiding alarm upon the nerves of the dear absentee. It seemed to have given a shake to memory, calling up notice after notice, of all the providential deliverances he had experienced in the course of his long and innocent life. Sitting up in my couch—my couch which, naked and void of furniture hitherto, for the salutary repose which it administered, shall be honoured with costly valance, at some price, and henceforth be a state-bed at Colebrooke,—he discoursed of marvellous escapes—by carelessness of nurses—by pails of gelid, and kettles of the boiling element, in infancy—by orchard pranks, and snapping twigs, in schoolboy frolics —by descent of tiles at Trumpington, and of heavier tomes at Pembroke—by studious watchings, inducing frightful vigilance—by want, and the fear of want, and all the sore throbbings of the learned head.—Anon, he would

[1] a half furlong] a furlong and a half 1823.

burst out into little fragments of chaunting—of songs long ago—ends of deliverance-hymns, not remembered before since childhood, but coming up now, when his heart was made tender as a child's—for the *tremor cordis*, in the retrospect of a recent deliverance, as in a case of impending danger, acting upon an innocent heart, will produce a self-tenderness, which we should do ill to christen cowardice ; and Shakspeare, in the latter crisis, has made his good Sir Hugh to remember the sitting by Babylon, and to mutter of shallow rivers.

Waters of Sir Hugh Middleton—what a spark you were like to have extinguished for ever ! Your salubrious streams to this City, for now near two centuries, would hardly have atoned for what you were in a moment washing away. Mockery of a river—liquid artifice—wretched conduit ! henceforth rank with canals, and sluggish aqueducts. Was it for this, that, smit in boyhood with the explorations of that Abyssinian traveller, I paced the vales of Amwell to explore your tributary springs, to trace your salutary waters sparkling through green Hertfordshire and cultured Enfield parks ?—Ye have no swans—no Naiads—no river God—or did the benevolent hoary aspect of my friend tempt ye to suck him in, that ye also might have the tutelary genius of your waters ?

Had he been drowned in Cam there would have been some consonancy in it ; but what willows had ye to wave and rustle over his moist sepulture ?—or, having no *name*, besides that unmeaning assumption of *eternal novity*, did ye think to get one by the noble prize, and henceforth to be termed the STREAM DYERIAN ?

> And could such spacious virtue find a grave
> Beneath the imposthumed bubble of a wave ?

I protest, George, you shall not venture out again—no, not by daylight—without a sufficient pair of spectacles— in your musing moods especially. Your absence of mind we have borne, till your presence of body came to be called in question by it. You shall not go wandering into Euripus with Aristotle, if we can help it. Fie, man, to turn dipper at your years, after your many tracts in favour of sprinkling only !

I have nothing but water in my head o' nights since
this frightful accident. Sometimes I am with Clarence in
his dream. At others, I behold Christian beginning to
sink, and crying out to his good brother Hopeful (that is
[1]to me), 'I sink in deep waters; the billows go over my
head, all the waves go over me. Selah.' Then I have
before me Palinurus, just letting go the steerage. I cry
out too late to save. Next follow—a mournful procession
—*suicidal faces*, saved against their wills from drowning;
dolefully trailing a length of reluctant gratefulness, with
ropy weeds pendant from locks of watchet hue—constrained
Lazari—Pluto's half-subjects—stolen fees from the grave
—bilking Charon of his fare. At their head Arion—or is it
G. D. ?—in his singing garments marcheth singly, with
harp in hand, and votive garland, which Machaon (or Dr.
Hawes) snatcheth straight, intending to suspend it to the
stern God of Sea. Then follow dismal streams of Lethe,
in which the half-drenched on earth are constrained to
drown downright, by wharfs where Ophelia twice acts her
muddy death.

And, doubtless, there is some notice in that invisible
world, when one of us approacheth (as my friend did so
lately) to their inexorable precincts. When a soul knocks
once, twice, at death's door, the sensation aroused within
the palace must be considerable; and the grim Feature,
by modern science so often dispossessed of his prey, must
have learned by this time to pity Tantalus.

A pulse assuredly was felt along the line of the Elysian
shades, when the near arrival of G. D. was announced by
no equivocal indications. From their seats of Asphodel
arose the gentler and the graver ghosts—poet, or historian
—of Grecian or of Roman lore—to crown with unfading
chaplets the half-finished love-labours of their unwearied
scholiast. Him Markland expected—him Tyrwhitt hoped
to encounter—him the sweet lyrist of Peter House, whom
he had barely seen upon earth,[a] with newest airs prepared
to greet —— ; and, patron of the gentle Christ's boy,—
who should have been his patron through life—the mild

[a] GRAIUM *tantum vidit.*

[1] to *omit* 1823.

Askew, with longing aspirations, leaned foremost from his venerable Æsculapian chair, to welcome into that happy company the matured virtues of the man, whose tender scions in the boy he himself upon earth had so prophetically fed and watered.

SOME SONNETS OF SIR PHILIP SYDNEY

[Printed, under the title *Nugæ Criticæ*: *By the Author of Elia. No. I. Defence of the Sonnets of Sir Philip Sydney*, in *The London Magazine*, vol. viii, no. xlv, p. 248; signed *L*. Collected under above title in *The Last Essays of Elia*, 1833. Text of 1833.]

SYDNEY'S Sonnets—I speak of the best of them—are among the very best of their sort. They fall below the plain moral dignity, the sanctity, and high yet modest spirit of self-approval, of Milton, in his compositions of a similar structure. They are in truth what Milton, censuring the Arcadia, says of that work (to which they are a sort of after-tune or application), ' vain and amatorious ' enough, yet the things in their kind (as he confesses to be true of the romance) may be ' full of worth and wit '. They savour of the Courtier, it must be allowed, and not of the Commonwealthsman. But Milton was a Courtier when he wrote the Masque at Ludlow Castle, and still more a Courtier when he composed the Arcades. When the national struggle was to begin, he becomingly cast these vanities behind him ; and if the order of time had thrown Sir Philip upon the crisis which preceded the Revolution, there is no reason why he should not have acted the same part in that emergency, which has glorified the name of a later Sydney. He did not want for plainness or boldness of spirit. His letter on the French match may testify, he could speak his mind freely to Princes. The times did not call him to the scaffold.

The Sonnets which we oftenest call to mind of Milton were the compositions of his maturest years. Those of Sydney, which I am about to produce, were written in the very hey-day of his blood. They are stuck full of amorous fancies—far-fetched conceits, befitting his occupation ; for True Love thinks no labour to send out Thoughts upon

the vast, and more than Indian voyages, to bring home
rich pearls, outlandish wealth, gums, jewels, spicery, to
sacrifice in self-depreciating similitudes, as shadows of
true amiabilities in the Beloved. We must be Lovers—or at
least the cooling touch of time, the *circum præcordia frigus*,
must not have so damped our faculties, as to take away our
recollection that we were once so—before we can duly
appreciate the glorious vanities, and graceful hyperboles,
of the passion. The images which lie before our feet (though
by some accounted the only natural) are least natural for
the high Sydnean love to express its fancies by. They
may serve for the loves of Tibullus, or the dear Author of
the Schoolmistress ; for passions that creep and whine in
Elegies and Pastoral Ballads. I am sure Milton never
loved at this rate. I am afraid some of his addresses (*ad
Leonoram* I mean) have rather erred on the farther side ;
and that the poet came not much short of a religious inde-
corum, when he could thus apostrophise a singing-girl :—

Angelus unicuique suus (sic credite gentes)
  Obtigit aetheriis ales ab ordinibus.
Quid mirum, Leonora, tibi si gloria major,
  Nam tua praesentem vox sonat ipsa Deum ?
Aut Deus, aut vacui certè mens tertia coeli,
  Per tua secretô guttura serpit agens ;
Serpit agens, facilisque docet mortalia corda
  Sensim immortali assuescere posse sono.
QUOD SI CUNCTA QUIDEM DEUS EST, PER CUNCTAQUE FUSUS,
  IN TE UNÂ LOQUITUR, CAETERA MUTUS HABET.

This is loving in a strange fashion ; and it requires some
candour of construction (besides the slight darkening of
a dead language) to cast a veil over the ugly appearance of
something very like blasphemy in the last two verses.
I think the Lover would have been staggered, if he had
gone about to express the same thought in English. I am
sure, Sydney has no flights like this. His extravaganzas
do not strike at the sky, though he takes leave to adopt the
pale Dian into a fellowship with his mortal passions.

I

With how sad steps, O Moon, thou climb'st the skies ;
How silently ; and with how wan a face !
What ! may it be, that even in heavenly place
That busy Archer his sharp arrows tries ?

Sure, if that long-with-love-acquainted eyes
Can judge of love, thou feel'st a lover's case;
I read it in thy looks; thy languisht grace
To me, that feel the like, thy state descries.
Then, even of fellowship, O Moon, tell me,
Is constant love deem'd there but want of wit?
Are beauties there as proud as here they be?
Do they above love to be loved, and yet
Those lovers scorn, whom that love doth possess?
Do they call *virtue* there—*ungratefulness?*

The last line of this poem is a little obscured by trans-
position. He means, Do they call ungratefulness there
a virtue?

II

Come, Sleep, O Sleep, the certain knot of peace,
The baiting place of wit, the balm of woe,
The poor man's wealth, the prisoner's release,
The indifferent judge between the high and low;
With shield of proof shield me from out the prease [a]
Of those fierce darts despair at me doth throw;
O make in me those civil wars to cease:
I will good tribute pay, if thou do so.
Take thou of me sweet pillows, sweetest bed;
A chamber deaf to noise, and blind to light;
A rosy garland, and a weary head.
And if these things, as being thine by right,
Move not thy heavy grace, thou shalt in me,
Livelier than elsewhere, STELLA's image see.

III

The curious wits, seeing dull pensiveness
Bewray itself in my long-settled eyes,
Whence those same fumes of melancholy rise,
With idle pains, and missing aim, do guess.
Some, that know how my spring I did address,
Deem that my Muse some fruit of knowledge plies;
Others, because the Prince my service tries,
Think, that I think state errors to redress;
But harder judges judge, ambition's rage,
Scourge of itself, still climbing slippery place,
Holds my young brain captiv'd in golden cage.
O fools, or over-wise! alas, the race
Of all my thoughts hath neither stop nor start,
But only STELLA's eyes, and STELLA's heart.

[a] Press.

IV

Because I oft in dark abstracted guise
Seem most alone in greatest company,
With dearth of words, or answers quite awry,
To them that would make speech of speech arise;
They deem, and of their doom the rumour flies,
That poison foul of bubbling *Pride* doth lie
So in my swelling breast, that only I
Fawn on myself, and others do despise;
Yet *Pride*, I think, doth not my Soul possess,
Which looks too oft in his unflattering glass:
But one worse fault—*Ambition*—I confess,
That makes me oft my best friends overpass,
Unseen, unheard—while Thought to highest place
Bends all his powers, even unto STELLA'S grace.

V

Having this day, my horse, my hand, my lance,
Guided so well that I obtained the prize,
Both by the judgment of the English eyes,
And of some sent from that *sweet enemy*,—France;
Horsemen my skill in horsemanship advance;
Townsfolk my strength; a daintier judge applies
His praise to sleight, which from good use doth rise;
Some lucky wits impute it but to chance;
Others, because of both sides I do take
My blood from them, who did excel in this,
Think Nature me a man of arms did make.
How far they shot awry! the true cause is,
STELLA look'd on, and from her heavenly face
Sent forth the beams which made so fair my race.

VI

In martial sports I had my cunning tried,
And yet to break more staves did me address,
While with the people's shouts (I must confess)
Youth, luck, and praise, even fill'd my veins with pride
When Cupid, having me (his slave) descried
In Mars's livery, prancing in the press,
'What now, Sir Fool!' said he; 'I would no less:
Look here, I say.' I look'd, and STELLA spied,
Who hard by made a window send forth light.
My heart then quak'd, then dazzled were mine eyes;
One hand forgot to rule, th'other to fight;
Nor trumpet's sound I heard, nor friendly cries.
My foe came on, and beat the air for me—
Till that her blush made me my shame to see.

VII

No more, my dear, no more these counsels try;
O give my passions leave to run their race;
Let Fortune lay on me her worst disgrace;
Let folk o'er-charged with brain against me cry;
Let clouds bedim my face, break in mine eye;
Let me no steps, but of lost labour, trace;
Let all the earth with scorn recount my case—
But do not will me from my love to fly.
I do not envy Aristotle's wit,
Nor do aspire to Cæsar's bleeding fame;
Nor aught do care, though some above me sit;
Nor hope, nor wish, another course to frame,
But that which once may win thy cruel heart:
Thou art my wit, and thou my virtue art.

VIII

Love still a boy, and oft a wanton, is,
School'd only by his mother's tender eye;
What wonder then, if he his lesson miss,
When for so soft a rod dear play he try?
And yet my Star, because a sugar'd kiss
In sport I suck'd, while she asleep did lie,
Doth lour, nay chide, nay threat, for only this.
Sweet, it was saucy Love, not humble I.
But no 'scuse serves; she makes her wrath appear
In beauty's throne—see now, who dares come near
Those scarlet judges, threat'ning bloody pain?
O heav'nly Fool, thy most kiss-worthy face
Anger invests with such a lovely grace,
That anger's self I needs must kiss again.

IX

I never drank of Aganippe well,
Nor ever did in shade of Tempe sit,
And Muses scorn with vulgar brains to dwell;
Poor lay-man I, for sacred rites unfit.
Some do I hear of Poets' fury tell,
But (God wot) wot not what they mean by it;
And this I swear by blackest brook of hell,
I am no pick-purse of another's wit.
How falls it then, that with so smooth an ease
My thoughts I speak, and what I speak doth flow
In verse, and that my verse best wits doth please?
Guess me the cause—what is it thus?—fye, no.
Or so?—much less. How then? sure thus it is,
My lips are sweet, inspired with Stella's kiss.

X

Of all the kings that ever here did reign,
Edward, named Fourth, as first in praise I name,
Not for his fair outside, nor well-lined brain—
Although less gifts imp feathers oft on Fame.
Nor that he could, young-wise, wise-valiant, frame
His sire's revenge, join'd with a kingdom's gain;
And, gain'd by Mars could yet mad Mars so tame,
That Balance weigh'd what Sword did late obtain.
Nor that he made the Floure-de-luce so 'fraid,
Though strongly hedged of bloody Lions' paws
That witty Lewis to him a tribute paid.
Nor this, nor that, nor any such small cause—
But only, for this worthy knight durst prove
To lose his crown rather than fail his love.

XI

O happy Thames, that didst my STELLA bear,
I saw thyself, with many a smiling line
Upon thy cheerful face, Joy's livery wear,
While those fair planets on thy streams did shine;
The boat for joy could not to dance forbear,
While wanton winds, with beauty so divine
Ravish'd, stay'd not, till in her golden hair
They did themselves (O sweetest prison) twine.
And fain those Æol's youth there would their stay
Have made; but, forced by nature still to fly,
First did with puffing kiss those locks display.
She, so dishevell'd, blush'd; from window I
With sight thereof cried out, O fair disgrace,
Let honour's self to thee grant highest place!

XII

Highway, since you my chief Parnassus be;
And that my Muse, to some ears not unsweet,
Tempers her words to trampling horses' feet,
More soft than to a chamber melody,—
Now blessed You bear onward blessed Me
To Her, where I my heart safe left shall meet,
My Muse and I must you of duty greet
With thanks and wishes, wishing thankfully.
Be you still fair, honour'd by public heed,
By no encroachment wrong'd, nor time forgot;
Nor blam'd for blood, nor shamed for sinful deed.
And that you know, I envy you no lot
Of highest wish, I wish you so much bliss,
Hundreds of years you STELLA's feet may kiss.

SONNETS OF SIR PHILIP SYDNEY 85

Of the foregoing, the first, the second, and the last sonnet, are my favourites. But the general beauty of them all is, that they are so perfectly characteristical. The spirit of 'learning and of chivalry',—of which union, Spenser has entitled Sydney to have been the 'president', —shines through them. I confess I can see nothing of the 'jejune' or 'frigid' in them ; much less of the 'stiff' and 'cumbrous'—which I have sometimes heard objected to the Arcadia. The verse runs off swiftly and gallantly. It might have been tuned to the trumpet ; or tempered (as himself expresses it) to 'trampling horses' feet'. They abound in felicitous phrases—

> O heav'nly Fool, thy most kiss-worthy face—
>> *8th Sonnet.*

> ——Sweet pillows, sweetest bed ;
> A chamber deaf to noise, and blind to light ;
> A rosy garland, and a weary head.
>> *2nd Sonnet.*

> ——That sweet enemy,—France—
>> *5th Sonnet.*

But they are not rich in words only, in vague and unlocalised feelings—the failing too much of some poetry of the present day—they are full, material, and circumstantiated. Time and place appropriates every one of them. It is not a fever of passion wasting itself upon a thin diet of dainty [1]words, but a transcendent passion pervading and illuminating action, pursuits, studies, feats of arms, the opinions of contemporaries and his judgment of them. An historical thread runs through them, which almost affixes a date to them ; marks the *when* and *where* they were written.

I have dwelt the longer upon what I conceive the merit of these poems, because I have been hurt by the wantonness (I wish I could treat it by a gentler name) with which [2]W. H. takes every occasion of insulting the memory of Sir Philip Sydney. But the decisions of the Author of Table Talk, &c., (most profound and subtle where they are, as for the most part, just) are more safely to be relied upon, on subjects and authors he has a partiality for, than

---

[1] *For a footnote of 1823, here omitted, see Editor's Notes.* [2] W. H.] a favourite critic of our day 1823.

on such as he has conceived an accidental prejudice against.
Milton wrote sonnets, and was a king-hater; and it was
congenial perhaps to sacrifice a courtier to a patriot. But
I was unwilling to lose a *fine idea* from my mind. The
noble images, passions, sentiments, and poetical delicacies
of character, scattered all over the Arcadia (spite of some
stiffness and encumberment), justify to me the character
which his contemporaries have left us of the writer. I cannot
think with [1]the Critic, that Sir Philip Sydney was that
opprobrious thing which a foolish nobleman in his insolent
hostility chose to term him. I call to mind the epitaph
[2]made on him, to guide me to juster thoughts of him; and
I repose upon the beautiful lines in the ' Friend's Passion
for his Astrophel ', printed with the Elegies of Spenser
and others.

> You knew—who knew not Astrophel ?
> (That I should live to say I knew,
> And have not in possession still !)—
> Things known permit me to renew—
>   Of him you know his merit such,
>   I cannot say—you hear—too much.

> Within these woods of Arcady
> He chief delight and pleasure took ;
> And on the mountain Partheny,
> Upon the crystal liquid brook,
>   The Muses met him every day,
>   That taught him sing, to write, and say.

> When he descended down the mount,
> His personage seemed most divine :
> A thousand graces one might count
> Upon his lovely chearful eyne,
>   To hear him speak, and sweetly smile,
>   You were in Paradise the while.

> *A sweet attractive kind of grace ;*
> *A full assurance given by looks ;*
> *Continual comfort in a face,*
> *The lineaments of Gospel books—*
>   *I trow that count'nance cannot lye,*
>   *Whose thoughts are legible in the eye.*
> *   *   *   *   *   *

---

[1] the Critic] Mr. Hazlitt 1823.   [2] made of Lord Brooke 1823.

Above all others this is he,
Which erst approved in his song,
That love and honour might agree,
And that pure love will do no wrong.
    Sweet saints, it is no sin or blame
    To love a man of virtuous name.

Did never Love so sweetly breathe
In any mortal breast before :
Did never Muse inspire beneath
A Poet's brain with finer store.
    He wrote of Love with high conceit,
    And Beauty rear'd above her height.

Or let any one read the deeper sorrows (grief running into rage) in the Poem,—the last in the collection accompanying the above,—which from internal testimony I believe to be Lord Brooke's,—beginning with ' Silence augmenteth grief',—and then seriously ask himself, whether the subject of such absorbing and confounding regrets could have been *that thing* which Lord Oxford termed him.

NEWSPAPERS THIRTY-FIVE YEARS AGO

[Printed under the title, *Peter's Net.   By the Author of ' Elia '.
No. II.—On the Total Defect of the faculty of Imagination, observable in
the works of modern British Artists*, in *The Englishman's Magazine,*
vol. ii, no. ii, p. 137 (Oct., 1831). See *Recollections of a late Royal
Academician*, p. 429 above. Collected under above title in *The Last
Essays of Elia*, 1833.   Text of 1833.]

DAN STUART once told us, that he did not remember that he ever deliberately walked into the Exhibition at Somerset House in his life. He might occasionally have escorted a party of ladies across the way that were going in ; but he never went in of his own head. Yet the office of the Morning Post newspaper stood then just where it does now—we are carrying you back, Reader, some thirty years [1] or more—with its gilt-globe-topt front facing that emporium of our artists' grand Annual Exposure. We sometimes wish, that we had observed the same abstinence with Daniel.

A word or two of D. S. He ever appeared to us one of the finest tempered of Editors. Perry, of the Morning

[1] or more *omit* 1831.

Chronicle, was equally pleasant, with a dash, no slight one either, of the courtier. S. was frank, plain, and English all over. We have worked for both these gentlemen.

It is soothing to contemplate the head of the Ganges; to trace the first little bubblings of a mighty river;

> With holy reverence to approach the rocks,
> Whence glide the streams renowned in ancient song.

Fired with a perusal of the Abyssinian Pilgrim's exploratory ramblings after the cradle of the infant Nilus, we well remember on one fine summer holyday (a ' whole day's leave ' we called it at Christ's Hospital) sallying forth at rise of sun, not very well provisioned either for such an undertaking, to trace the current of the New River— Middletonian stream !—to its scaturient source, as we had read, in meadows by fair Amwell. Gallantly did we commence our solitary quest—for it was essential to the dignity of a DISCOVERY, that no eye of schoolboy, save our own, should beam on the detection. By flowery spots, and verdant lanes, skirting Hornsey, Hope trained us on in many a baffling turn; endless, hopeless meanders, as it seemed; or as if the jealous waters had *dodged* us, reluctant to have the humble spot of their nativity revealed; till spent, and nigh famished, before set of the same sun, we sate down somewhere by Bowes Farm, near Tottenham, with a tithe of our proposed labours only yet accomplished; sorely convinced in spirit, that that Brucian enterprise was as yet too arduous for our young shoulders.

Not more refreshing to the thirsty curiosity of the traveller is the tracing of some mighty waters up to their shallow fontlet, than it is to a pleased and candid reader to go back to the inexperienced essays, the first callow flights in authorship, of some established name in literature; from the Gnat which preluded to the Æneid, to the Duck which Samuel Johnson trod on.

[1]In those days every Morning Paper, as an essential retainer to its establishment, kept an author, who was

---

[1] *In* 1831 *this paragraph begins :*—We ourself—PETER—in whose inevitable NET already Managers and R. A.s lie caught and floundering— and more peradventure shall flounder—were, in the humble times to which we have been recurring, small Fishermen indeed, essaying upon minnows ; angling for quirks, not *men*. In those days *etc.*

bound to furnish daily a quantum of witty paragraphs. Sixpence a joke—and it was thought pretty high too—was Dan Stuart's settled remuneration in these cases. The chat of the day, scandal, but, above all, *dress*, furnished the material. The length of no paragraph was to exceed seven lines. Shorter they might be, but they must be poignant.

A fashion of *flesh*, or rather *pink*-coloured hose for the ladies, luckily coming up at the juncture, when we were on our probation for the place of Chief Jester to S.'s Paper, established our reputation in that line. We were pronounced a ' capital hand '. O the conceits which we varied upon *red* in all its prismatic differences ! from the trite and obvious flower of Cytherea, to the [1]flaming costume of the lady that has her sitting upon ' many waters '. Then there was the collateral topic of ancles. What an occasion to a truly chaste writer, like ourself, of touching that nice brink, and yet never tumbling over it, of a seemingly ever approximating something ' not quite proper ' ; while, like a skilful posture-master, balancing betwixt decorums and their opposites, he keeps the line, from which a hair's-breadth deviation is destruction ; hovering in the confines of light and darkness, or where 'both seem either' ; a hazy uncertain delicacy ; Autolycus-like in the Play, still putting off his expectant auditory with ' Whoop, do me no harm, good man ! ' But, above all, that conceit arrided us most at [2]that time, and still tickles our midriff to remember, where, allusively to the flight of Astræa—*ultima Cœlestûm terras reliquit*—we pronounced—in reference to the stockings still—that MODESTY TAKING HER FINAL LEAVE OF MORTALS, HER LAST BLUSH WAS VISIBLE IN HER ASCENT TO THE HEAVENS BY THE TRACT OF THE GLOWING INSTEP. This might be called the crowning conceit ; and was esteemed tolerable writing in those days.

But the fashion of jokes, with all other things, passes away ; as did the transient mode which had so favoured us. The ancles of our fair friends in a few weeks began to reassume their whiteness, and left us scarce a leg to stand upon. Other female whims followed, but none,

[1] flaming] flaunting 1831.   [2] that] the 1831.

methought, so pregnant, so invitatory of shrewd conceits, and more than single meanings.

Somebody has said, that to swallow six cross-buns daily consecutively for a fortnight would surfeit the stoutest digestion. But to have to furnish as many jokes daily, and that not for a fortnight, but for a long twelvemonth, as we were constrained to do, was a little harder [1]execution. 'Man goeth forth to his work until the evening'—from a reasonable hour in the morning, we presume it was meant. Now as our main occupation took us up from eight till five every day in the City ; and as our evening hours, at that time of life, had generally to do with any thing rather than business, it follows, that the only time we could spare for this manufactory of jokes—our supplementary livelihood, that supplied us in every want beyond mere bread and cheese—was exactly that part of the day which (as we have heard of No Man's Land) may be fitly denominated No Man's Time ; that is, no time in which a man ought to be up, and awake, in. To speak more plainly, it is that time, of an hour, or an hour and a half's duration, in which a man, whose occasions call him up so preposterously, has to wait for his breakfast.

O those headaches at dawn of day, when at five, or half-past-five in summer, and not much later in the dark seasons, we were compelled to rise, having been perhaps not above four hours in bed—(for we were no go-to-beds with the lamb, though we anticipated the lark ofttimes in her [2]rising—we liked a parting cup at midnight, as all young men did before these effeminate times, and to have our friends about us—we were not constellated under Aquarius, that watery sign, and therefore incapable of Bacchus, cold, washy, bloodless—we were none of your Basilian water-sponges, nor had taken our degrees at Mount Ague— we were right toping Capulets, jolly companions, we and they)—but to have to get up, as we said before, curtailed of half our fair sleep, fasting, with only a dim vista of refreshing Bohea in the distance—to be necessitated to rouse ourselves at the detestable rap of an old hag of a domestic, who seemed to take a diabolical pleasure in her announcement that it was 'time to rise'; and whose

[1] execution] exaction 1831.   [2] rising] risings 1831.

chappy knuckles we have often yearned to amputate, and
string them up at our chamber door, to be a terror to all
such unseasonable rest-breakers in future—

'Facil' and sweet, as Virgil sings, had been the 'descending ' of the over-night, balmy the first sinking of the heavy
head upon the pillow ; but to get up, as he goes on to say,

—revocare gradus, superasque evadere ad auras—

and to get up moreover to make jokes with malice prepended—there was the ' labour ', there the ' work '.

No Egyptian taskmaster ever devised a slavery like to
that, our slavery. No fractious operants ever turned out
for half the tyranny, which this necessity exercised upon
us. Half a dozen jests in a day (bating Sundays too), why,
it seems nothing ! We make twice the number every day
in our lives as a matter of course, and claim no Sabbatical
exemptions. But then they come into our head. But
when the head has to go out to them—when the mountain
must go to Mahomet—

Reader, try it for once, only for one short twelvemonth.

It was not every week that a fashion of pink stockings
came up ; but mostly, instead of it, some rugged, untract-
able subject ; some topic impossible to be contorted into
the risible ; some feature, upon which no smile could play ;
some flint, from which no process of ingenuity could procure
a distillation. There they lay ; there your appointed tale
of brick-making was set before you, which you must
finish, with or without straw, as it happened. The craving
Dragon—*the Public*—like him in Bel's temple—must be
fed ; it expected its daily rations ; and Daniel, and ourselves, to do us justice, did the best we could on this side
bursting [1]him.

While we were wringing out coy sprightliness for the
Post, and writhing under the toil of what is called ' easy
writing', Bob Allen, our *quondam* schoolfellow, was tapping
his impracticable brains in a like service for the 'Oracle'.
Not that Robert troubled himself much about wit. If his
paragraphs had a sprightly air about them, it was sufficient.
He carried this nonchalance so far at last, that a matter of

[1] him.] him ; ' taking pitch, and fat, and hair, and seething them
together, and making lumps thereof '.   1831.

intelligence, and that no very important one, was not
seldom palmed upon his employers for a good jest ; for
example sake—' *Walking yesterday morning casually down
Snow Hill, who should we meet but Mr. Deputy Humphreys !
we rejoice to add, that the worthy Deputy appeared to enjoy
a good state of health. We do not remember ever to have seen
him look better.*' This gentleman, so surprisingly met upon
Snow Hill, from some peculiarities in gait or gesture, was
a constant butt for mirth to the small paragraph-mongers
of the day ; and our friend thought that he might have
his fling at him with the rest. We met A. in Holborn
shortly after this extraordinary rencounter, which he told
with tears of satisfaction in his eyes, and chuckling at the
anticipated effects of its announcement next day in the
paper. We did not quite comprehend where the wit of it
lay at the time ; nor was it easy to be detected, when the
thing came out, advantaged by type and letter-press.
He had better have met any thing that morning than a
Common Council Man. His services were shortly after
dispensed with, on the plea that his paragraphs of late
had been deficient in point. The one in question, it must
be owned, had an air, in the opening especially, proper to
awaken curiosity ; and the sentiment, or moral, wears the
aspect of humanity, and good neighbourly feeling. But
somehow the conclusion was not judged altogether to
answer to the magnificent promise of the premises. We
traced our friend's pen afterwards in the ' True Briton ',
the ' Star ', the ' Traveller ',—from all which he was successively dismissed, the Proprietors having ' no further
occasion for his services '. Nothing was easier than to detect
him. When wit failed, or topics ran low, there constantly
appeared the following—' *It is not generally known that
the three Blue Balls at the Pawnbrokers' shops are the ancient
arms of Lombardy. The Lombards were the first money-
brokers in Europe.*' Bob has done more to set the public
right on this important point of blazonry, than the whole
College of Heralds.

The appointment of a regular wit has long ceased to be
a part of the economy of a Morning Paper. Editors find
their own jokes, or do as well without them. Parson Este,
and Topham, brought up the set custom of ' witty para-

graphs' first in the 'World'. Boaden was a reigning
paragraphist in his day, and succeeded poor Allen in the
Oracle. But, as we said, the fashion of jokes passes away;
and it would be difficult to discover in the Biographer of
Mrs. Siddons, any traces of that vivacity and fancy which
charmed the whole town at the commencement of the
present century. Even the prelusive delicacies of the
present writer—the curt 'Astræan allusion'—would be
thought pedantic, and out of date, in these days.

From the office of the Morning Post (for we may as well
exhaust our Newspaper Reminiscences at once) by change
of property in the paper, we were transferred, mortifying
exchange! to the office of the Albion Newspaper, late
Rackstrow's Museum, in Fleet-street. What a transition
—from a handsome apartment, from rose-wood desks, and
silver-inkstands, to an office—no office, but a *den* rather,
but just redeemed from the occupation of dead monsters,
of which it seemed redolent—from the centre of loyalty
and fashion, to a focus of vulgarity and sedition! Here
in murky closet, inadequate from its square contents to
the receipt of the two bodies of Editor, and humble para-
graph-maker, together at one time, sat in the discharge of
his new Editorial functions (the 'Bigod' of Elia) the
redoubted John Fenwick.

F., without a guinea in his pocket, and having left not
many in the pockets of his friends whom he might command, had purchased (on tick doubtless) the whole and
sole Editorship, Proprietorship, with all the rights and
titles (such as they were worth) of the Albion, from one
Lovell; of whom we know nothing, save that he had
stood in the pillory for a libel on the Prince of Wales.
With this hopeless concern—for it had been sinking ever
since its commencement, and could now reckon upon not
more than a hundred subscribers—F. resolutely determined upon pulling down the Government in the first
instance, and making both our fortunes by way of corollary.
For seven weeks and more did this infatuated Democrat
go about borrowing seven shilling pieces, and lesser coin,
to meet the daily demands of the Stamp Office, which
allowed no credit to publications of that side in politics.
An outcast from politer bread, we attached our small

talents to the forlorn fortunes of our friend. Our occupation now was to write treason.

Recollections of feelings—which were all that now
remained from our first boyish heats kindled by the French
Revolution, when if we were misled, we erred in the company of some, who are accounted very good men now—
rather than any tendency at this time to Republican
doctrines—assisted us in assuming a style of writing, while
the paper lasted, consonant in no very under-tone to the
right earnest fanaticism of F. Our cue was now to insinu-
ate, rather than recommend, possible abdications. Blocks,
axes, Whitehall tribunals, were covered with [1]flowers of so
cunning a periphrasis—as Mr. Bayes says, never naming
the *thing* directly—that the keen eye of an Attorney
General was insufficient to detect the lurking snake among
them. There were times, indeed, when we sighed for our
more gentleman-like occupation under Stuart. But with
change of masters it is ever change of service. Already
one paragraph, and another, as we learned afterwards
from a gentleman at the Treasury, had begun to be marked
at that office, with a view of its being submitted at least
to the attention of the proper Law Officers—when an
unlucky, or rather lucky epigram from our pen, aimed at
Sir J——s M——h, who was on the eve of departing for
India to reap the fruits of his apostacy, as F. pronounced
it, (it is hardly worth particularising), happening to offend
the nice sense of Lord, or, as he then delighted to be called,
Citizen Stanhope, deprived F. at once of the last hopes
of a guinea from the last patron that had stuck by us ;
and breaking up our establishment, left us to the safe,
but somewhat mortifying, neglect of the Crown Lawyers.—
It was about this time, or a little earlier, that Dan. Stuart
made that curious confession to us, that he had ' never
deliberately walked into an Exhibition at Somerest House
in his [2]life '.

---

[1] flowers] the flowers 1831.   [2] life '.] life '.—(To be continued.)
1831.

BARRENNESS OF THE IMAGINATIVE FACULTY IN THE PRODUCTIONS OF MODERN ART

[Written in 1831 for insertion—under the heading *Peter's Net. No. III.*
—in the November issue of *The Englishman's Magazine*, as a sequel to
the essay afterwards entitled *Newspapers Thirty-five Years ago* (see
prefatory note to this Essay, p. 87 above). Printed in part—*The
Englishman's Magazine* having ceased with the October number—in
The Reflector (Moxon's weekly), no. ii (week ending Dec. 22, 1832);
and, lastly, printed under the title, *On the Total Defect of the Quality
of Imagination observable in the Works of Modern British Artists. By
the Author of the Essays signed ' Elia'*, in *The Athenæum*, Jan. 12, 19,
26, and Feb. 2, 1833. Collected in *The Last Essays of Elia*, 1833. Text
of *Last Essays*.]

[1]HOGARTH excepted, can we produce any one painter
within the last fifty years, or since the humour of exhibiting
began, that has treated a story *imaginatively* ? By this
we mean, upon whom his subject has so acted, that it has
seemed to direct *him*—not to be arranged by him ?   Any
upon whom its leading or collateral points have impressed
themselves so tyrannically, that he dared not treat it
otherwise, lest he should falsify a revelation ?   Any that
has imparted to his compositions, not merely so much
truth as is enough to convey a story with clearness, but
that individualising property, which should keep the subject so treated distinct in feature from every other subject,
however similar, and to common apprehensions almost
identical ; so as that we might say, this and this part could
have found an appropriate place in no other picture in the
world but this ?   Is there anything in modern art—we will
not demand that it should be equal—but in any way
analogous to what Titian has effected, in that wonderful
bringing together of two times in the ' Ariadne ', in the
National Gallery ?   Precipitous, with his reeling Satyr rout
about him, re-peopling and re-illuming suddenly the
waste places, drunk with a new fury beyond the grape,
Bacchus, born in fire, fire-like flings himself at the Cretan.
This is the time present.   With this telling of the story an
artist, and no ordinary one, might remain richly proud.

---

[1] *The first three paragraphs appeared in* THE ATHEN., *Jan.* 12, p. 26.

Guido, in his harmonious version of it, saw no further.
But from the depths of the imaginative spirit Titian has
recalled past time, and laid it contributory with the present
to one simultaneous effect. With the desert all ringing
with the mad cymbals of his followers, made lucid with the
presence and new offers of a god,—as if unconscious of
Bacchus, or but idly casting her eyes as upon some unconcerning pageant—her soul undistracted from Theseus—
Ariadne is still pacing the solitary shore, in as much heart-
silence, and in almost the same local solitude, with which
she awoke at day-break to catch the forlorn last glances of
the sail that bore away the Athenian.

Here are two points miraculously co-uniting ; fierce
society, with the feeling of solitude still absolute ; noon-day
revelations, with the accidents of the dull grey dawn
unquenched and lingering ; the *present* Bacchus, with the
past Ariadne ; two stories, with double Time ; separate,
and harmonising. Had the artist made the woman one
shade less indifferent to the God ; still more, had she
expressed a rapture at his advent, where would have been
the story of the mighty desolation of the heart previous ?
merged in the insipid accident of a flattering offer met with
a welcome acceptance. The broken heart for Theseus was
not lightly to be pieced up by a God.

We have before us a fine rough print, from a picture by
Raphael in the Vatican. It is the Presentation of the new-
born Eve to Adam by the Almighty. A fairer mother of
mankind we might imagine, and a goodlier sire perhaps of
men since born. But these are matters subordinate to
the conception of the *situation*, displayed in this extraordinary production. A tolerably modern artist would
have been satisfied with tempering certain raptures of
connubial anticipation, with a suitable acknowledgment
to the Giver of the blessing, in the countenance of the first
bridegroom ; something like the divided attention of the
child (Adam was here a child man) between the given toy,
and the mother who had just blest it with the bauble. This
is the obvious, the first-sight view, the superficial. An
artist of a higher grade, considering the awful presence they
were in, would have taken care to subtract something from
the expression of the more human passion, and to heighten

the more spiritual one. This would be as much as an
exhibition-goer, from the opening of Somerset House to last
year's show, has been encouraged to look for. It is obvious
to hint at a lower expression yet, in a picture, that for
respects of drawing and colouring, might be deemed not
wholly inadmissible within these art-fostering walls, in
which the raptures should be as ninety-nine, the gratitude
as one, or perhaps Zero ! By neither the one passion nor the
other has Raphael expounded the situation of Adam. Singly
upon his brow sits the absorbing sense of wonder at the
created miracle. The *moment* is seized by the intuitive
artist, perhaps not self-conscious of his art, in which neither
of the conflicting emotions—a moment how abstracted—
have had time to spring up, or to battle for indecorous
mastery.—We have seen a landscape of a justly admired
neoteric, in which he aimed at delineating a fiction, one of
the most severely beautiful in antiquity—the gardens of
the Hesperides. To do Mr. —— justice, he had painted
a laudable orchard, with fitting seclusion, and a veritable
dragon (of which a Polypheme by Poussin is somehow
a fac-simile for the situation), looking over into the world
shut out backwards, so that none but a ' still-climbing
Hercules ' could hope to catch a peep at the admired
Ternary of Recluses. No conventual porter could keep
his keys better than this custos with the ' lidless eyes '.
He not only sees that none *do* intrude into that privacy, but,
as clear as daylight, that none but *Hercules aut Diabolus*
by any manner of means *can*. So far all is well. We have
absolute solitude here or nowhere. *Ab extra* the damsels
are snug enough. But here the artist's courage seems to
have failed him. He began to pity his pretty charge, and,
to comfort the irksomeness, has peopled their solitude with
a bevy of fair attendants, maids of honour, or ladies of the
bed-chamber, according to the approved etiquette at a court
of the nineteenth century ; giving to the whole scene the
air of a *fête champêtre*, if we will but excuse the absence of
the gentlemen. This is well, and Watteauish. But what
is become of the solitary mystery—the

> Daughters three,
> That sing around the golden tree ?

H

[1]This is not the way in which Poussin would have treated this subject.

[2]The paintings, or rather the stupendous architectural designs, of [3]a modern artist, have been urged as objections to the theory of our motto. They are of a character, we confess, to stagger it. His towered structures are of the highest order of the material sublime. Whether they were dreams, or transcripts of some elder workmanship—Assyrian ruins old—restored by this mighty artist, they satisfy our most stretched and craving conceptions of the glories of the antique world. It is a pity that they were ever peopled. On that side, the imagination of the artist halts, and appears defective. Let us examine the point of the story in the ' Belshazzar's Feast '. We will introduce it by an apposite anecdote.

The court historians of the day record, that at the first dinner given by the late King (then Prince Regent) at the Pavilion, the following characteristic frolic was played off. The guests were select and admiring ; the banquet profuse and admirable ; the lights lustrous and oriental ; the eye was perfectly dazzled with the display of plate, among which the great gold salt-cellar, brought from the regalia in the Tower for this especial purpose, itself a tower ! stood conspicuous for its magnitude. And now the Rev. * * * * the then admired court Chaplain, was proceeding with the grace, when, at a signal given, the lights were suddenly overcast, and a huge transparency was discovered, in which glittered in golden letters—

' BRIGHTON—EARTHQUAKE—SWALLOW-UP-ALIVE ! '

Imagine the confusion of the guests ; the Georges and garters, jewels, bracelets, moulted upon the occasion ! The fans dropt, and picked up the next morning by the sly court pages ! Mrs. Fitz-what's-her-name fainting, and the Countess of * * * * holding the smelling bottle, till the good-humoured Prince caused harmony to be restored by calling in fresh candles, and declaring that the whole was nothing but a pantomime *hoax*, got up by the ingenious

---

[1] This] Now this *Athen.*, *Jan.* 12.   [2] *This and the nine following*
paragraphs appeared on Jan. 19, p. 42.   [3] a modern artist] M——
Athen., *Jan.* 19.

Mr. Farley, of Covent Garden, from hints which his Royal Highness himself had furnished ! Then imagine the infinite applause that followed, the mutual rallyings, the declarations that ' they were not much frightened ', of the assembled galaxy.

The point of time in the picture exactly answers to the appearance of the transparency in the anecdote. The huddle, the flutter, the bustle, the escape, the alarm, and the mock alarm ; the prettinesses heightened by consternation ; the courtier's fear which was flattery, and the lady's which was affectation ; all that we may conceive to have taken place in a mob of Brighton courtiers, sympathising with the well-acted surprise of their sovereign ; all this, and no more, is exhibited by the well-dressed lords and ladies in the Hall of Belus. Just this sort of consternation we have seen among a flock of disquieted wild geese at the report only of a gun having gone off !

But is this vulgar fright, this mere animal anxiety for the preservation of their persons,—such as we have witnessed at a theatre, when a slight alarm of fire has been given—an adequate exponent of a supernatural terror ? the way in which the finger of God, writing judgments, would have been met by the withered conscience ? There is a human fear, and a divine fear. The one is disturbed, restless, and bent upon escape. The other is bowed down, effortless, passive. When the spirit appeared before Eliphaz in the visions of the night, and the hair of his flesh stood up, was it in the thoughts of the Temanite to ring the bell of his chamber, or to call up the servants ? But let us see in the text what there is to justify all this huddle of vulgar consternation.

From the words of Daniel it appears that Belshazzar had made a great feast to a thousand of his lords, and drank wine before the thousand. The golden and silver vessels are gorgeously enumerated, with the princes, the king's concubines, and his wives. Then follows—

' In the same hour came forth fingers of a man's hand, and wrote over against the candlestick upon the plaster of the wall of the king's palace ; and the *king* saw the part of the hand that wrote. Then the *king's* countenance was changed, and his thoughts troubled him, so that the joints of his loins were loosened, and his knees smote one against another.'

This is the plain text. By no hint can it be otherwise inferred, but that the appearance was solely confined to the fancy of Belshazzar, that his single brain was troubled. Not a word is spoken of its being seen by any else there present, not even by the queen herself, who merely undertakes for the interpretation of the phenomenon, as related to her, doubtless, by her husband. The lords are simply said to be astonished ; *i.e.* at the trouble and the change of countenance in their sovereign. Even the prophet does not appear to have seen the scroll, which the king saw. He recalls it only, as Joseph did the Dream to the King of Egypt. ' Then was the part of the hand sent from him [the Lord], and this writing was written.' He speaks of the phantasm as past.

Then what becomes of this needless multiplication of the miracle ? this message to a royal conscience, singly expressed—for it was said, ' thy kingdom is divided,'—simultaneously impressed upon the fancies of a thousand courtiers, who were implied in it neither directly nor grammatically ?

But admitting the artist's own version of the story, and that the sight was seen also by the thousand courtiers—let it have been visible to all Babylon—as the knees of Belshazzar were shaken, and his countenance troubled, even so would the knees of every man in [1]Babylon, and their countenances, as of an individual man, have been troubled ; bowed, bent down, so would they have remained, stupor-fixed, with no thought of struggling with that inevitable judgment.

Not all that is optically possible to be seen, is to be shown in every picture. The eye delightedly dwells upon the brilliant individualities in a ' Marriage at Cana ', by Veronese, or Titian, to the very texture and colour of the wedding garments, the ring glittering upon the bride's finger, the metal and fashion of the wine pots ; for at such seasons there is leisure and luxury to be curious. But in a ' day of judgment ', or in a ' day of lesser horrors, yet divine ', as at the impious feast of Belshazzar, the eye should see, as

[1] Babylon,] Babylon have shook, *Athen.*, *Jan.* 19.

the actual eye of an agent or patient in the immediate scene would see, only in masses and indistinction. Not only the female attire and jewelry exposed to the critical eye of [1]the fashion, as minutely as the dresses in a lady's magazine, in [2]the criticised picture,—but perhaps the curiosities of anatomical science, and [3]studied diversities of posture, in the falling angels and sinners of Michael Angelo,—have no business in their great subjects. There was no leisure [4]of them.

[5]By a wise falsification, the great masters of painting got at their true conclusions ; by not showing the actual appearances, that is, all that was to be seen at any given moment by an indifferent eye, but only what the eye might be supposed to see in the doing or suffering of some portentous action. Suppose the moment of the swallowing up of Pompeii. There they were to be seen—houses, columns, architectural proportions, differences of public and private buildings, men and women at their standing occupations, the diversified thousand postures, attitudes, dresses, in some confusion truly, but physically they were visible. But what eye saw them at that eclipsing moment, which reduces confusion to a kind of unity, and when the senses are upturned from their proprieties, when sight and hearing are a feeling only ? A thousand years have passed, and we are at leisure to contemplate the weaver fixed standing at his shuttle, the baker at his oven, and to turn over with antiquarian coolness the pots and pans of Pompeii.

' Sun, stand thou still upon Gibeah, and thou, Moon, in the valley of Ajalon.' Who, in reading this magnificent Hebraism, in his conception, sees aught but the heroic son of Nun, with the outstretched arm, and the greater and lesser [6]light obsequious ? Doubtless there were to be seen hill and dale, and chariots and horsemen, on open plain, or winding by secret defiles, and all the circumstances and stratagems of war. But whose eyes would have been conscious of this array at the interposition of the synchronic miracle ? Yet in the picture of this subject by the artist of

<hr>

[1] the omit Athen.   [2] the criticised] Mr. M.'s Athen.   [3] studied diversities] individuality Athen.   [4] of] for Athen.   [5] This and the three following paragraphs appeared on Jan. 26, p. 57.   [6] light] lights Athen.

the ' Belshazzar's Feast '—no ignoble work [1]either—the mar-
shalling and landscape of the war is everything, the miracle
sinks into an anecdote of the day; and the eye may 'dart
through rank and file traverse ' for some minutes, before it
shall discover, among his armed followers, *which is Joshua!*
Not modern art alone, but ancient, where only it is to be
found if anywhere, can be detected erring, from defect of
this imaginative faculty. The world has nothing to show
of the preternatural in painting, transcending the figure of
Lazarus bursting his grave-clothes, in the great picture at
Angerstein's. It seems a thing between two beings. A
ghastly horror at itself struggles with newly-apprehending
gratitude at second life bestowed. It cannot forget that
it was a ghost. It has hardly felt that it is a body. It has
to tell of the world of spirits.—Was it from a feeling, that
the crowd of half-impassioned by-standers, and the still
more irrelevant herd of passers-by at a distance, who have
not heard or but faintly have been told of the passing
miracle, admirable as they are in design and hue—for it
is a glorified work—do not respond adequately to the
action—that the single figure of the Lazarus has been attributed to Michael Angelo, and the mighty Sebastian
unfairly robbed of the fame of the greater half of the
interest ? Now that there were not indifferent passers-by
within actual scope of the eyes of those present at the
miracle, to whom the sound of it had but faintly, or not at
all, reached, it would be hardihood to deny; but would they
see them ? or can the mind in the conception of it admit
of such unconcerning objects ? can it think of them at all ?
or what associating league to the imagination can there be
between the seers, and the seers not, of a presential miracle ?

Were an artist to paint upon demand a picture of a
Dryad, we will ask whether, in the present low state of
expectation, the patron would not, or ought not to be fully
satisfied with a beautiful naked figure recumbent under
wide-stretched oaks ? Disseat those woods, and place the
same figure among fountains, and falls of pellucid water,
and you have a—Naiad ! Not so in a rough print we have
seen after Julio Romano, we think—for it is long since—
there, by no process, with mere change of scene, could the

---

[1] either] neither *Athen.*

figure have reciprocated characters. Long, grotesque, fantastic, yet with a grace of her own, beautiful in convolution
and distortion, linked to her connatural tree, co-twisting
with its limbs her own, till both seemed either—these,
animated branches ; those, disanimated members—yet the
animal and vegetable lives sufficiently kept distinct—*his*
Dryad lay—an approximation of two natures, which to
conceive, it must be seen ; analogous to, not the same
with, the delicacies of Ovidian transformations.

To the lowest subjects, and, to a superficial comprehen-
sion, the most barren, the Great Masters gave loftiness and
fruitfulness. The large eyes of genius saw in the meanness
of present objects their capabilities of treatment from their
relations to some grand Past or Future. How has Raphael
—we must still linger about the Vatican—treated the
humbler craft of the ship-builder, in *his* ' Building of the
Ark ' ? It is in that scriptural series, to which we have referred, and which, judging from some fine rough old graphic
sketches of them which we possess, seem to be of a higher
and more poetic grade than even the cartoons. The dim of
sight are the timid and the shrinking. There is a cowardice
in modern art. As the Frenchmen, of whom Coleridge's
friend made the prophetic guess at Rome, from the beard
and horns of the Moses of Michael Angelo collected no
inferences beyond that of a He Goat and a Cornuto ; so
from this subject, of mere mechanic promise, it would instinctively turn away, as from one incapable of investiture
with any grandeur. The dock-yards at Woolwich would
object derogatory associations. The depôt at Chatham
would be the mote and the beam in its intellectual eye. But
not to the nautical preparations in the ship-yards of Civita
Vecchia did Raphael look for instructions, when he imagined
the Building of the Vessel that was to be conservatory of
the wrecks of the species of drowned mankind. In the
intensity of the action, he keeps ever out of sight the
meanness of the operation. There is the Patriarch, in calm
forethought, and with holy prescience, [1]giving directions.
And there are his agents—the solitary but sufficient Three—
hewing, sawing, every one with the might and earnestness
of a Demiurgus ; under some instinctive rather than tech-

[1] giving] giving, as guided by heaven, *Athen.*

nical guidance ; giant-muscled ; every one a Hercules, or
liker to those Vulcanian Three, that in [1]sounding caverns
under Mongibello wrought in fire—Brontes, and black
Steropes, and Pyracmon. So work the workmen that
should repair a world !

[2]Artists again err in the confounding of *poetic* with
pictorial subjects. In the latter, the exterior accidents are
nearly everything, the unseen qualities as nothing. Othello's
colour—the infirmities and corpulence of a Sir John Falstaff
—do they haunt us perpetually in the reading ? or are they
obtruded upon our conceptions one time for ninety-nine
that we are lost in admiration at the respective moral or
intellectual attributes of the character ? But in a picture
Othello is *always* a Blackamore ; and the other only Plump
Jack. Deeply corporealised, and enchained hopelessly in the
grovelling fetters of externality, must be the mind, to which,
in its better moments, the image of the high-souled, high-
intelligenced Quixote—the errant Star of Knighthood, made
more tender by eclipse—has never presented itself, divested
from the unhallowed accompaniment of a Sancho, or a
rabblement at the heels of Rosinante. That man has read
his book by halves ; he has laughed, mistaking his author's
purport, which was—tears. The artist that pictures
Quixote (and it is in this degrading point that he is every
season held up at our Exhibitions) in the shallow hope of
exciting mirth, would have joined the rabble at the heels
of his starved steed. We wish not to see *that* counterfeited,
which we would not have wished to see in the reality.
Conscious of the heroic insight of the noble Quixote, who,
on hearing that his withered person was passing, would
have stepped over his threshold to gaze upon his forlorn
habiliments, and the ' strange bed-fellows which misery
brings a man acquainted with ' ? Shade of Cervantes !
who in thy Second Part could put into the mouth of thy
Quixote those high aspirations of a super-chivalrous gal-
lantry, where he replies to one of the shepherdesses, appre-
hensive that he would spoil their pretty net-works, and
inviting him to be a guest with them, in accents like these :
' Truly, fairest Lady, Actæon was not more astonished

---

[1] sounding] the sounding *Athen.*   [2] *This and the next paragraph
appeared on Feb. 2, p. 73.*

when he saw Diana bathing herself [1]at the fountain, than
I have been in beholding your beauty : I commend the
manner of your pastime, and thank you for your kind offers ;
and, if I may serve you, so I may be sure you will be obeyed,
you may command me : for my profession is this, To show
myself thankful, and a doer of good to all sorts of people,
especially of the rank that your person shows you to be ;
and if those nets, as they take up but a little piece of ground,
should take up the whole world, I would seek out new
worlds to pass through, rather than break them : and (he
adds,) that you may give credit to this my exaggeration,
behold at least he that promiseth you this, is Don Quixote
de la Mancha, if haply this name hath come to your hearing.'
Illustrious Romancer ! were the ' fine frenzies', which possessed the brain of thy own Quixote, a fit subject, as in
this second Part, to be exposed to the jeers of Duennas and
Serving Men ? to be monstered, and shown up at the heartless banquets of great men ? Was that pitiable infirmity,
which in thy First Part misleads him, *always from within*,
into half-ludicrous, but more than half-compassionable and
admirable errors, not infliction enough from heaven, that
men by studied artifices must devise and practise upon the
humour, to inflame where they should soothe it ? Why,
Goneril would have blushed to practise upon the abdicated
king at this rate, and the she-wolf Regan not have endured
to play the pranks upon his fled wits, which thou hast made
thy Quixote suffer in Duchesses' halls, and at the hands of
that unworthy nobleman.[a]

In the First Adventures, even, it needed all the art of
the most consummate artist in the Book way that the
world hath yet seen, to keep up in the mind of the reader
the heroic attributes of the character without relaxing ;
so as absolutely that they shall suffer no alloy from the
debasing fellowship of the clown. If it ever obtrudes itself
as a disharmony, are we inclined to laugh ; or not, rather,
to indulge a contrary emotion ?—Cervantes, stung, perchance, by the relish with which *his* Reading Public had

[a] Yet from this Second Part, our cried-up pictures are mostly selected ;
the waiting-women with beards, &c.

---

[1] at] in *Athen.*

received the fooleries of the man, more to their palates
than the generosities of the master, in the sequel let his pen
run riot, lost the harmony and the balance, and sacrificed
a great idea to the taste of his contemporaries.   We know
that in the present day the Knight has fewer admirers than
the Squire.   Anticipating, what did actually happen to him
—as afterwards it did to his scarce inferior follower, the
Author of ' Guzman de Alfarache '—that some less knowing
hand would prevent him by a spurious Second Part : and
judging, that it would be easier for his competitor to out-bid
him in the comicalities, than in the *romance*, of his work,
he abandoned his Knight, and has fairly set up the Squire
for his Hero.   For what else has he unsealed the eyes of
Sancho ; and instead of that twilight state of semi-insanity
—the madness at second-hand—the contagion, caught from
a stronger mind infected—that war between native cunning,
and hereditary deference, with which he has hitherto accompanied his master—two for a pair almost—does he substitute a downright Knave, with open eyes, for his own
ends only following a confessed Madman ; and offering at
one time to lay, if not actually laying, hands upon him !
From the moment that Sancho loses his reverence, Don
Quixote is become a—treatable lunatic.   Our artists handle
him accordingly.

REJOICINGS UPON THE NEW YEAR'S COMING OF AGE

[Printed in *The Morning Chronicle*, Jan. 1, 1823 ; reprinted in *The
London Magazine* (Jan., 1823 ; signed *Elia's Ghost*, see *Preface*, p. 1
above). Collected in *The Last Essays of Elia*, 1833. Text of 1833.]

THE *Old Year* being dead, and the *New Year* coming of
age, which he does, by Calendar Law, as soon as the breath
is out of the old gentleman's body, nothing would serve the
young spark but he must give a dinner upon the occasion,
to which all the *Days* in the year were invited.   The
Festivals, whom he deputed as his stewards, were mightily
taken with the notion.   They had been engaged time out
of mind, they said, in providing mirth and good cheer for
mortals below ; and it was time they should have a taste of

their own bounty. It was stiffly debated among them, whether the *Fasts* should be admitted Some said, the appearance of such lean, starved guests, with their mortified faces, would pervert the ends of the meeting. But the objection was overruled by *Christmas Day*, who had a design upon *Ash Wednesday* (as you shall hear), and a mighty desire to see how the old Domine would behave himself in his cups. Only the *Vigils* were requested to come with their lanterns, to light the gentlefolks home at night.

All the *Days* came to their day. Covers were provided for three hundred and sixty-five guests at the principal table ; with an occasional knife and fork at the side-board for the *Twenty Ninth of February*.

I should have told you, that cards of invitation had been issued. The carriers were the *Hours ;* twelve little, merry, whirligig foot-pages, as you should desire to see, that went all round, and found out the persons invited well enough, with the exception of *Easter Day*, *Shrove Tuesday*, and a few such *Moveables*, who had lately shifted their quarters.

Well, they all met at last, foul *Days*, fine *Days*, all sorts of *Days*, and a rare din they made of it. There was nothing but, Hail ! fellow *Day*,—well met—brother *Day*—sister *Day*, —only *Lady Day* kept a little on the aloof, and seemed somewhat scornful. Yet some said, *Twelfth Day* cut her out and out, for she came in a tiffany suit, white and gold, like a queen on a frost-cake, all royal, glittering, and *Epiphanous*. The rest came, some in green, some in white— but old *Lent and his family* were not yet out of mourning. Rainy *Days* came in, dripping ; and sun-shiny *Days* helped them to change their stockings. *Wedding Day* was there in his marriage finery, a little the worse for wear. *Pay Day* came late, as he always does ; and *Doomsday* sent word—he might be expected.

April Fool (as my young lord's jester) took upon himself to marshal the guests, and wild work he made of it. It would have posed old Erra Pater to have found out any given *Day* in the year, to erect a scheme upon—good *Days*, bad *Days*, were so shuffled together, to the confounding of all sober horoscopy.

He had stuck the *Twenty First of June* next to the *Twenty*

Second of December, and the former looked like a Maypole siding a marrow-bone. *Ash Wednesday* got wedged in (as was concerted) betwixt *Christmas* and *Lord Mayor's Days*. Lord ! how he laid about him ! Nothing but barons of beef and turkeys would go down with him—to the great greasing and detriment of his new sackcloth bib and tucker. And still *Christmas Day* was at his elbow, plying him with the wassail-bowl, till he roared, and hiccup'd, and protested there was no faith in dried ling, but commended it to the devil for a sour, windy, acrimonious, censorious, hy-po-crit-crit-critical mess, and no dish for a gentleman. Then he dipt his fist into the middle of the great custard that stood before his *left-hand neighbour*, and daubed his hungry beard all over with it, till you would have taken him for the *Last Day in December*, it so hung in icicles.

At another part of the table, *Shrove Tuesday* was helping the *Second of September* to some cock broth,—which courtesy the latter returned with the delicate thigh of a hen pheasant —so there was no love lost for that matter. The *Last of Lent* was spunging upon *Shrovetide's* pancakes; which *April Fool* perceiving, told him he did well, for pancakes were proper to a *good fry-day*.

In another part, a hubbub arose about the *Thirtieth of January*, who, it seems, being a sour puritanic character, that thought nobody's meat good or sanctified enough for him, had smuggled into the room a ¹calf's head, which he had had cooked at home for that purpose, thinking to feast thereon incontinently ; but as it lay in the dish, *March Manyweathers*, who is a very fine lady, and subject to the megrims, ²screamed out there was a ' human head in the platter ', and raved about Herodias' daughter to that degree, that the obnoxious viand was obliged to be removed ; nor did she recover her stomach till she had gulped down a *Restorative*, confected of *Oak Apple*, which the merry *Twenty Ninth of May* always carries about with him for that purpose.

The King's health[a] being called for after this, a notable dispute arose between the *Twelfth of August* (a zealous old

[a] The late King [1833].

---

¹ calf's] calves' 1823.   ² screamed] suddenly screamed 1823.

Whig gentlewoman,) and the *Twenty Third of April* (a new-fangled lady of the Tory stamp,) as to which of them should have the honour to propose it. *August* grew hot upon the matter, affirming time out of mind the prescriptive right to have lain with her, till her rival had basely supplanted her; whom she represented as little better than a *kept* mistress, who went about in *fine clothes*, while she (the legitimate BIRTHDAY) had scarcely a rag, &c.

April Fool, being made mediator, confirmed the right in the strongest form of words to the appellant, but decided for peace' sake that the exercise of it should remain with the present possessor. At the same time, he slily rounded the first lady in the ear, that an action might lie against the Crown for *bi-geny*.

It beginning to grow a little duskish, *Candlemas* lustily bawled out for lights, which was opposed by all the *Days*, who protested against burning daylight. Then fair water was handed round in silver ewers, and the *same lady* was observed to take an unusual time in *Washing* herself.

May Day, with that sweetness which is peculiar to her, in a neat speech proposing the health of the founder, crowned her goblet (and by her example the rest of the company) with garlands. This being done, the lordly *New Year* from the upper end of the table, in a cordial but somewhat lofty tone, returned thanks. He felt proud on an occasion of meeting so many of his worthy father's late tenants, pro-mised to improve their farms, and at the same time to abate (if any thing was found unreasonable) in their rents.

At the mention of this, the four *Quarter Days* involuntarily looked at each other, and smiled; *April Fool* whistled to an old tune of ' New Brooms '; and a surly old rebel at the farther end of the table (who was discovered to be no other than the *Fifth of November*,) muttered out, distinctly enough to be heard by the whole company, words to this effect, that, ' when the old one is gone, he is a fool that looks for a better.' Which rudeness of his, the guests re-senting, unanimously voted his expulsion; and the male-content was thrust out neck and heels into the cellar, as the properest place for such a *boutefeu* and firebrand as he had shown himself to be.

Order being restored—the young lord (who to say truth,

had been a little ruffled, and put beside his oratory) in as few, and yet as obliging words as possible, assured them of entire welcome ; and, with a graceful turn, singling out poor *Twenty Ninth of February*, that had sate all this while mumchance at the side-board, begged to couple his health with that of the good company before him—which he drank accordingly ; observing, that he had not seen his honest face any time these four years, with a number of endearing expressions besides. At the same time, removing the solitary *Day* from the forlorn seat which had been assigned him, he stationed him at his own board, somewhere between the *Greek Calends* and *Latter Lammas*.

Ash Wednesday, being now called upon for a song, with his eyes fast stuck in his head, and as well as the Canary he had swallowed would give him leave, struck up a Carol, which *Christmas Day* had taught him for the nonce ; and was followed by the latter, who gave ' Miserere ' in fine style, hitting off the mumping notes and lengthened drawl of *Old Mortification* with infinite humour. *April Fool* swore they had exchanged conditions : but *Good Friday* was observed to look extremely grave ; and *Sunday* held her fan before her face, that she might not be seen to smile.

Shrove-tide, *Lord Mayor's Day*, and *April Fool*, next joined in a glee—

Which is the properest day to drink ?

in which all the *Days* chiming in, made a merry burden.

They next fell to quibbles and conundrums. The question being proposed, who had the greatest number of followers —the *Quarter Days* said, there could be no question as to that ; for they had all the creditors in the world dogging their heels. But *April Fool* gave it in favour of the *Forty Days before Easter ;* because the debtors in all cases outnumbered the creditors, and they kept *lent* all the year.

All this while, *Valentine's Day* kept courting pretty *May*, who sate next him, slipping amorous *billets-doux* under the table, till the *Dog Days* (who are naturally of a warm constitution) began to be jealous, and to bark and rage exceedingly. *April Fool*, who likes a bit of sport above measure, and had some pretensions to the lady besides, as being but a cousin once removed,—clapped and halloo'd

them on ; and as fast as their indignation cooled, those
mad wags, the *Ember Days*, were at it with their bellows,
to blow it into a flame ; and all was in a ferment : till old
Madam *Septuagesima* (who boasts herself the *Mother of the
Days*) wisely diverted the conversation with a tedious tale
of the lovers which she could reckon when she was young ;
and of one Master *Rogation Day* in particular, who was for
ever putting the *question* to her ; but she kept him at a
distance, as the chronicle would tell—by which I apprehend she meant the Almanack.   Then she rambled on to
the *Days that were gone*, the *good old Days*, and so to the
Days before the Flood—which plainly showed her old head
to be little better than crazed and doited.

Day being ended, the *Days* called for their cloaks and
great coats, and took their leaves.   *Lord Mayor's Day* went
off in a mist, as usual ; *Shortest Day* in a deep black Fog,
that wrapt the little gentleman all round like a hedge-hog.
Two *Vigils*—so watchmen are called in heaven—saw *Christmas Day* safe home—they had been used to the business
before.   Another *Vigil*—a stout, sturdy patrole, called the
Eve of St. Christopher—seeing *Ash Wednesday* in a condition
little better than he should be—e'en whipt him over his
shoulders, pick-a-back fashion, and *Old Mortification* went
floating home, singing—

On the bat's back do I fly,

and a number of old snatches besides, between drunk and
sober, but very few Aves or Penitentiaries (you may believe
me) were among them.   *Longest Day* set off westward in
beautiful crimson and gold—the rest, some in one fashion,
some in another ; but *Valentine* and pretty *May* took their
departure together in one of the prettiest silvery twilights
a Lover's Day could wish to set in.

THE WEDDING

[Printed in *The London Magazine, New Series*, vol. ii, no. vi, p. 217
(June, 1825).   Collected in *The Last Essays of Elia*, 1833.   Text of
1833.]

I DO not know when I have been better pleased than at
being invited last week to be present at the wedding of

a friend's daughter.   I like to make one at these ceremonies,
which to us old people give back our youth in a manner,
and restore our gayest season, in remembrance of our own
success, or the regrets, scarcely less tender, of our own
youthful disappointments, in this point of a settlement.
On these occasions I am sure to be in good-humour for a
week or two after, and enjoy a reflected honey-moon. Being
without a family, I am flattered with these temporary
adoptions into a friend's family ; I feel a sort of cousin-
hood, or uncleship, for the season ; I am inducted into
degrees of affinity ; and, in the participated socialities of
the little community, I lay down for a brief while my solitary
bachelorship.   I carry this humour so far, that I take it
unkindly to be left out, even when a funeral is going on in
the house of a dear friend.   But to my subject.——

The union itself had been long settled, but its celebration
had been hitherto deferred, to an almost unreasonable state
of suspense in the lovers, by some invincible prejudices
which the bride's father had unhappily contracted upon
the subject of the too early marriages of females.   He
has been lecturing any time these five years—for to that
length the courtship has been protracted—upon the pro-
priety of putting off the solemnity, till the lady should have
completed her five-and-twentieth year. We all began to be
afraid that a suit, which as yet had abated of none of its
ardours, might at last be lingered on, till passion had come
to cool, and love go out in the experiment. But a little
wheedling on the part of his wife, who was by no means
a party to these overstrained notions, joined to some serious
expostulations on that of his friends, who, from the growing
infirmities of the old gentleman, could not promise ourselves
many years' enjoyment of his company, and were anxious
to bring matters to a conclusion during his life-time, at
length prevailed ; and on Monday last the daughter of my
old friend, Admiral ——, having attained the *womanly* age
of nineteen, was conducted to the church by her pleasant
cousin J——, who told some few years older.

Before the youthful part of my female readers express
their indignation at the abominable loss of time occasioned
to the lovers by the preposterous notions of my old friend,
they will do well to consider the reluctance which a fond

parent naturally feels at parting with his child. To this unwillingness, I believe, in most cases may be traced the difference of opinion on this point between child and parent, whatever pretences of interest or prudence may be held out to cover it. The hard-heartedness of fathers is a fine theme for romance writers, a sure and moving topic ; but is there not something untender, to say no more of it, in the hurry which a beloved child is sometimes in to tear herself from the parental stock, and commit herself to strange graftings ? The case is heightened where the lady, as in the present instance, happens to be an only child. I do not understand these matters experimentally, but I can make a shrewd guess at the wounded pride of a parent upon these occasions. It is no new observation, I believe, that a lover in most cases has no rival so much to be feared as the father. Certainly there is a jealousy in *unparallel subjects*, which is little less heart-rending than the passion which we more strictly christen by that name. Mother's scruples are more easily got over ; for this reason, I suppose, that the protection transferred to a husband is less a derogation and a loss to their authority than to the paternal. Mothers, besides, have a trembling foresight, which paints the inconveniences (impossible to be conceived in the same degree by the other parent) of a life of forlorn celibacy, which the refusal of a tolerable match may entail upon their child. Mothers' instinct is a surer guide here, than the cold reasonings of a father on such a topic. To this instinct may be imputed, and by it alone may be excused, the unbeseeming artifices, by which some wives push on the matrimonial projects of their daughters, which the husband, however approving, shall entertain with comparative indifference. A little shamelessness on this head is pardonable. With this explanation, forwardness becomes a grace, and maternal importunity receives the name of a virtue.—But the parson stays, while I preposterously assume his office ; I am preaching while the bride is on the threshold.

Nor let any of my female readers suppose that the sage reflections which have just escaped me have the obliquest tendency of application to the young lady, who, it will be seen, is about to venture upon a change in her condition, at a *mature and competent age*, and not without the fullest

I

approbation of [1]all parties. I only deprecate *very hasty marriages.*

It had been fixed that the ceremony should be gone through at an early hour, to give time for a little *déjeuné* afterwards, to which a select party of friends had been invited. We were in church a little before the clock struck eight.

Nothing could be more judicious or graceful than the dress of the bride-maids—the three charming Miss Foresters—on this morning. To give the bride an opportunity of shining singly, they had come habited all in green. I am ill at describing female apparel ; but, while *she* stood at the altar in vestments white and candid as her thoughts, a sacrificial whiteness, *they* assisted in robes, such as [2]might become Diana's nymphs—Foresters indeed—as such who had not yet come to the resolution of putting off cold virginity. These young maids, not being so blest as to have a mother living, I am told, keep single for their father's sake, and live altogether so happy with their remaining parent, that the hearts of their lovers are [3]ever broken with the prospect (so inauspicious to their hopes) of such uninterrupted and provoking home-comfort. Gallant girls ! each a victim worthy of Iphigenia !

I do not know what business I have to be present in solemn places. I cannot divest me of an unseasonable disposition to levity upon the most awful occasions. I was never cut out for a public functionary. Ceremony and I have long shaken hands ; but I could not resist the importunities of the young lady's father, whose gout unhappily confined him at home, to act as parent on this occasion, and *give away the bride.* Something ludicrous occurred to me at this most serious of all moments—a sense of my unfitness to have the disposal, even in imagination, of the sweet young creature beside me. I fear I was betrayed to some lightness, for the awful eye of the parson—and the rector's eye of Saint Mildred's in the Poultry is no trifle of a rebuke—was upon me in an instant, souring my incipient jest to the tristful severities of a funeral.

This was the only misbehaviour which I can plead to

[1] all parties] both parents 1825.   [2] might] might have 1825.   [3] ever] even 1825.

upon this solemn occasion, unless what was objected to me
after the ceremony by one of the handsome [1]Miss T——s,
be accounted a solecism. She was pleased to say that she
had never seen a gentleman before me give away a bride in
black. Now black has been my ordinary apparel so long—
indeed I take it to be the proper costume of an author—
the stage sanctions it—that to have appeared in some
lighter [2]colour would have raised more mirth at my expense,
than the anomaly had created censure. But I could perceive that the bride's mother, and some elderly ladies
present (God bless them !), would have been well content,
if I had come in any other colour than that. But I got
over the omen by a lucky apologue, which I remembered
out of Pilpay, or some Indian author, of all the birds being
invited to the linnets' wedding, at which, when all the rest
came in their gayest feathers, the raven alone apologised
for his cloak because ' he had no other '. This tolerably
reconciled the elders. But with the young people all was
merriment, and shaking of hands, and congratulations, and
kissing away the bride's tears, and kissings from her in
return, till a young lady, who assumed some experience in
these matters, having worn the nuptial bands some four or
five weeks longer than her friend, rescued her, archly
observing, with half an eye upon the bridegroom, that at
this rate she would have ' none left '.

My friend the admiral was in fine wig and buckle on this
occasion—a striking contrast to his usual neglect of personal
appearance. He did not once shove up his borrowed locks
(his custom ever at his morning studies) to betray the few
grey stragglers of his own beneath them. He wore an
aspect of thoughtful satisfaction. I trembled for the hour,
which at length approached, when after a protracted *breakfast* of three hours—if stores of cold fowls, tongues, hams,
botargoes, dried fruits, wines, cordials, &c., can deserve so
meagre an appellation—the coach was announced, which
was come to carry off the bride and bridegroom for a season,
as custom has sensibly ordained, into the country ; upon
which design, wishing them a felicitous journey, let us
return to the assembled guests.

[1] T——s] Turners 1825.   [2] colour would] colours—a pea-green
coat, for instance, like the bridegroom's—would 1825.

As when a well-graced actor leaves the stage,
The eyes of men
Are idly bent on him that enters next,

so idly did we bend our eyes upon one another, when the
chief performers in the morning's pageant had vanished.
None told his tale. None sipt her glass. The poor Admiral
made an effort—it was not much. I had anticipated so far.
Even the infinity of full satisfaction, that had betrayed
itself through the prim looks and quiet deportment of his
lady, began to wane into something of misgiving. No one
knew whether to take their leaves or stay. We seemed
assembled upon a silly occasion. In this crisis, betwixt
tarrying and departure, I must do justice to a foolish talent
of mine, which had otherwise like to have brought me into
disgrace in the fore-part of the day ; I mean a power, in
any emergency, of thinking and giving vent to all manner
of strange nonsense. In this awkward dilemma I found it
sovereign. I rattled off some of my most excellent absurdi-
ties. All were willing to be relieved, at any expense of
reason, from the pressure of the intolerable vacuum which
had succeeded to the morning bustle. By this means I was
fortunate in keeping together the better part of the company to a late hour : and a rubber of whist (the Admiral's
favourite game) with some rare strokes of chance as well
as skill, which came opportunely on his side—lengthened out
till midnight—dismissed the old gentleman at last to his
bed with comparatively easy spirits.

I have been at my old friend's various times since. I do
not know a visiting place where every guest is so perfectly
at his ease ; nowhere, where harmony is so strangely the
result of confusion. Every body is at cross purposes, yet
the effect is so much better than uniformity. Contradictory
orders ; servants pulling one way ; master and mistress
driving some other, yet both diverse ; visitors huddled up
in corners ; chairs unsymmetrised : candles disposed by
chance ; meals at odd hours, tea and supper at once, or
the latter preceding the former ; the host and the guest
conferring, yet each upon a different topic, each understanding himself, neither trying to understand or hear the
other ; draughts and politics, chess and political economy,
cards and conversation on nautical matters, going on at

once, without the hope, or indeed the wish, of distinguishing them, make it altogether the most perfect *concordia discors* you shall meet with. Yet somehow the old house is not quite what it should be. The Admiral still enjoys his pipe, but he has no Miss Emily to fill it for him. The instrument stands where it stood, but she is gone, whose delicate touch could sometimes for a short minute appease the warring elements. He has learnt, as Marvel expresses it, to ' make his destiny his choice '. He bears bravely up, but he does not come out with his flashes of wild wit so thick as formerly. His sea songs seldomer escape him. His wife, too, looks as if she wanted some younger body to scold and set to rights. We all miss a junior presence. It is wonderful how one young maiden freshens up, and keeps green, the paternal roof. Old and young seem to have an interest in her, so long as she is not absolutely disposed of. The youthfulness of the house is flown. Emily is married.

THE CHILD ANGEL

A Dream

[Printed in *The London Magazine*, vol. vii, no. xlii, p. 677 (June, 1823). Collected in *The Last Essays of Elia*, 1833. Text of 1833.]

I CHANCED upon the prettiest, oddest, fantastical thing of a dream the other night, that you shall hear of. I had been reading the ' Loves of the Angels ', and went to bed with my head full of speculations, suggested by that extraordinary legend. It had given birth to innumerable conjectures ; and, I remember, the last waking thought, which I gave expression to on my pillow, was a sort of wonder, ' what could come of it.'

I was suddenly transported, how or whither I could scarcely make out—but to some celestial region. It was not the real heavens neither—not the downright Bible heaven—but a kind of fairyland heaven, about which a poor human fancy may have leave to sport and air itself, I will hope, without presumption.

Methought—what wild things dreams are !—I was present —at what would you imagine ?—at an angel's gossiping.

Whence it came, or how it came, or who bid it come, or whether it came purely of its own head, neither you nor I know—but there lay, sure enough, wrapped in its little cloudy swaddling bands—a Child Angel.

Sun-threads—filmy beams—ran through the celestial napery of what seemed its princely cradle. All the winged orders hovered round, watching when the new-born should open its yet closed eyes ; which, when it did, first one, and then the other—with a solicitude and apprehension, yet not such as, stained with fear, dims the expanding eye-lids of mortal infants, but as if to explore its path in those its unhereditary palaces—what an inextinguishable titter that time spared not celestial visages ! Nor wanted there to my seeming—O the inexplicable simpleness of dreams !— bowls of that cheering nectar,

—which mortals *caudle* call below—

Nor were wanting faces of female ministrants,—stricken in years, as it might seem,—so dexterous were those heavenly attendants to counterfeit kindly similitudes of earth, to greet with terrestrial child-rites the young *present*, which earth had made to heaven.

Then were celestial harpings heard, not in full symphony as those by which the spheres are tutored ; but, as loudest instruments on earth speak oftentimes, muffled ; so to accommodate their sound the better to the weak ears of the imperfect-born. And, with the noise of those subdued soundings, the Angelet sprang forth, fluttering its rudiments of pinions—but forthwith flagged and was recovered into the arms of those full-winged angels. And a wonder it was to see how, as years went round in heaven—a year in dreams is as a day—continually its white shoulders put forth buds of wings, but, wanting the perfect angelic nutriment, anon was shorn of its aspiring, and fell fluttering—still caught by angel hands—for ever to put forth shoots, and to fall fluttering, because its birth was not of the unmixed vigour of heaven.

And a name was given to the Babe Angel, and it was to be called *Ge-Urania*, because its production was of earth and heaven.

And it could not taste of death, by reason of its adoption

into immortal palaces : but it was to know weakness, and
reliance, and the shadow of human imbecility ; and it went
with a lame gait; but in its goings it exceeded all mortal
children in grace and swiftness. Then pity first sprang up
in angelic bosoms ; and yearnings (like the human) touched
them at the sight of the immortal lame one.

And with pain did then first those Intuitive Essences,
with pain and strife to their natures (not grief), put back
their bright intelligences, and reduce their ethereal minds,
schooling them to degrees and slower processes, so to adapt
their lessons to the gradual illumination (as must needs be)
of the half-earth-born ; and what intuitive notices they
could not repel (by reason that their nature is, to know all
things at once), the half-heavenly novice, by the better
part of its nature, aspired to receive into its understanding ;
so that Humility and Aspiration went on even-paced in the
instruction of the glorious Amphibium.

But, by reason that Mature Humanity is too gross to
breathe the air of that super-subtle region, its portion was,
and is, to be a child for ever.

And because the human part of it might not press into
the heart and inwards of the palace of its adoption, those
full-natured angels tended it by turns in the purlieus of the
palace, where were shady groves and rivulets, like this
green earth from which it came : so Love, with Voluntary
Humility, waited upon the entertainment of the new-
adopted.

And myriads of years rolled round (in dreams Time is
nothing), and still it kept, and is to keep, perpetual childhood, and is the Tutelar Genius of Childhood upon earth,
and still goes lame and lovely.

By the banks of the river Pison is seen, lone-sitting by
the grave of the terrestrial [1]Adah, whom the angel Nadir
loved, a Child ; but not the same which I saw in heaven.
A [2]mournful hue overcasts its lineaments ; nevertheless,
a correspondency is between the child by the grave, and
that celestial orphan, whom I saw above ; and the dimness
of the grief upon the heavenly, is as a shadow or emblem of
that which stains the beauty of the terrestrial. And this
correspondency is not to be understood but by dreams.

[1] Adah] Mirzah 1823.   [2] mournful] pensive 1823.

And in the archives of heaven I had grace to read, how
that once the angel Nadir, being exiled from his place for
mortal passion, upspringing on the wings of parental love
(such power had parental love for a moment to suspend
the else-irrevocable law) appeared for a brief instant in his
station ; and, depositing a wondrous Birth, straightway
disappeared, and the palaces knew him no more.   And this
charge was the self-same Babe, who goeth lame and lovely
—but [1]Adah sleepeth by the river Pison.

A DEATH-BED

In a Letter to R. H. Esq. of B——

[Printed in Hone's *Table Book*, vol. i, cols. 425–6 ; signed *L.*, and
dated *London, February* 10, 1827.   Composed originally as a letter
(dated Jan. 20, 1827) addressed to H. Crabb Robinson of Bury St. Edmund's on the death of Randal Norris, sub-treasurer of the Inner Temple.
Collected in *The Last Essays of Elia*, 1833, 1st ed., but replaced by the
Confessions of a Drunkard (p. 168 above) in the second edition, 1835.
Text of 1833.]

I called upon you this morning, and found that you
were gone to visit a dying friend.   I had been upon a like
errand.   Poor [2]N. R. has lain dying now for almost a week ;
such is the penalty we pay for having enjoyed [3]through
life a strong constitution.   Whether he knew me or not,
I know not, or whether he saw me through his poor glazed
eyes ; but the group I saw about him I shall not forget.
Upon the bed, or about it, were assembled his Wife, [4]their
two Daughters, and poor deaf Robert, looking doubly
stupified.   There they were, and seemed to have been
sitting all the week.   I could only reach out a hand to
Mrs. [5]R.   Speaking was impossible in that mute chamber.
By this time [6]it must be all over with him.   In him I have
a loss the world cannot make up.   He was my friend, and
my father's friend, [7]for all the life that I can remember.

[1] Adah] Mirzah 1823.   [2] N. R. has lain] Norris has been lying
Jan., 1827.   [3] through life *omit Jan.*, 1827.   [4] , their . . . Robert]
and two daughters, and poor deaf Richard, his son, *Jan.*, 1827.
[5] R.] Norris *Jan.*, 1827.   [6] it must be] I hope it is *Jan.*, 1827.   [7] for
omit Jan., 1827.

I seem to have made foolish friendships [1]since. Those are
the friendships, which [2]outlast a second generation. Old
as I am [3]getting, in his eyes I was still the child he [4]knew
me. To the last he called me [5]Jemmy. I have none to call
me [5]Jemmy now. He was the last link that bound me to
[6]B——. You are but of yesterday. In him [7]I seem to
have lost the old plainness of manners and singleness of
heart. [8]Lettered he was not ; his reading scarcely exceeded
the Obituary of the old Gentleman's Magazine, to which he
has never failed of having recourse for these last fifty years.
Yet there was the pride of literature about him from that
slender perusal ; and moreover from his office of archive-
keeper to your ancient city, in which he must needs pick
up some equivocal Latin ; which, among his less literary
friends, assumed the air of a very pleasant pedantry. Can
I forget the erudite look with which, having tried to puzzle
out the text of a Black-lettered Chaucer in your Corporation
Library, to which he was a sort of Librarian, he gave it up
with this consolatory reflection—' Jemmy,' said he, ' I do
not know what you find in these very old books, but I
observe, there is a deal of very indifferent spelling in them.'
His jokes (for he had some) are ended ; but they were old
Perennials, staple, and always as good as new. He had
one Song, that spake of the ' flat bottoms of our foes coming
over in darkness ', and alluded to a threatened Invasion,
many years since blown over ; this he reserved to be sung
on Christmas Night, which we always passed with him,
and he sang it with the freshness of an impending event.
How his eyes would sparkle when he came to the passage :—

> We'll still make 'em run, and we'll still make 'em sweat,
> In spite of the devil and Brussels' Gazette !

What is the Brussels' Gazette now ? I cry, while I endite
these trifles. His poor girls who are, I believe, compact
of solid goodness, will have to receive their afflicted mother
at an unsuccessful home in a petty village in ——shire,
where for years they have been struggling to raise a Girls'

---

[1] since] ever since *Jan.* 1827.   [2] outlast] outlive *Jan.*, 1827.
[2] getting] waxing *Jan.*, 1827.   [4] knew] first knew *Jan.*, 1827.
[5] Jemmy] Charley *Jan.*, 1827.   [6] B——] the Temple, *Jan.*, 1827.
[7] I . . . lost] seem to have died *Jan.*, 1827.   [8] *For the remainder of*
the letter of Jan., 1827 *see Editor's Notes.*

School with no effect. Poor deaf Robert (and the less
hopeful for being so) is thrown upon a deaf world, without
the comfort to his father on his death-bed of knowing him
provided for. They are left almost provisionless. Some
life assurance there is ; but, I fear, not exceeding ——.
Their hopes must be from your Corporation, which their
father has served for fifty years. Who or what are your
Leading Members now, I know not. Is there any, to whom
without impertinence, you can represent the true circumstances of the family ? You cannot say good enough of
poor R., and his poor wife. Oblige me and the dead, if
you can.

OLD CHINA

[Printed in *The London Magazine*, vol. vii, no. xxxix, p. 269 (March,
1823). Collected in *The Last Essays of Elia*, 1833. Text of 1833.]

I HAVE an almost feminine partiality for old china.
When I go to see any great house, I inquire for the china-
closet, and next for the picture gallery. I cannot defend
the order of preference, but by saying, that we have all
some taste or other, of too ancient a date to admit of our
remembering distinctly that it was an acquired one. I can
call to mind the first play, and the first exhibition, that
I was taken to ; but I am not conscious of a time when
china jars and saucers were introduced into my imagination.

I had no repugnance then—why should I now have ?—
to those little, lawless, azure-tinctured grotesques, that
under the notion of men and women, float about, uncircumscribed by any element, in that world before perspective
—a china tea-cup.

I like to see my old friends—whom distance cannot
diminish—figuring up in the air (so they appear to our
optics), yet on *terra firma* still—for so we must in courtesy
interpret that speck of deeper blue, which the decorous
artist, to prevent absurdity, has made to spring up beneath
their sandals.

I love the men with women's faces, and the women, if
possible, with still more womanish expressions.

Here is a young and courtly Mandarin, handing tea to
a lady from a salver—two miles off. See how distance

seems to set off respect ! And here the same lady, or another—for likeness is identity on tea-cups—is stepping into a little fairy boat, moored on the hither side of this calm garden river, with a dainty mincing foot, which in a right angle of incidence (as angles go in our world) must infallibly land her in the midst of a flowery mead—a furlong off on the other side of the same strange stream !

Farther on—if far or near can be predicated of their world—see horses, trees, pagodas, dancing the hays.

Here—a cow and rabbit couchant, and co-extensive— so objects show, seen through the lucid atmosphere of fine Cathay.

I was pointing out to my cousin last evening, over our Hyson (which we are old fashioned enough to drink unmixed still of an afternoon) some of these *speciosa miracula* upon a set of extraordinary old blue china (a recent purchase) which we were now for the first time using ; and could not help remarking, how favourable circumstances had been to us of late years, that we could afford to please the eye sometimes with trifles of this sort—when a passing sentiment seemed to over-shade the brows of my companion. I am quick at detecting these summer clouds in Bridget.

'I wish the good old times would come again', she said, ' when we were not quite so rich. I do not mean, that I want to be poor ; but there was a middle state ; '—so she was pleased to ramble on,—' in which I am sure we were a great deal happier. A purchase is but a purchase, now that you have money enough and to spare. Formerly it used to be a triumph. When we coveted a cheap luxury (and, O ! how much ado I had to get you to consent in those times !) we were used to have a debate two or three days before, and to weigh the *for* and *against*, and think what we might spare it out of, and what saving we could hit upon, that should be an equivalent. A thing was worth buying then, when we felt the money that we paid for it.

' Do you remember the brown suit, which you made to hang upon you, till all your friends cried shame upon you, it grew so thread-bare—and all because of that folio Beaumont and Fletcher, which you dragged home late at night from Barker's in Covent-garden ? Do you remember how we eyed it for weeks before we could make up our minds to the purchase, and had not come to a determination till it was near ten o'clock of the Saturday night, when you set off from Islington, fearing you should be too late—and when the old bookseller with some grumbling opened his shop, and by the twinkling taper (for he was setting bedwards) lighted out the relic from his dusty treasures—and when you lugged it home, wishing it were twice as cumbersome—and when you presented it to me—and when we were exploring the perfectness of it (*collating* you called it)— and while I was repairing some of the loose leaves with paste, which your impatience would not suffer to be left till day-break—was there no pleasure in being a poor man ? or can those neat black clothes which you wear now, and are so careful to keep brushed, since we have become rich and finical, give you half the honest vanity, with which you flaunted it about in that over-worn suit—your old corbeau —for four or five weeks longer than you should have done, to pacify your conscience for the mighty sum of fifteen— or sixteen shillings was it ?—a great affair we thought it then—which you had lavished on the old folio. Now you can afford to buy any book that pleases you, but I do not see that you ever bring me home any nice old purchases now.

' When you came home with twenty apologies for laying out a less number of shillings upon that print after Lionardo, which we christened the " Lady Blanch " ; when you looked at the purchase, and thought of the money—and thought of the money, and looked again at the picture— was there no pleasure in being a poor man ? Now, you have nothing to do but to walk into [1]Colnaghi's, and buy a wilderness of Lionardos. Yet do you ?

' Then, do you remember our pleasant walks to Enfield, and Potter's Bar, and Waltham, when we had a holyday— holydays, and all other fun, are gone, now we are rich— and the little hand-basket in which I used to deposit our day's fare of savoury cold lamb and salad—and how you would pry about at noon-tide for some decent house, where we might go in, and produce our store—only paying for the ale that you must call for—and speculate upon the looks of the landlady, and whether she was likely to allow us a table-cloth—and wish for such another honest hostess, as

[1] Colnaghi's] Colnaghi's (as W—— calls it) 1823.

Izaak Walton has described many a one on the pleasant banks of the Lea, when he went a fishing—and sometimes they would prove obliging enough, and sometimes they would look grudgingly upon us—but we had cheerful looks still for one another, and would eat our plain food savorily, scarcely grudging Piscator his Trout Hall ? Now, when we go out a day's pleasuring, which is seldom moreover, we *ride* part of the way—and go into a fine inn, and order the best of dinners, never debating the expense—which, after all, never has half the relish of those chance country snaps, when we were at the mercy of uncertain usage, and a precarious welcome.

' You are too proud to see a play anywhere now but in the [1]pit. Do you remember where it was we used to sit, when we saw the Battle of Hexham, and the Surrender of Calais, and Bannister and Mrs. Bland in the Children in the Wood—when we squeezed out our shillings a-piece to sit three or four times in a season in the one-shilling gallery—where you felt all the time that you ought not to have brought me—and more strongly I felt obligation to you for having brought me—and the pleasure was the better for a little shame—and when the curtain drew up, what cared we for our place in the house, or what mattered it where we were sitting, when our thoughts were with Rosalind in Arden, or with Viola at the Court of Illyria ? You used to say, that the gallery was the best place of all for enjoying a play socially—that the relish of such exhibitions must be in proportion to the infrequency of going—that the company we met there, not being in general readers of plays, were obliged to attend the more, and did attend, to what was going on, on the stage—because a word lost would have been a chasm, which it was impossible for them to fill up. With such reflections we consoled our pride then—and I appeal to you, whether, as a woman, I met generally with less attention and accommodation, than I have done since in more expensive situations in the house ? The getting in indeed, and the crowding up those inconvenient staircases, was bad enough,—but there was still a law of civility to women recognised to quite as great an extent as we ever found in the other passages—and how a little difficulty over-

[1] pit.] pit or boxes. 1823.

come heightened the snug seat, and the play, afterwards!
Now we can only pay our money, and walk in. You
cannot see, you say, in the galleries now. I am sure we
saw, and heard too, well enough then—but sight, and all,
I think, is gone with our poverty.

'There was pleasure in eating strawberries, before they
became quite common—in the first dish of peas, while they
were yet dear—to have them for a nice supper, a treat.
What treat can we have now ? If we were to treat ourselves now—that is, to have dainties a little above our
means, it would be selfish and wicked. It is the very little
more that we allow ourselves beyond what the actual poor
can get at, that makes what I call a treat—when two
people living together, as we have done, now and then
indulge themselves in a cheap luxury, which both like ;
while each apologises, and is willing to take both halves
of the blame to his single share. I see no harm in people
making much of themselves in that sense of the word.
It may give them a hint how to make much of others.
But now—what I mean by the word—we never do make
much of ourselves. None but the poor can do it. I do
not mean the veriest poor of all, but persons as we were,
just above poverty.

'I know what you were going to say, that it is mighty
pleasant at the end of the year to make all meet—and much
ado we used to have every Thirty-first Night of December
to account for our exceedings—many a long face did you
make over your puzzled accounts, and in contriving to
make it out how we had spent so much—or that we had
not spent so much—or that it was impossible we should
spend so much next year—and still we found our slender
capital decreasing—but then, betwixt ways, and projects,
and compromises of one sort or another, and talk of curtail-
ing this charge, and doing without that for the future—and
the hope that youth brings, and laughing spirits (in which
you were never poor till now,) we pocketed up our loss,
and in conclusion, with " lusty brimmers " (as you used to
quote it out of *hearty cheerful Mr. Cotton*, as you called
him), we used to welcome in the " coming guest ". Now
we have no reckoning at all at the end of [1]the old year—

                    [1] the] an 1823.

no flattering promises about the new year doing better
for us.'

Bridget is so sparing of her speech on most occasions,
that when she gets into a rhetorical vein, I am careful how
I interrupt it. I could not help, however, smiling at the
phantom of wealth which her dear imagination had conjured up out of a clear income of poor — hundred pounds
a year. ' It is true we were happier when we were poorer,
but we were also younger, my cousin. I am afraid we must
put up with the excess, for if we were to shake the superflux
into the sea, we should not much mend ourselves. That
we had much to struggle with, as we grew up together, we
have reason to be most thankful. It strengthened, and
knit our compact closer. We could never have been what
we have been to each other, if we had always had the
sufficiency which you now complain of. The resisting power—
those natural dilations of the youthful spirit, which circumstances cannot straiten—with us are long since passed
away. Competence to age is supplementary youth ;
a sorry supplement indeed, but I fear the best that is to
be had. We must ride, where we formerly walked : live
better, and lie softer—and shall be wise to do so—than we
had means to do in those good old days you speak of.
Yet could those days return—could you and I once more
walk our thirty miles a-day—could Bannister and Mrs. Bland
again be young, and you and I be young to see them—could
the good old one-shilling gallery days return—they are
dreams, my cousin, now—but could you and I at this
moment, instead of this quiet argument, by our well-
carpeted fire-side, sitting on this luxurious sofa—be once
more struggling up those inconvenient stair-cases, pushed
about, and squeezed, and elbowed by the poorest rabble
of poor gallery scramblers—could I once more hear those
anxious shrieks of yours—and the delicious *Thank God, we
are safe*, which always followed when the topmost stair,
conquered, let in the first light of the whole cheerful theatre
down beneath us—I know not the fathom line that ever
touched a descent so deep as I would be willing to bury
more wealth in than Crœsus had, or the great Jew R——
is supposed to have, to purchase it. And now do just look
at that merry little Chinese waiter holding an umbrella,

big enough for a bed-tester, over the head of that pretty
insipid half-Madonna-ish chit of a lady in that very blue
summer-house.'

POPULAR FALLACIES

I.—THAT A BULLY IS ALWAYS A COWARD

[This and the eight following articles appeared in *The New Monthly
Magazine*, Jan., 1826, pp. 25-9, and were collected, with the remaining
seven here printed, in *The Last Essays of Elia*, 1833. See *The Genteel
Style in Writing, Sanity of True Genius*, and *That a Deformed Person is
a Lord*, pp. 61 and 46 above. Text of 1833.]

THIS axiom contains a principle of compensation, which
disposes us to admit the truth of it. But there is no safe
trusting to dictionaries and definitions. We should more
willingly fall in with this popular language, if we did not
find *brutality* sometimes awkwardly coupled with *valour* in
the same vocabulary. The comic writers, with their
poetical justice, have contributed not a little to mislead us
upon this point. To see a hectoring fellow exposed and
beaten upon the stage, has something in it wonderfully
diverting. Some people's share of animal spirits is
notoriously low and defective. It has not strength to raise
a vapour, or furnish out the wind of a tolerable bluster.
These love to be told that huffing is no part of valour.
The truest courage with them is that which is the least
noisy and obtrusive. But confront one of these silent heroes
with the swaggerer of real life, and his confidence in the
theory quickly vanishes. Pretensions do not uniformly
bespeak non-performance. A modest inoffensive deportment does not necessarily imply [1]valour ; neither does the
absence of it justify us in denying that quality. Hickman
wanted modesty—we do not mean *him* of Clarissa—but
who ever doubted his [2]courage ? Even the poets—upon
whom this equitable distribution of qualities should be
most binding—have thought it agreeable to nature to
depart from the rule upon occasion. Harapha, in the
' Agonistes ', is indeed a bully upon the received notions.
Milton has made him at once a blusterer, a giant, and
a dastard. But Almanzor, in Dryden, talks of driving

[1] valour] courage 1826.   [2] courage] pluck 1826.

armies singly before him—and does it. Tom Brown had a shrewder insight into this kind of character than either of his predecessors. He divides the palm more equably, and allows his hero a sort of dimidiate pre-eminence :— 'Bully Dawson kicked by half the town, and half the town kicked by Bully Dawson.' This was true distributive justice.

II.—THAT ILL-GOTTEN GAIN NEVER PROSPERS

The weakest part of mankind have this saying commonest in their [1]mouth. It is the trite consolation administered to the easy dupe, when he has been tricked out of his money or estate, that the acquisition of it will do the owner *no good*. But the rogues of this world—the prudenter part of them, at least—know better ; and, if the observation had been as true as it is old, would not have failed by this time to have discovered it. They have pretty sharp distinctions of the fluctuating and the permanent. 'Lightly come, lightly go,' is a proverb, which they can very well afford to leave, when they leave little else, to the losers. They do not always find manors, got by rapine or chicanery, insensibly to melt away, as the poets will have it ; or that all gold glides, like thawing snow, from the thief's hand that grasps it. Church land, alienated to lay uses, was formerly denounced to have this slippery quality. But some portions of it somehow always stuck so fast, that the denunciators have been fain to postpone the prophecy of refundment to a late posterity.

III.—THAT A MAN MUST NOT LAUGH AT HIS OWN JEST

The severest exaction surely ever invented upon the self-denial of poor human nature ! This is to expect a gentleman to give a treat without partaking of it ; to sit esurient at his own table, and commend the flavour of his venison upon the absurd strength of his never touching it himself. On the contrary, we love to see a wag *taste* his own joke to his party ; to watch a quirk, or a merry conceit, flickering upon the lips some seconds before the tongue is delivered

[1] mouth] mouths 1826.

of it. If it be good, fresh, and racy—begotten of the occasion ; if he that utters it never thought it before, he is naturally the first to be tickled with it ; and any suppression of such complacence we hold to be churlish and insulting. What does it seem to imply, but that your company is weak or foolish enough to be moved by an image or a fancy, that shall stir you not at all, or but faintly ? This is exactly the humour of the fine gentleman in Mandeville, who, while he dazzles his guests with the display of some costly toy, affects himself to ' see nothing considerable in it '.

IV.—THAT SUCH A ONE SHOWS HIS BREEDING.—THAT IT IS EASY TO PERCEIVE HE IS NO GENTLEMAN

A speech from the poorer sort of people, which always indicates that the party vituperated is a gentleman. The very fact which they deny, is that which galls and exasperates them to use this language. The forbearance with which it is usually received, is a proof what interpretation the bystander sets upon it. Of a kin to this, and still less politic, are the phrases with which, in their street rhetoric, they ply one another more grossly :—*He is a poor creature.*— *He has not a rag to cover*——*&c. ;* though this last, we confess, is more frequently applied by females to females. They do not perceive that the satire glances upon themselves. A poor man, of all things in the world, should not upbraid an antagonist with poverty. Are there no other topics— as, to tell him his father was hanged—his sister, &c.——, without exposing a secret, which should be kept snug between them ; and doing an affront to the order to which they have the honour equally to belong ? All this while they do not see how the wealthier man stands by and laughs in his sleeve at both.

V.—THAT THE POOR COPY THE VICES OF THE RICH

A smooth text to the latter ; and, preached from the pulpit, is sure of a docile audience from the pews lined with satin. It is twice sitting upon velvet to a foolish squire to be told, that *he*—and not *perverse nature,* as the homilies would make us imagine, is the true cause of all the irregularities in his parish. This is striking at the root of free-will indeed, and denying the originality of sin in any sense. But men are not such implicit sheep as this comes to. If the abstinence from evil on the part of the upper classes is to derive itself from no higher principle, than the apprehension of setting ill patterns to the lower, we beg leave to discharge them from all squeamishness on that score : they may even take their fill of pleasures, where they can find them. The Genius of Poverty, hampered and straitened as it is, is not so barren of invention but it can trade upon the staple of its own vice, without drawing upon their capital. The poor are not quite such servile imitators as they take them for. Some of them are very clever artists in their way. Here and there we find an original. Who taught the poor to steal, to pilfer ? They did not go to the great for schoolmasters in these faculties surely. It is well if in some vices they allow us to be—no copyists. In no other sense is it true that the poor copy them, than as servants may be said to *take after* their masters and mistresses, when they succeed to their reversionary cold meats. If the master, from indisposition or some other cause, neglect his food, the servant dines notwithstanding.

' O, but (some will say) the force of example is great.' We knew a lady who was so scrupulous on this head, that she would put up with the calls of the most impertinent visitor, rather than let her servant say she was not at home, for fear of teaching her maid to tell an untruth ; and this in the very face of the fact, which she knew well enough, that the wench was one of the greatest liars upon the earth without teaching ; so much so, that her mistress possibly never heard two words of consecutive truth from her in her life. But nature must go for nothing : example must be every thing. This liar in grain, who never opened her mouth without a lie, must be guarded against a remote inference, which she (pretty casuist !) might possibly draw from a form of words—literally false, but essentially deceiving no one—that under some circumstances a fib might not be so exceedingly sinful—a fiction, too, not at all in her own way, or one that she could be suspected of adopting, for few servant-wenches care to be denied to visitors.

K 2

This word *example* reminds us of another fine word which is in use upon these occasions—*encouragement*. ' People in our sphere must not be thought to give encouragement to such proceedings.' To such a frantic height is this principle capable of being carried, that we have known individuals who have thought it within the scope of their influence to sanction despair, and give *éclat* to—suicide. A domestic in the family of a county member lately deceased, for love, or some unknown cause, cut his throat, but not successfully. The poor fellow was otherwise much loved and respected ; and great interest was used in his behalf, upon his recovery, that he might be permitted to retain his place; his word being first pledged, not without some substantial sponsors to promise for him, that the like should never happen again. His master was inclinable to keep him, but his mistress thought otherwise ; and John in the end was dismissed, her ladyship declaring that she ' could not think of encouraging any such doings in the county '.

VI.—THAT ENOUGH IS AS GOOD AS A FEAST

Not a man, woman, or child in ten miles round Guildhall, who really believes this saying. The inventor of it did not believe it himself. It was made in revenge by somebody, who was disappointed of a regale. It is a vile cold-scrag-of-mutton sophism ; a lie palmed upon the palate, which knows better things. If nothing else could be said for a feast, this is sufficient, that from the superflux there is usually something left for the next day. Morally interpreted, it belongs to a class of proverbs, which have a tendency to make us undervalue *money*. Of this cast are those notable observations, that money is not health ; riches cannot purchase every thing : the metaphor which makes gold to be mere muck, with the morality which traces fine clothing to the sheep's back, and denounces pearl as the unhandsome excretion of an oyster. Hence, too, the phrase which imputes dirt to acres—a sophistry so barefaced, that even the literal sense of it is true only in a wet season. This, and abundance of similar sage saws assuming to inculcate *content*, we verily believe to have been the invention of some cunning borrower, who had designs upon the purse of

his wealthier neighbour, which he could only hope to carry
by force of these verbal jugglings. Translate any one of
these sayings out of the artful metonyme which envelops it,
and the trick is apparent. Goodly legs and shoulders of
mutton, exhilarating cordials, books, pictures, the oppor-
tunities of seeing foreign countries, independence, heart's
ease, a man's own time to himself, are not *muck*—however
we may be pleased to scandalise with that appellation the
faithful metal that provides them for us.

VII.—OF TWO DISPUTANTS, THE WARMEST IS GENERALLY IN THE WRONG

Our experience would lead us to quite an opposite conclusion. Temper, indeed, is no test of truth ; but warmth
and earnestness are a proof at least of a man's own conviction of the rectitude of that which he maintains. Coolness
is as often the result of an unprincipled indifference to truth
or falsehood, as of a sober confidence in a man's own side
in a dispute. Nothing is more insulting sometimes than
the appearance of this philosophic temper. There is little
Titubus, the stammering law-stationer in Lincoln's Inn—
we have seldom known this shrewd little fellow engaged in
an argument where we were not convinced he had the best
of it, if his tongue would but fairly have seconded him.
When he has been spluttering excellent broken sense for an
hour together, writhing and labouring to be delivered of the
point of dispute—the very gist of the controversy knocking
at his teeth, which like some obstinate iron-grating still
obstructed its deliverance—his puny frame convulsed, and
face reddening all over at an unfairness in the logic which
he wanted articulation to expose, it has moved our gall to
see a smooth portly fellow of an adversary, that cared not
a button for the merits of the question, by merely laying
his hand upon the head of the stationer, and desiring him
to be *calm* (your tall disputants have always the advantage),
with a provoking sneer carry the argument clean from him
in the opinion of all the bystanders, who have gone away
clearly convinced that Titubus must have been in the wrong,
because he was in a passion ; and that Mr. ——, meaning
his opponent, is one of the fairest, and at the same time
one of the most dispassionate arguers breathing.

VIII.—THAT VERBAL ALLUSIONS ARE NOT WIT, BECAUSE THEY WILL NOT BEAR A TRANSLATION

The same might be said of the wittiest local allusions. A custom is sometimes as difficult to explain to a foreigner as a pun. What would become of a great part of the wit of the last age, if it were tried by this test ? How would certain topics, as aldermanity, cuckoldry, have sounded to a Terentian auditory, though Terence himself had been alive to translate them ? *Senator urbanus*, with *Curruca* to boot for a synonime, would but faintly have done the business. Words, involving notions, are hard enough to render ; it is too much to expect us to translate a sound, and give an elegant version to a jingle. The Virgilian harmony is not translatable, but by substituting harmonious sounds in another language for it. To Latinise a pun, we must seek a pun in Latin, that will answer to it ; as, to give an idea of the double endings in Hudibras, we must have recourse to a similar practice in the old monkish doggerel. Dennis, the fiercest oppugner of puns in ancient or modern times, professes himself highly tickled with the ' a stick ' chiming to ' ecclesiastic '. Yet what is this but a species of pun, a verbal consonance ?

IX.—THAT THE WORST PUNS ARE THE BEST

If by worst be only meant the most far-fetched and startling, we agree to it. A pun is not bound by the laws which limit nicer wit. It is a pistol let off at the ear ; not a feather to tickle the intellect. It is an antic which does not stand upon manners, but comes bounding into the presence, and does not show the less comic for being dragged in sometimes by the head and shoulders. What though it limp a little, or prove defective in one leg—all the better. A pun may easily be too curious and artificial. Who has not at one time or other been at a party of professors (himself perhaps an old offender in that line), where, after ringing a round of the most ingenious conceits, every man contributing his shot, and some there the most expert shooters of the day ; after making a poor *word* run the gauntlet till it is ready to drop ; after hunting and [1]winding

[1] winding] sending 1826.

it through all the possible ambages of similar sounds ; after
squeezing, and hauling, and tugging at it, till the very milk
of it will not yield a drop further,—suddenly some obscure,
unthought-of fellow in a corner, who was never 'prentice
to the trade, whom the company for very pity passed over,
as we do by a known poor man when a money-subscription
is going round, no one calling upon him for his quota—has
all at once come out with something so whimsical, yet so
pertinent ; so brazen in its pretensions, yet so impossible
to be denied ; so exquisitely good, and so deplorably bad,
at the same time,—that it has proved a Robin Hood's shot ;
any thing ulterior to that is despaired of ; and the party
breaks up, unanimously voting it to be the very worst (that
is, best) pun of the evening. This species of wit is the better
for not being perfect in all its parts. What it gains in
completeness, it loses in naturalness. The more exactly it
satisfies the critical, the less hold it has upon some other
faculties. The puns which are most entertaining are those
which will least bear an analysis. Of this kind is the following, recorded, with a sort of stigma, in one of Swift's
Miscellanies.

An Oxford scholar, meeting a porter who was carrying
a hare through the streets, accosts him with this extraordinary question : 'Prithee, friend, is that thy own hare,
or a wig ? '

There is no excusing this, and no resisting it. A man
might blur ten sides of paper in attempting a defence of it
against a critic who should be laughter-proof. The quibble
in itself is not considerable. It is only a new turn given,
by a little false pronunciation, to a very common, though
not very courteous inquiry. Put by one gentleman to
another at a dinner-party, it would have been vapid ; to
the mistress of the house, it would have shown much less
wit than rudeness. We must take in the totality of time,
place, and person ; the pert look of the inquiring scholar,
the desponding looks of the puzzled porter ; the one
stopping at leisure, the other hurrying on with his burthen ;
the innocent though rather abrupt tendency of the first
member of the question, with the utter and inextricable
irrelevancy of the second ; the place—a public street, not
favourable to frivolous investigations ; the affrontive

quality of the primitive inquiry (the common question) invidiously transferred to the derivative (the new turn given to it) in the implied satire ; namely, that few of that tribe are expected to eat of the good things which they carry, they being in most countries considered rather as the temporary trustees than owners of such dainties,—which the fellow was beginning to understand ; but then the *wig* again comes in, and he can make nothing of it : all put together constitute a picture : Hogarth could have made it intelligible on canvass.

Yet nine out of ten critics will pronounce this a very bad pun, because of the defectiveness in the concluding member, which is its very beauty, and constitutes the surprise. The same persons shall cry up for admirable the cold quibble from Virgil about the broken Cremona;[a] because it is made out in all its parts, and leaves nothing to the imagination. We venture to call it cold ; because of thousands who have admired it, it would be difficult to find one who has heartily chuckled at it. As appealing to the judgment merely (setting the risible faculty aside,) we must pronounce it a monument of curious felicity. But as some stories are said to be too good to be true, it may with equal truth be asserted of this bi-verbal[1] allusion, that it is too good to be natural. One cannot help suspecting that the incident was invented to fit the line. It would have been better had it been less perfect. Like some Virgilian hemistichs, it has suffered by filling up. The *nimium Vicina* was enough in conscience ; the *Cremonœ* afterwards loads it. It is in fact a double pun ; and we have always observed that a superfœtation in this sort of wit is dangerous. When a man has said a good thing, it is seldom politic to follow it up. We do not care to be cheated a second time ; or, perhaps, the mind of man (with reverence be it spoken) is not capacious enough to lodge two puns at a time. The impression, to be forcible, must be simultaneous and undivided.

[a] Swift. [Mantua vae miserae nimium vicina Cremonae.—1826 *only.*]

[1] allusion, that] allusion applied by Swift to a lady's dress, or mantua (as it was then termed) coming in contact with one of those fiddles called Cremonas, that 1826.

X.—THAT HANDSOME IS THAT HANDSOME DOES

[This ' *Fallacy* ', followed by *That my Lord Shaftesbury*, &c. (see *The Genteel Style in Writing*, p. 61 above) and No. XII of the present series, appeared in *The New Monthly Magazine*, March, 1826, pp. 258–65.]

Those who use this proverb can never have seen Mrs. Conrady.

The soul, if we may believe Plotinus, is a ray from the celestial beauty. As she partakes more or less of this heavenly light, she informs, with corresponding characters, the fleshly tenement which she chooses, and frames to herself a suitable mansion.

All which only proves that the soul of Mrs. Conrady, in her pre-existent state, was no great judge of architecture.

To the same effect, in a Hymn in honour of Beauty, divine Spenser, *platonizing*, sings :—

> ——' Every spirit as it is more pure,
> And hath in it the more of heavenly light,
> So it the fairer body doth procure
> To habit in, and it more fairly dight
> With cheerful grace and amiable sight.
> For of the soul the body form doth take:
> For soul is form, and doth the body make.'

But Spenser, it is clear, never saw Mrs. Conrady.

These poets, we find, are no safe guides in philosophy ; for here, in his very next stanza but one, is a saving clause, which throws us all out again, and leaves us as much to seek as ever :—

> ' Yet oft it falls, that many a gentle mind
> Dwells in deformed tabernacle drown'd,
> Either by chance, against the course of kind,
> Or through unaptness in the substance found,
> Which it assumed of some stubborn ground,
> That will not yield unto her form's direction,
> But is perform'd with some foul imperfection.'

From which it would follow, that Spenser had seen somebody like Mrs. Conrady.

The spirit of this good lady—her previous *anima*—must have stumbled upon one of these untoward tabernacles which he speaks of. A more rebellious commodity of clay for a ground, as the poet calls it, no gentle mind—and sure her's is one of the gentlest—ever had to deal with.

Pondering upon her inexplicable visage—inexplicable,

we mean, but by this modification of the theory—we have
come to a conclusion that, if one must be plain, it is better
to be plain all over, than, amidst a tolerable residue of
features, to hang out one that shall be exceptionable.   No
one can say of Mrs. Conrady's countenance, that it would
be better if she had but a nose.   It is impossible to pull her
to pieces in this manner.   We have seen the most malicious
beauties of her own sex baffled in the attempt at a selection.
The *tout ensemble* defies particularising.   It is too complete
—too consistent, as we may say—to admit of these invidious
reservations.   It is not as if some Apelles had picked out
here a lip—and there a chin—out of the collected ugliness
of Greece, to frame a model by.   It is a symmetrical whole.
We challenge the minutest connoisseur to cavil at any part
or parcel of the countenance in question ; to say that this,
or that, is improperly placed.   We are convinced that true
ugliness, no less than is affirmed of true beauty, is the result
of harmony.   Like that too it reigns without a competitor.
No one ever saw Mrs. Conrady, without pronouncing her
to be the plainest woman that he ever met with in the
course of his life.   The first time that you are indulged
with a sight of her face, is an era in your existence ever
after.   You are glad to have seen it—like Stonehenge.   No
one can pretend to forget it.   No one ever apologised to
her for meeting her in the street on such a day and not
knowing her : the pretext would be too bare.   Nobody
can mistake her for another.   Nobody can say of her,
' I think I have seen that face somewhere, but I cannot call
to mind where.'   You must remember that in [1]such a
parlour it first struck you—like a bust.   You wondered
where the owner of the house had picked it up.   You
wondered more when it began to move its lips—so mildly
too !   No one ever thought of asking her to sit for her
picture.   Lockets are for remembrance ; and it would be
clearly superfluous to hang an image at your heart, which,
once seen, can never be out of it.   It is not a mean face
[2]either ; its entire originality precludes that.   Neither is it
of that order of plain faces which improve upon acquaintance.   Some very good but ordinary people, by an unwearied perseverance in good offices, put a cheat upon our

[1] such] such or such 1826.   [2] either] neither 1826.

eyes : juggle our senses out of their natural impressions ;
and set us upon discovering good indications in a countenance, which at first sight promised nothing less.   We
detect gentleness, which had escaped us, lurking about an
under lip.   But when Mrs. Conrady has done you a service,
her face remains the same ; when she has done you a thousand, and you know that she is ready to double the number,
still it is that individual face.   Neither can you say of it,
that it would be a good face if it was not marked by the
small-pox—a compliment which is always more admissive
than excusatory—for either Mrs. Conrady never had the
small-pox ; or, as we say, took it kindly.   No, it stands
upon its own merits fairly.   There it is.   It is her mark,
her token ; that which she is known by.

XI.—THAT WE MUST NOT LOOK A GIFT-HORSE IN THE MOUTH

[Printed in *The New Monthly Magazine*, April, 1826, p. 418.]

Nor a lady's age in the parish register.   We hope we
have more delicacy than to do either : but some faces spare
us the trouble of these *dental* inquiries.   And what if the
beast, which my friend would force upon my acceptance,
prove, upon the face of it, a sorry Rozinante, a lean, ill-
favoured jade, whom no gentleman could think of setting
up in his stables ?   Must I, rather than not be obliged to
my friend, make her a companion to Eclipse or Lightfoot ?
A horse-giver, no more than a horse-seller, has a right to
palm his spavined article upon us for good ware.   An
equivalent is expected in either case ; and, with my own
good will, I would no more be cheated out of my thanks,
than out of my money.   Some people have a knack of
putting upon you gifts of no real value, to engage you to
substantial gratitude.   We thank them for nothing.   Our
friend Mitis carries this humour of never refusing a present,
to the very point of absurdity—if it were possible to couple
the ridiculous with so much mistaken delicacy, and real
good-nature.   Not an apartment in his fine house (and he
has a true taste in household decorations), but is stuffed up
with some preposterous print or mirror—the worst adapted
to his panels that may be —the presents of his friends that
know his weakness ; while his noble Vandykes are displaced,

to make room for a set of daubs, the work of some wretched
artist of his acquaintance, who, having had them returned
upon his hands for bad likenesses, finds his account in
bestowing them here gratis. The good creature has not the
heart to mortify the painter at the expense of an honest
refusal. It is pleasant (if it did not vex one at the same
time) to see him sitting in his dining parlour, surrounded
with obscure aunts and cousins to God knows whom, while
the true Lady Marys and Lady Bettys of his own honourable family, in favour to these adopted frights, are con-
signed to the staircase and the lumber-room. In like manner his goodly shelves are one by one stript of his favourite
old authors, to give place to a collection of presentation
copies—the flower [? flour] and bran of modern poetry. A presentation copy, reader—if haply you are yet innocent of such
favours—is a copy of a book which does not sell, sent you
by the author, with his foolish autograph at the beginning
of it ; for which, if a stranger, he only demands your friendship ; if a brother author, he expects from you a book of
yours which does sell, in return. We can speak to experience, having by us a tolerable assortment of these gift-
horses. Not to ride a metaphor to death—we are willing
to acknowledge, that in some gifts there is sense. A
duplicate out of a friend's library (where he has more than
one copy of a rare author) is intelligible. There are favours,
short of the pecuniary—a thing not fit to be hinted at
among gentlemen—which confer as much grace upon the
acceptor as the offerer : the kind, we confess, which is
most to our palate, is of those little conciliatory missives,
which for their vehicle generally choose a hamper—little
odd presents of game, fruit, perhaps wine—though it is
essential to the delicacy of the latter that it be home-made.
We love to have our friend in the country sitting thus at
our table by proxy ; to apprehend his presence (though
a hundred miles may be between us) by a turkey, whose
goodly aspect reflects to us his ' plump corpusculum ' ; to
taste him in grouse or woodcock ; to feel him gliding down
in the toast peculiar to the latter ; to concorporate him in
a slice of Canterbury brawn. This is indeed to have him
within ourselves ; to know him intimately : such participation is methinks unitive, as the old theologians phrase it.

For these considerations we should be sorry if certain restrictive regulations, which are thought to bear hard upon the peasantry of this country, were entirely done away with. A hare, as the law now stands, makes many friends. Caius conciliates Titius (knowing his *goût*) with a leash of partridges. Titius (suspecting his partiality for them) passes them to Lucius; who in his turn, preferring his friend's relish to his own, makes them over to Marcius; till in their ever widening progress, and round of unconscious circum-migration, they distribute the seeds of harmony over half a parish. We are well disposed to this kind of sensible remembrances; and are the less apt to be taken by those little airy tokens—inpalpable to the palate—which, under the names of rings, lockets, keep-sakes, amuse some people's fancy mightily. We could never away with these indigestible trifles. They are the very kickshaws and foppery of friendship.

XII.—THAT HOME IS HOME THOUGH IT IS NEVER SO HOMELY

[See No. X of this series.]

[1]Homes there are, we are sure, that are no homes: the home of the very poor man, and another which we shall speak to presently. Crowded places of cheap entertainment, and the benches of ale-houses, if they could speak, might bear mournful testimony to the [2]first. To them the very poor man resorts for an image of the home, which he cannot find at home. For a starved grate, and a scanty firing, that is not enough to keep alive the natural heat in the fingers of so many shivering children with their mother, he finds in the depth of winter always a blazing hearth, and a hob to warm his pittance of beer by. Instead of the clamours of a wife, made gaunt by famishing, he meets with a cheerful attendance beyond the merits of the trifle which he can afford to spend. He has companions which his home denies him, for the very poor man [3]has no visitors. He can look into the goings on of the world, and speak a little to politics. At home there are no politics stirring, but the domestic. All interests, real or imaginary, all topics

---

[1] Homes] Two homes 1826.   [2] first.] first of our assertions. 1826.
[3] has] can ask 1826.

that should expand the mind of man, and connect him to
a sympathy with general existence, are crushed in the
absorbing consideration of food to be obtained for the
family.   Beyond the price of bread, news is senseless and
impertinent.   At home there is no larder.   Here there is
at least a show of plenty ; and while he cooks his lean scrap
of butcher's meat before the common bars, or munches his
humbler cold viands, his relishing bread and cheese with an
onion, in a corner, where no one reflects upon his poverty,
he has sight of the substantial joint providing for the land-
lord and his family.   He takes an interest in the dressing
of it ; and while he assists in removing the trivet from the
fire, he feels that there is such a thing as beef and cabbage,
which he was beginning to forget at home.   All this while
he deserts his wife and children.   But what wife, and what
children ?   Prosperous men, who object to this desertion,
image to themselves some clean contented family like that
which they go home to.   But look at the countenance of
the poor wives who follow and persecute their good man to
the door of the public house, which he is about to enter,
when something like shame would restrain him, if stronger
misery did not induce him to pass the threshold.   That
face, ground by want, in which every cheerful, every
conversable lineament has been long effaced by misery,—
is that a face to stay at home with ? is it more a woman, or
a wild cat ? alas ! it is the face of the wife of his youth,
that once smiled upon him.   It can smile no longer.   What
comforts can it share ? what burthens can it lighten ? Oh,
'tis a fine thing to talk of the humble meal shared together !
But what if there be no bread in the cupboard ? The
innocent prattle of his children takes out the sting of a
man's poverty.   But the children of the very poor do not
prattle.   It is none of the least frightful features in that
condition, that there is no childishness in its dwellings.
Poor people, said a sensible old nurse to us once, do not
bring up their children ; they drag them up.   The little
careless darling of the wealthier nursery, in their hovel is
transformed betimes into a premature reflecting person.
No one has time to dandle it, no one thinks it worth while
to coax it, to soothe it, to toss it up and down, to humour
it.   There is none to kiss away its tears.   If it cries, it can

only be beaten. It has been prettily said that 'a babe is fed with milk and praise'. But the ailment of this poor babe was thin, unnourishing ; the return to its little baby-tricks, and efforts to engage attention, bitter ceaseless objurgation. It never had a toy, or knew what a coral meant. It grew up without the lullaby of nurses, it was a stranger to the patient fondle, the hushing caress, the attracting novelty, the costlier plaything, or the cheaper off-hand contrivance to divert the child ; the prattled nonsense (best sense to it), the wise impertinences, the wholesome lies, the apt story interposed, that puts a stop to present sufferings, and awakens the passion of young wonder. It was never sung to—no one ever told to it a tale of the nursery. It was dragged up, to live or to die as it happened. It had no young dreams. It broke at once into the iron realities of life. A child exists not for the very poor as any object of dalliance ; it is only another mouth to be fed, a pair of little hands to be betimes inured to labour. It is the rival, till it can be the co-operator, for food with the parent. It is never his mirth, his diversion, his solace ; it never makes him young again, with recalling his young times. The children of the very poor have no young times. It makes the very heart to bleed to overhear the casual street-talk between a poor woman and her little girl, a woman of the better sort of poor, in a condition rather above the squalid beings which we have been contemplating. It is not of toys, of nursery books, of summer holidays (fitting that age) ; of the promised sight, or play ; of praised sufficiency at school. It is of mangling and clear-starching, of the price of coals, or of potatoes. The questions of the child, that should be the very outpourings of curiosity in idleness, are marked with forecast and melancholy providence. It has come to be a woman, before it was a child. It has learned to go to market ; it chaffers, it haggles, it envies, it murmurs ; it is knowing, acute, sharpened ; it never prattles. Had we not reason to say, that the home of the very poor is no home ?

There is yet another home, which we are constrained to deny to be one. It has a larder, which the home of the poor man wants ; its fireside conveniences, of which the poor dream not. But with all this, it is no home. It is—

the house of the man that is infested with many visitors.
May we be branded for the veriest churl, if we deny our
heart to the many noble-hearted friends that at times
exchange their dwelling for our poor roof ! It is not of
guests that we complain, but of endless, purposeless visitants ; droppers in, as they are called. We sometimes
wonder from what sky they fall. It is the very error of
the position of our lodging ; its horoscopy was ill calculated,
being just situate in a medium—a plaguy suburban mid-
space—fitted to catch idlers from town or country. We
are older than we were, and age is easily put out of its way.
We have fewer sands in our glass to reckon upon, and we
cannot brook to see them drop in endlessly succeeding
impertinences. At our time of life, to be alone sometimes
is as needful as sleep. It is the refreshing sleep of the [1]day.
The growing infirmities of age manifest themselves in nothing
more strongly, than in an inveterate dislike of interruption.
The thing which we are doing, we wish to be permitted to do.
We have neither much knowledge nor devices ; but there
are fewer in the place to which we hasten. We are not
willingly put out of our way, even at a game of nine-pins.
While youth was, we had vast reversions in time future ;
we are reduced to a present pittance, and obliged to econo-
mise in that article. We bleed away our moments now
as hardly as our ducats. We cannot bear to have our thin
wardrobe eaten and fretted into by moths. We are willing to
barter our good time with a friend, who gives us in exchange
his own. Herein is the distinction between the genuine
guest and the visitant. This latter takes your good time,
and gives you his bad in exchange. The guest is domestic
to you as your good cat, or household bird ; the visitant
is your fly, that flaps in at your window, and out again,
leaving nothing but a sense of disturbance, and victuals
spoiled. The inferior functions of life begin to move heavily.
We cannot concoct our food with interruptions. Our chief
meal, to be nutritive, must be solitary. With difficulty

[1] day.] day. O the comfort of sitting down heartily to an old folio,
and thinking surely that the next hour or two will be your own—and the
misery of being defeated by the useless call of somebody, who is come to
tell you that he is just come from hearing Mr. Irving ! What is that to
you ? Let him go home, and digest what the good man has said to him.
You are at your chapel, in your oratory.—1826.

we can eat before a guest ; and never understood what the
relish of public feasting meant.   Meats have no sapor, nor
digestion fair play, in a crowd.   The unexpected coming in
of a visitant stops the machine.   There is a punctual
generation who time their calls to the precise commencement of your dining-hour—not to eat—but to see you eat.
Our knife and fork drop instinctively, and we feel that we
have swallowed our latest morsel.   Others again show their
genius, as we have said, in knocking the moment you have
just sat down to a book.   They have a peculiar compas-
sionating sneer, with which they ' hope that they do not
interrupt your studies '.   Though they flutter off the next
moment, to carry their impertinences to the nearest student
that they can call their friend, the tone of the book is spoiled;
we shut the leaves, and, with Dante's lovers, read no more
that day.   It were well if the effect of intrusion were simply
co-extensive with its presence ; but it mars all the good
hours afterwards.   These scratches in appearance leave an
orifice that closes not hastily.   ' It is a prostitution of the
bravery of friendship ', says worthy Bishop Taylor, ' to
spend it upon impertinent people, who are, it may be, loads
to their families, but can never ease my loads.'   This is
the secret of their gaddings, their visits, and morning calls.
They too have homes, which are—no homes.

XIII.—THAT YOU MUST LOVE ME, AND LOVE MY DOG

[This and the two following *Fallacies* appeared in their present order
in *The New Monthly Magazine*, Feb., 1826, pp. 224-9.]

' Good sir, or madam, as it may be—we most willingly
embrace the offer of your friendship.   We long have known
your excellent qualities.   We have wished to have you
nearer to us ; to hold you within the very innermost fold
of our heart.   We can have no reserve towards a person of
your open and noble nature.   The frankness of your humour
suits us exactly.   We have been long looking for such a
friend.   Quick—let us disburthen our troubles into each
other's bosom—let us make our single joys shine by redupli-
cation—But *yap, yap, yap!*—what is this confounded cur ?
he has fastened his tooth, which is none of the bluntest, just
in the fleshy part of my leg.'

' It is my dog, sir. You must love him for my sake. Here, Test—Test—Test ! '

' But he has bitten me.'

' Ay, that he is apt to do, till you are better acquainted with him. I have had him three years. He never bites me.'

Yap, yap, yap !—' He is at it again.'

' Oh, sir, you must not kick him. He does not like to be kicked. I expect my dog to be treated with all the respect due to myself.'

' But do you always take him out with you, when you go a friendship-hunting ? '

' Invariably. 'Tis the sweetest, prettiest, best-conditioned animal. I call him my *test*—the touchstone by which I try a friend. No one can properly be said to love me, who does not love him.'

' Excuse us, dear sir—or madam aforesaid—if upon further consideration we are obliged to decline the otherwise invaluable offer of your friendship. We do not like dogs.'

' Mighty well, sir—you know the conditions—you may have worse offers. Come along, Test.'

The above dialogue is not so imaginary, but that, in the intercourse of life, we have had frequent occasions of breaking off an agreeable intimacy by reason of these canine appendages. They do not always come in the shape of dogs ; they sometimes wear the more plausible and human character of kinsfolk, near acquaintances, my friend's friend, his partner, his wife, or his children. We could never yet form a friendship—not to speak of more delicate correspondences—however much to our taste, without the intervention of some third anomaly, some impertinent clog affixed to the relation—the understood *dog* in the proverb. The good things of life are not to be had singly, but come to us with a mixture ; like a schoolboy's holiday, with a task affixed to the tail of it. What a delightful companion is * * * *, if he did not always bring his tall cousin with him ! He seems to grow with him ; like some of those double births, which we remember to have read of with such wonder and delight in the old ' Athenian Oracle ', where Swift commenced author by writing Pindaric Odes (what a beginning for him !) upon Sir William Temple. There is the picture of the brother, with the little brother

peeping out at his shoulder ; a species of fraternity, which
we have no name of kin close enough to comprehend.
When * * * * comes, poking in his head and shoulders into
your room, as if to feel his entry, you think, surely you
have now got him to yourself—what a three hours' chat we
shall have !—but, ever in the haunch of him, and before his
diffident body is well disclosed in your apartment, appears
the haunting shadow of the cousin, over-peering his modest
kinsman, and sure to over-lay the expected good talk with
his insufferable procerity of stature, and uncorresponding
dwarfishness of observation. Misfortunes seldom come
alone. 'Tis hard when a blessing comes accompanied.
Cannot we like Sempronia, without sitting down to chess
with her eternal brother ? or know Sulpicia, without knowing all the round of her card-playing relations ? must my
friend's brethren of necessity be mine also ? must we be
hand and glove with Dick Selby the parson, or Jack Selby
the calico printer, because W. S., who is neither, but a ripe
wit and a critic, has the misfortune to claim a common
parentage with them ? Let him lay down his brothers ;
and 'tis odds but we will cast him in a pair of our's (we have
a superflux) to balance the concession. Let F. H. lay down
his garrulous uncle ; and Honorius dismiss his vapid wife,
and superfluous establishment of six boys—things between
boy and manhood—too ripe for play, too raw for conversation—that come in, impudently staring their father's old
friend out of countenance ; and will neither aid, nor let
alone, the conference : that we may once more meet upon
equal terms, as we were wont to do in the disengaged state
of bachelorhood.

It is well if your friend, or mistress, be content with these
canicular probations. Few young ladies but in this sense
keep a dog. But when Rutilia hounds at you her tiger aunt;
or Ruspina expects you to cherish and fondle her viper
sister, whom she has preposterously taken into her bosom,
to try stinging conclusions upon your constancy ; they
must not complain if the house be rather thin of suitors.
Scylla must have broken off many excellent matches in her
time, if she insisted upon all, that loved her, loving her dogs
also.

An excellent story to this moral is told of Merry, of Della

Cruscan memory. In tender youth, he loved and courted
a modest appanage to the Opera, in truth a dancer, who
had won him by the artless contrast between her manners
and situation. She seemed to him a native violet, that
had been transplanted by some rude accident into that
exotic and artificial hotbed. Nor, in truth, was she less
genuine and sincere than she appeared to him. He wooed
and won this flower. Only for appearance' sake, and for
due honour to the bride's relations, she craved that she
might have the attendance of her friends and kindred at the
approaching solemnity. The request was too amiable not
to be conceded ; and in this solicitude for conciliating the
good will of mere relations, he found a presage of her
superior attentions to himself, when the golden shaft should
have ' killed the flock of all affections else '. The morning
came ; and at the Star and Garter, Richmond—the place
appointed for the breakfasting—accompanied with one
English friend, he impatiently awaited what reinforcements
the bride should bring to grace the ceremony. A rich
muster she had made. They came in six coaches—the
whole corps du ballet—French, Italian, men and women.
Monsieur de B., the famous *pirouetter* of the day, led his
fair spouse, but craggy, from the banks of the Seine. The
Prima Donna had sent her excuse. But the first and
second Buffa were there ; and Signor Sc—, and Signora
Ch—, and Madame V—, with a countless cavalcade besides
of chorusers, figurantes, at the sight of whom Merry afterwards declared, that ' then for the first time it struck him
seriously, that he was about to marry—a dancer '. But
there was no help for it. Besides, it was her day ; these
were, in fact, her friends and kinsfolk. The assemblage,
though whimsical, was all very natural. But when the
bride—handing out of the last coach a still more extraordinary figure than the rest—presented to him as her *father*—
the gentleman that was to *give her away*—no less a person
than Signor Delpini himself—with a sort of pride, as much
as to say, See what I have brought to do us honour !—the
thought of so extraordinary a paternity quite overcame
him ; and slipping away under some pretence from the bride
and her motley adherents, poor Merry took horse from the
back yard to the nearest sea-coast, from which, shipping

himself to America, he shortly after consoled himself with
a more congenial match in the person of Miss Brunton ;
relieved from his intended clown father, and a bevy of
painted Buffas for bridemaids.

XIV.—THAT WE SHOULD RISE WITH THE LARK

At what precise minute that little airy musician doffs his
night gear, and prepares to tune up his unseasonable matins,
we are not naturalists enough to determine. But for a mere
human gentleman—that has no orchestra business to call
him from his warm bed to such preposterous exercises—
we take ten, or half after ten (eleven, of course during this
Christmas solstice), to be the very earliest hour, at which
he can begin to think of abandoning his pillow. To think
of it, we say ; for to do it in earnest, requires another half-
hour's good consideration. Not but there are pretty sun-
risings, as we are told, and such like gawds, abroad in the
world, in summer time especially, some hours before what
we have assigned ; which a gentleman may see, as they
say, only for getting up. But, having been tempted once
or twice, in earlier life, to assist at those ceremonies, we
confess our curiosity abated. We are no longer ambitious
of being the sun's courtiers, to attend at his morning levees.
We hold the good hours of the dawn too sacred to waste
them upon such observances ; which have in them, besides,
something Pagan and Persic. To say truth, we never anticipated our usual hour, or got up with the sun (as 'tis called),
to go a journey, or upon a foolish whole day's pleasuring,
but we suffered for it all the long hours after in listlessness
and headachs; Nature herself sufficiently declaring her sense
of our presumption, in aspiring to regulate our frail waking
courses by the measures of that celestial and sleepless
traveller. We deny not that there is something sprightly
and vigorous, at the outset especially, in these break-of-day
excursions. It is flattering to get the start of a lazy world ;
to conquer death by proxy in his image. But the seeds of
sleep and mortality are in us ; and we pay usually in strange
qualms, before night falls, the penalty of the unnatural
inversion. Therefore, while the busy part of mankind are
fast huddling on their clothes, [1]are already up and about

---

[1] are] or are 1826.

their occupations, content to have swallowed their sleep by wholesale ; we choose to linger a-bed, and digest our dreams. It is the very time to recombine the wandering images, which night in a confused mass presented ; to snatch them from forgetfulness ; to shape, and mould them. Some people have no good of their dreams. Like fast feeders, they gulp them too grossly, to taste them curiously. We love to chew the cud of a foregone vision : to collect the scattered rays of a brighter phantasm, or act over again, with firmer nerves, the sadder nocturnal tragedies ; to drag into day-light a struggling and half-vanishing night-mare ; to handle and examine the terrors, or the airy solaces. We have too much respect for these spiritual communications, to let them go so lightly. We are not so stupid, or so careless, as that Imperial forgetter of his dreams, that we should need a seer to remind us of the form of them. They seem to us to have as much significance as our waking concerns ; or rather to import us more nearly, as more nearly we approach by years to the shadowy world, whither we [1]are hastening. We have shaken hands with the world's business ; we have done with it ; we have discharged ourself of it. Why should we get up ? we have neither suit to solicit, nor affairs to manage. The drama has shut in upon us at the fourth act. We have nothing here to expect, but in a short time a sick bed, and a dismissal. We delight to anticipate death by such shadows as night affords. We are already half acquainted with ghosts. We were never much in the world. Disappointment early struck a dark veil between us and its dazzling illusions. Our spirits showed grey before our hairs. The mighty changes of the world already appear as but the vain stuff out of which dramas are composed. We have asked no more of life than what the mimic images in play-houses present us with. Even those types have waxed fainter. Our clock appears to have struck. We are SUPERANNUATED. In this dearth of mundane satisfaction, we contract politic alliances with shadows. It is good to have friends at court. The abstracted media of dreams seem no ill introduction to that spiritual presence, upon which, in no long time, we expect to be thrown. We are trying to know a little of the usages of that colony ;

[1] are] are all 1826.

to learn the language, and the faces we shall meet with there, that we may be the less awkward at our first coming among them. We willingly call a phantom our fellow, as knowing we shall soon be of their dark companionship. Therefore. we cherish dreams. We try to spell in them the alphabet of the invisible world ; and think we know already, how it shall be with us. Those uncouth shapes, which, while we clung to flesh and blood, affrighted us, have become familiar. We feel attenuated into their meagre essences, and have given the hand of half-way approach to incorporeal being. We once thought life to be something ; but it has unaccountably fallen from us before its time. Therefore we choose to dally with visions. The sun has no purposes of ours to light us to. Why should we get up ?

XV.—THAT WE SHOULD LIE DOWN WITH THE LAMB

We could never quite understand the philosophy of this arrangement, or the wisdom of our ancestors in sending us for instruction to these woolly bedfellows. A sheep, when it is dark, has nothing to do but to shut his silly eyes, and sleep if he can. Man found out long sixes.—Hail, candle-light ! without disparagement to sun or moon, the kindliest luminary of the three—if we may not rather style thee their radiant deputy, mild viceroy of the moon !—We love to read, talk, sit silent, eat, drink, sleep, by candle-light. They are every body's sun and moon. This is our peculiar and household planet. Wanting it, what savage unsocial nights must our ancestors have spent, wintering in caves and unillumined fastnesses ! They must have lain about and grumbled at one another in the dark. What repartees could have passed, when you must have felt about for a smile, and handled a neighbour's cheek to be sure that he understood it ? This accounts for the seriousness of the elder poetry. It has a sombre cast (try Hesiod or Ossian), derived from the tradition of those unlantern'd nights. Jokes came in with candles. We wonder how they saw to pick up a pin, if they had any. How did they sup ? what a mélange of chance carving they must have made of it !—here one had got a leg of a goat, when he wanted a horse's shoulder—there another had dipt his scooped palm in a kid-skin of wild honey, when he meditated right mare's milk. There is neither good eating nor drinking in fresco. Who, even in these civilised times, has never experienced this, when at some economic table he has commenced dining after dusk, and waited for the flavour till the lights came ? The senses absolutely give and take reciprocally. Can you tell pork from veal in the dark ? or distinguish Sherris from pure Malaga ? Take away the candle from the smoking man ; by the glimmering of the left ashes, he knows that he is still smoking, but he knows it only by an inference ; till the restored light, coming in aid of the olfactories, reveals to both senses the full aroma. Then how he redoubles his puffs! how he burnishes!—There is absolutely no such thing as reading, but by a candle. We have tried the affectation of a book at noon-day in gardens, and in sultry arbours ; but it was labour thrown away. Those gay motes in the beam come about you, hovering and teazing, like so many coquets, that will have you all to their self, and are jealous of your abstractions. By the midnight taper, the writer digests his meditations. By the same light, we must approach to their perusal, if we would catch the flame, the odour. It is a mockery, all that is reported of the influential Phœbus. No true poem ever owed its birth to the sun's light. They are abstracted works—

> ' Things that were born, when none but the still night,
> And his dumb candle, saw his pinching throes.'

Marry, daylight—daylight might furnish the images, the crude material ; but for the fine shapings, the true turning and filing (as mine author hath it), they must be content to hold their inspiration of the candle. The mild internal light, that reveals them, like fires on the domestic hearth, goes out in the sunshine. Night and silence call out the starry fancies. Milton's Morning Hymn on Paradise, we would hold a good wager, was penned at midnight ; and Taylor's richer description of a ª sun-rise smells decidedly of the taper. Even ourself, in these our humbler lucubrations, tune our best measured cadences (Prose has her cadences) not unfrequently to the charm of the drowsier watchman, ' blessing the doors ; ' or the wild sweep of winds at mid-

ª Holy Dying [1826 *only*].

night. Even now a loftier speculation than we have yet attempted, courts our endeavours. We would indite something about the Solar System.—*Betty, bring the candles.*

XVI.—THAT A SULKY TEMPER IS A MISFORTUNE

[Printed in *The New Monthly Magazine*, Sept., 1826, pp. 245-7.]

We grant that it is, and a very serious one—to a man's friends, and to all that have to do with him ; but whether the condition of the man himself is so much to be deplored, may admit of a question. We can speak a little to it, being ourself but lately recovered—we whisper it in confidence, reader—out of a long and desperate fit of the sullens. Was the cure a blessing ? The conviction which wrought it, came too clearly to leave a scruple of the fanciful injuries —for they were mere fancies—which had provoked the humour. But the humour itself was too self-pleasing, while it lasted—we know how bare we lay ourself in the confession—to be abandoned all at once with the grounds of it. We still brood over wrongs which we know to have been imaginary ; and for our old acquaintance, N——, whom we find to have been a truer friend than we took him for, we substitute some phantom—a Caius or a Titius—as like him as we dare to form it, to wreak our yet unsatisfied resentments on. It is mortifying to fall at once from the pinnacle of neglect ; to forego the idea of having been ill-used and contumaciously treated by an old friend. The first thing to aggrandise a man in his own conceit, is to conceive of himself as neglected. There let him fix if he can. To undeceive him is to deprive him of the most tickling morsel within the range of self-complacency. No flattery can come near it. Happy is he who suspects his friend of an injustice ; but supremely blest, who thinks all his friends in a conspiracy to depress and undervalue him. There is a pleasure (we sing not to the profane) far beyond the reach of all that the world counts joy—a deep, enduring satisfaction in the depths, where the superficial seek it not, of discontent. Were we to recite one half of this mystery, which we were let into by our late dissatisfaction, all the world would be in love with disrespect ; we should wear a slight for a bracelet, and neglects and contumacies would be the only

matter for courtship. Unlike to that mysterious book in
the Apocalypse, the study of this mystery is unpalatable
only in the commencement. The first sting of a suspicion
is grievous ; but wait—out of that wound, which to flesh
and blood seemed so difficult, there is balm and honey to be
extracted. Your friend passed you on such or such a day,—
having in his company one that you conceived worse than
ambiguously disposed towards you,—passed you in the
street without notice. To be sure he is something short-
sighted ; and it was in your power to have accosted *him*.
But facts and sane inferences are trifles to a true adept in
the science of dissatisfaction. He must have seen you ; and
S——, who was with him, must have been the cause of the
contempt. It galls you, and well it may. But have
patience. Go home, and make the worst of it, and you are
a made man from this time. Shut yourself up, and—
rejecting, as an enemy to your peace, every whispering
suggestion that but insinuates there may be a mistake—
reflect seriously upon the many lesser instances which you
had begun to perceive, in proof of your friend's disaffection
towards you. None of them singly was much to the
purpose, but the aggregate weight is positive ; and you
have this last affront to clench them. Thus far the process
is any thing but agreeable. But now to your relief comes
in the comparative faculty. You conjure up all the kind
feelings you have had for your friend ; what you have been
to him, and what you would have been to him, if he would
have suffered you ; how you defended him in this or that
place ; and his good name—his literary reputation, and
so forth, was always dearer to you than your own ! Your
heart, spite of itself, yearns towards him. You could weep
tears of blood but for a restraining pride. How say you ?
do you not yet begin to apprehend a comfort ? some allay
of sweetness in the bitter waters ? Stop not here, nor
penuriously cheat yourself of your reversions. You are on
vantage ground. Enlarge your speculations, and take in
the rest of your friends, as a spark kindles more sparks.
Was there one among them, who has not to you proved
hollow, false, slippery as water? Begin to think that the
relation itself is inconsistent with mortality. That the
very idea of friendship, with its component parts, as honour,

fidelity, steadiness, exists but in your single bosom. Image yourself to yourself, as the only possible friend in a world incapable of that communion. Now the gloom thickens. The little star of self-love twinkles, that is to encourage you through deeper glooms than this. You are not yet at the half point of your elevation. You are not yet, believe me, half sulky enough. Adverting to the world in general, (as these circles in the mind will spread to infinity) reflect with what strange injustice you have been treated in quarters where, (setting gratitude and the expectation of friendly returns aside as chimeras,) you pretended no claim beyond justice, the naked due of all men. Think the very idea of right and fit fled from the earth, or your breast the solitary receptacle of it, till you have swelled yourself into at least one hemisphere; the other being the vast Arabia Stony of your friends and the world aforesaid. To grow bigger every moment in your own conceit, and the world to lessen: to deify yourself at the expense of your species; to judge the world—this is the acme and supreme point of your mystery—these the true PLEASURES of SULKINESS. We profess no more of this grand secret than what ourself experimented on one rainy afternoon in the last week, sulking in our study. We had proceeded to the penultimate point, at which the true adept seldom stops, where the consideration of benefit forgot is about to merge in the meditation of general injustice—when a knock at the door was followed by the entrance of the very friend, whose not seeing of us in the morning, (for we will now confess the case our own), an accidental oversight, had given rise to so much agreeable generalization! To mortify us still more, and take down the whole flattering superstructure which pride had piled upon neglect, he had brought in his hand the identical S——, in whose favour we had suspected him of the contumacy. Asseverations were needless, where the frank manner of them both was convictive of the injurious nature of the suspicion. We fancied that they perceived our embarrassment; but were too proud, or something else, to confess to the secret of it. We had been but too lately in the condition of the noble patient in [1]Argos:

[1] Argos] Horace 1826.

Qui se credebat miros audire tragoedos,
In vacuo laetus sessor plausorque [1]theatro—

and could have exclaimed with equal reason against the
friendly [2]hands that cured us—

Pol me occidistis, amici,
Non servâstis, ait ; cui sic extorta voluptas,
Et demptus per vim mentis gratissimus error.

[1] theatro—] theatro— Ep. 2. 2. 130.   1826.   [2] hands] hand 1826.

EDITOR'S NOTES

[No word in the text which can be found in the *Pocket Oxford Dictionary* with an explanation in Lamb's sense has been annotated below. The reader, then, who does not find among these notes the explanation he wants is referred to that Dictionary, even for words or senses which he might not have expected to find there.

Shakespeare's plays are referred to by their titles only, or by the recognized abbreviations of their titles. The line numbers are as in the 'Oxford Poets' edition.

References to passages in Charles and Mary Lamb's writings other than the *Essays of Elia* are indicated only by their volume and page numbers in the two-volume Oxford Edition of *The Works of Charles and Mary Lamb*: thus 'ii. 379' refers to a story by Mary Lamb in 'Mrs. Leicester's School'.

The references to '*Elia*' with a page number indicate the companion volume of the first series of *The Essays of Elia* edited by Mr. O. C. Williams.

The present notes owe very much to the friendly censoring of Mr. Edmund Blunden, Mr. L. F. Powell, and others. I am conscious that they often go beyond the needs of scholars and their teachers. When they do so, it is usually to illustrate Lamb by himself, and thus to inventorize the furniture of his mind, for the delectation of my fellow Elians. F. P.]

PREFACE (PAGE 1)

BY A FRIEND OF THE LATE ELIA

Heading] The Preface is of course by Lamb himself. Bernard Barton (1784–1849) in a letter to James Keymer, 4 Jan. 1835, says: 'Perhaps Lamb's own account of himself, as given in the prefatory paper to the last Essays of Elia, is the best sketch of him we ever shall have'. R. B. Adam's *Catalogue of Johnsonian Collection* (1921).

1–7. The title and first two paragraphs in the *London Magazine* were as follows:

'A CHARACTER OF THE LATE ELIA

'BY A FRIEND

'This gentleman, who for some months past had been in a declining way, hath at length paid his final tribute to nature. He just lived long enough (it was what he wished) to see his papers collected into a volume. The pages of the *London Magazine* will henceforth know him no more.

'Exactly at twelve last night his queer spirit departed, and the bells of St. Bride's[1] rang him out with the old year. The mournful vibrations were caught in the dining-room of his friends T. and H.;[2] and the company, assembled there to welcome in another

---

[1] *St. Bride's*, Fleet Street, close to Ludgate Circus. Taylor and Hessey were at 33 Fleet Street.

[2] Messrs. Taylor and Hessey, the publishers of the *London Magazine*.

First of January, checked their carousals in mid-mirth and were silent. Janus[1] wept. The gentle P——r,[2] in a whisper, signified his intention of devoting an Elegy; and Allan C——,[3] nobly forget-ful of his countrymen's wrongs,[4] vowed a Memoir to his *manes*, full and friendly as a Tale of Lyddal-cross.'[5]

6. *a two years' and a half existence*, from Aug. 1820, when the *Essays of Elia* began in the *London Magazine*.

18. *a former Essay*: 'Christ's Hospital', *Elia*, p. 16.

21. *a country-boy*: S. T. Coleridge (1772–1834), from Ottery St. Mary in Devonshire.

23. *Imply*: Lamb (following Spenser and Chapman) is using it in the literal sense of the Latin *implicare*, to infold.

PAGE 2. 8. *My late friend*, &c.: this paragraph is largely modelled on Laurence Sterne's (1713–1768) character of Yorick in *Tristram Shandy* (1759), I, xi. (cf. *Elia*, p. 90, ll. 22–6).

PAGE 3. 6. *intimados*: formed from 'intimate', after Spanish words ending in 'ado'. Lamb found the word in Richardson's *Clarissa* (see note to p. 22, l. 27).

7. *a ragged regiment*: like Falstaff's in *1 Henry IV*, IV. ii. 27, 33; also preface to Milton's *Eikonoklastes* (see note on p. 79, l. 4).

13. *scandalised (and offences were sure to arise)*: cf. Luke xvii. I. The word for 'offences' in the Vulgate is 'scandala', and for 'offended' in verse 2, 'scandalizet': so Lamb may have had both the English and Latin versions in his mind.

19. *Indian weed*: tobacco from Virginia, once inhabited by Ameri-can Red Indians.

24. *proceeded*: technical use for taking one's degree (as B.A., M.A., etc.).

statist: politician, as in Wordsworth's poem, 'A Poet's Epitaph'.

33. *Shacklewell*: a north-eastern suburb of London.

school of industry: an Industrial school.

33–41. Cf. 'Oxford in the Vacation': *Elia*, p. 12, ll. 19–22.

PAGE 4. 1. *He herded always . . . with people younger than himself*: this was more noticeable in later years, with 'Barry Cornwall', Moxon, Forster, Emma Isola.

---

[1] *Janus*: a pseudonym of T. G. Wainewright (1794–1852), littérateur and afterwards a poisoner.

[2] Bryan Waller Procter ('Barry Cornwall'; 1787–1874), dramatist and song writer. 'P——r, candid and affectionate as his own poetry', Lamb called him in his letter to Southey, Oct. 1823 (i. 293).

[3] Allan Cunningham (1784–1842): poet and miscellaneous writer. 'Allan C., the large-hearted Scot' (i. 293).

[4] *Nobly forgetful of his countrymen's wrongs*, sc. at the hands of Lamb himself in his essay 'Imperfect Sympathies' (*Elia*, pp. 75–8).

[5] Cunningham contributed six out of a proposed 'Twelve Tales of Lyddal-cross' to the *London Magazine*, Jan.–June 1822.

5. *toga virilis*: garb of manhood (among the Romans).
9. In the *London Magazine* the essay proceeds:

'He left little property behind him. Of course, the little that is left (chiefly in India bonds) devolves upon his cousin Bridget.[1] A few critical dissertations were found in his escritoire, which have been handed over to the Editor of this Magazine, in which it is to be hoped they will shortly appear, retaining his accustomed signature.

'He has himself not obscurely hinted that his employment lay in a public office.[2] The gentlemen in the Export Department of the East India House will forgive me, if I acknowledge the readiness with which they assisted me in the retrieval of his few manuscripts. They pointed out in a most obliging manner the desk, at which he had been planted for forty years; showed me ponderous tomes of figures, in his own remarkably neat hand, which, more properly than his few printed tracts, might be called his "Works". They seemed affectionate to his memory, and universally commended his expertness in book-keeping. It seems he was the inventor of some ledger, which should combine the precision and certainty of the Italian double entry (I think they call it) with the brevity and facility of some newer German system—but I am not able to appreciate the worth of the discovery. I have often heard him express a warm regard for his associates in office, and how fortunate he considered himself in having his lot thrown in amongst them. There is more sense, more discourse, more shrewdness, and even talent, among these clerks (he would say) than in twice the number of authors by profession that I have conversed with. He would brighten up sometimes upon the "old days of the India House", when he consorted with Woodroffe, and Wissett,[3] and Peter Corbet (a descendant and worthy representative, bating the point of sanctity, of old facetious Bishop Corbet[4]), and Hoole[5] who translated Tasso,[6] and Bartlemy

[1] Bridget Elia, throughout Lamb's essays, is his sister Mary (1764–1847).
[2] The India House; the head office of the Honourable East India Company. It was situated in Leadenhall Street.
[3] Not identified.
[4] Richard Corbet (1582–1635), Bishop of Oxford and Norwich. The song, 'Farewell, Rewards and Fairies' is his.
[5] John Hoole (1727–1803), translated Tasso's *Jerusalem Delivered*, 1763: 'I wished to gain some idea of Tasso from this Mr. Hoole, the great boast and ornament of the India House, but soon desisted. I found him more vapid than smallest small beer sun-vinegared' (Lamb to Coleridge, 5 Feb. 1797). Hoole entered the service of the East India House at the age of seventeen.
[6] The dedication of which to the Queen was written by Dr. Johnson. It was so 'happily conceived and elegantly expressed' that Boswell could

Brown[1] whose father (God assoil him therefore !) modernised Walton[2]—and sly warm-hearted old Jack Cole (King Cole they called him in those days), and Campe, and Fombelle[3]—and a world of choice spirits, more than I can remember to name, who associated in those days with Jack Burrell[3] (the *bon vivant* of the South Sea House[4]), and little Eyton[3] (said to be a *facsimile* of Pope—he was a miniature of a gentleman) that was cashier under him, and Dan Voight[3] of the Custom House, that left the famous library.

'Well, Elia is gone—for aught I know, to be reunited with them—and these poor traces of his pen are all we have to show for it. How little survives of the wordiest authors ! Of all they said or did in their lifetime, a few glittering words only ! His essays found some favourers, as they appeared separately; they shuffled their way in the crowd well enough singly; how they will *read*, now they are brought together, is a question for the publishers, who have thus ventured to draw out into one piece his "weaved-up follies".[5]   'PHIL-ELIA.'[6]

In the *L.M.* for March, 1823, there appeared a notice contradicting the announcement of his death made in the foregoing *Character*.

BLAKESMOOR IN H——SHIRE (PAGE 4)

This is Blakesware, about four miles north-east of Ware, in Hertfordshire, where was the 'large old family mansion' of the Plumers, and where Lamb's grandmother, Mary Field, had been housekeeper for fifty or sixty years. Here as a boy Lamb sometimes spent his holidays. With Lamb's reminiscences of Blakesware (both in this essay and in 'Dream Children', *Elia*, p. 127), may be compared Mary Lamb's reminiscences of the same place in the story 'The Young Mahometan' in *Mrs. Leicester's School*. The parallels are quoted below with the references ii. 378–9.

not refrain from bringing it to the peculiar notice of his readers by reprinting it in the *Life of Johnson*, *sub anno* 1763.

[1] *Whose father*: Moses Brown (1704–87), edited the *Compleat Angler* in 1750, altering the text to suit the taste of the age. He tells us in his first edition (1750), that he undertook the employment of editing Walton 'at the instigation of an ingenious and learned Friend, whose Judgment of Men and Books is sufficiently established, by his own writings, in the Opinion of the World'. This friend was Samuel Johnson. A second edition was called for in 1759. See Boswell, n. e., ii. 363, note ad loc.

[2] Izaak Walton (1593–1683), author of *The Compleat Angler* (1653).

[3] None of these names have been identified.

[4] *South Sea House*: see *Elia*, pp. 1–10.

[5] *Richard II*, iv. i. 229.   [6] i.e. A friend of Elia.

15. *beauty of holiness*: Psalms xxix. 2, xcvi. 9.

22. *motionless as the marble effigies*: cf. 'Forget thyself to Marble', Milton, *Il Penseroso*, l. 42.

PAGE 5. 2. *had lately pulled it down*: in 1822. In 1827 (three years after the essay) Lamb saw the site of the house and gardens covered with corn.

3. *could not all have perished*: cf. p. 9, ll. 12–15, and note.

21. *Cowley*, Abraham (1618–67), poet and essayist. Cowley, in his essay 'Of My Self', has similarly described how as a child he sat in his mother's parlour and read Spenser.

26. *The tapestried bedrooms*: according to Mary Lamb (ii. 379) the 'tapestry hangings . . . were full of Bible history. The subject of the one which chiefly attracted my attention, was Hagar and her son Ishmael'. In a letter to Southey, 31 Oct. 1799, just after a visit to Blakesware, Lamb mentions 'The Judgment of Solomon' as a companion panel to the 'Actaeon'.

32. *Ovid*: Publius Ovidius Naso (43 B.C.–A.D. 18), Roman poet. The references are to his *Metamorphoses*, Books III, VI.

33. *Actaeon*: a hunter, turned into a stag, and torn to pieces by dogs, for having seen Artemis bathing.

in mid sprout: his horns are sprouting.

35. *Dan*: lord, or sir, from the Latin 'dominus'.

36. *Marsyas*: the Phrygian satyr, who challenged Phoebus Apollo to a contest in music, on condition that the victor might do what he would with the vanquished. Apollo was the victor, and flayed Marsyas alive.

37. *Mrs. Battle*: here probably Mrs. Elizabeth Plumer. Mrs. Battle the whist-player (*Elia*, pp. 41–8) is supposed to have been Mrs. Burney, the wife of Admiral Burney (see note below on p. 112, l. 28), but in the world of Elia the one Mrs. Battle may represent both Mrs. Burney and Mrs. Plumer. Certainly the Mrs. Battle who is Mrs. Burney has for maternal uncle the Walter Plumer who (*Elia*, p. 9) was of the Plumers of Hertfordshire, and (*ib.*, p. 44) she had a 'gallery at Sandham', with Vandykes and Paul Potters in the anteroom, which we may perhaps identify with the gallery at 'Blakesmoor' (p. 8).

40, 41. '*How shall they build it up again?*': this is italicized as a rhetorical question. Actually the furnishings of Blakesware were being used for Gilston (see 'Dream-Children', *Elia*, p. 127), and the intended answer to the rhetorical question may be that this effort to recreate the atmosphere of Blakesmoor was a vain one. But, taken in conjunction with line 3 above and the last three lines of this essay, it seems more likely that Lamb meant to suggest that Blakesware could only be rebuilt for others in his (and his sister's) memories.

PAGE **6.** 4–5. *battledores . . . shuttlecocks*: Mary Lamb also commemorates these (ii. 379).

19. *Lacus Incognitus*: 'unknown lake', such as might have been marked on an early map of Africa.

27. *that garden-loving poet*: Andrew Marvell (1621–78), '(whose poems by the way I am just going to possess)' Lamb to Godwin, 14 Dec., 1800; poet, satirist, member of Parliament for Hull, and joint Latin Secretary with Milton under Cromwell.

29. *gadding vines*: Marvell was plagiarizing his fellow secretary's *Lycidas*, l. 40.

38. *these were the conditions of my birth*: ' I was born, and passed the first seven years of my life, in the Temple' (*Elia*, p. 104).

PAGE **7.** 5. *importunate*: since '*noblesse oblige*'.

6. *coatless antiquary*: a student of heraldry, himself without a coat of arms.

7. *Mowbray*: the present baron is the twenty-fourth since 1283. Before that there were De Mowbrays, who 'came over with William the Conqueror'.

8. *De Clifford*: the present baron is the twenty-sixth since 1299. 'Fair Rosamond' was a De Clifford.

12. *trenchant*: here 'capable of being cut'. A reminiscence of *Macbeth*, v. vii. 38.

hacked off as a spur: part of the ceremonial degradation of a knight.

13. *torn away like a . . . garter*, from a disgraced Knight of the Garter. *tarnished garter*, belonging to a knight who had disgraced the Order.

16. *capitulatory*: recapitulatory.

24. '*Resurgam*': (Lat.) 'I shall rise again'.

25. *peasantry*: rusticity: Lamb supposes that his ancestors were peasants.

36. *Damœtas*: 'one that keeps other people's sheep' (Lamb to Coleridge, 9 June, 1796).

37. *Lincoln*: Lamb's father came from Lincoln (see p. 14, l. 19). In a letter of 1810 Lamb pretends to assume the title of Baron Lamb of Stamford 'where my family came from'.

39. *Aegon*: the master of Damœtas, in Virgil, Eclogue iii.

PAGE **8.** 3. *a newer trifle*: Gilston House (itself pulled down in 1851) near Harlow in the same county.

6. *W——s*: the initial is fictitious and represents the Plumers.

7–8. *old waste places*: cf. Isaiah, lxi. 4.

9. *that gallery of good old family portraits*, &c.: ' . . . some were old men and women, and some were children. I used to long to have a fairy's power to call the children down from their frames to play with me' (ii. 379).

16–17. *That Beauty, with . . . a lamb*: 'One little girl in particular, who hung by the side of a glass door which opened into the garden, I often invited to walk there with me, but she still kept her station—one arm round a little lamb's neck, and in her hand a large bunch of roses' (ii. 379).

18. *bright yellow H——shire hair*: not characteristic of Hertfordshire, but proper to the 'Alice' of the next line: in two early sonnets (ii. 522, 526) he speaks of a 'fair-hair'd maid', in 'New Year's Eve' (*Elia*, p. 35) she has 'fair hair', in his 'Dream-Children' (*Elia*, p. 130) she has 'bright hair'; his 'Rosamund Gray' (i. 8) has 'yellow hair', and in his imitation of Burton (i. 38), the lovesick youth's Glycera has hair lustrous and *smiling*.

watchet: pale blue. (It is a favourite word with Lamb: he found it in Spenser and Drayton.)

19. *Alice*: Lamb's first love, the Alice W(interto)n' of 'New Year's Eve' and 'Dream-Children' (*Elia*, pp. 35, 130), whose real name was Ann Simmons. Lamb met her at Blakesware when he was seventeen, and (at least according to those two essays) courted her for seven years. She married a pawnbroker, Bartrum, of Leicester Square.

20. *Mildred Elia*: not to be identified among Lamb's kindred.

21. *thy noble Marble Hall*: 'a very large hall, which, from being paved with marble, was called the marble hall' (ii. 378).

22. *its Twelve Caesars*: from Julius Caesar to Domitian. 'The heads of the twelve Caesars were hung round the hall . . . Hogarth's prints were below the Caesars' (ii. 378). It is odd that Lamb omits to mention these here, although he does mention them in the letter to Southey, 31 Oct. 1799.

25. *Nero*: (A.D. 37–68), proverbial for cruelty.

26. *Galba* (3 B.C.–A.D. 69) Roman emperor after Nero from June 68 to Jan. 69.

28. *Justice Hall*: the owners of Blakesware had been Justices of the Peace: in a letter to Bernard Barton (10 Aug. 1827) Lamb implies that Blakesware was 'peopled with the spirits of deceased members for the County and Justices of the Quorum'.

32. *thy costly fruit-garden*: 'his Lordship's magnificent fruit-garden' of 'The Last Peach' (i. 359).

32–3. *its sunbaked southern wall*: 'the South wall (can I forget the hot feel of the brickwork?)'—ib. i. 360.

Footnote] *The poem* HELEN [ii. 550]: 'How do you like this little epigram? It is not my writing, nor had I any finger in it. If you concur with me in thinking it very elegant and very original, I shall be tempted to name the author to you. I will just hint that it is almost or quite a first attempt.' Lamb to Coleridge, 26 Aug. 1800. The poem was his sister's.

PAGE 9. 3. *thy firry wilderness*: cf. 'Rosamund Gray' (i. 30), 'In this

Wilderness . . . Its stately fir trees were yet standing, with all
their luxuriant company of underwood—the squirrel was there,
and the melancholy cooings of the wood-pigeon.'

7. *Sylvanus*: Roman god of fields and forests (*silva*, a wood).

9. *Was it for this, that,* i.e. 'Was it because'. For similar construc-
tions, cf. pp. 73, l. 34 and 77, l. 17.

12. *plough . . . pleasant places*: cf. Isaiah xiii. 22 and Hosea ix. 6.

13. *do not die all*: cf. Horace, *Odes*, III. xxx. 6: 'Non omnis moriar',
'I shall not wholly die'.

POOR RELATIONS (PAGE 9)

Paragraphs 1–3: The detached phrases and the terminations in -'eth'
show that Lamb is consciously imitating the 'character'-writers
of the seventeenth century,—Canon Ainger suggests Fuller (see
note on p. 29, l. 35) but Miss Gwendolen Murphy's *Cabinet of
Characters* makes it clear that the resemblance is general rather
than particular. In a letter to Coleridge, 11 Oct. 1802, Lamb
says '"Bishop Hall's Characters" I know nothing about, having
never seen them': we may be sure he took Coleridge's hint, and
read them, and was influenced by their style.

3. *preposterous*: Lamb always uses this in its etymological sense of
'hindforemost'. A shadow lengthens at eventide, and is shortest
at noon.

8. *blot on your 'scutcheon*: the earliest use of the phrase recorded in
O.E.D. is 1683. It seems not to be a technical phrase in heraldry.

9. *a death's head at your banquet*: an old Egyptian custom, a reminder of one's last end. Cf. *1 Henry IV*, III. iii. 34.

10. *Agathocles' pot*: a reminder of one's lowly descent. The father of
Agathocles, tyrant of Syracuse, was a potter.
Mordecai: Esther iii. 2.
Lazarus: Luke xvi. 20.

11. *lion in your path*: 1 Kings xiii. 24.
frog in your chamber: Exodus viii. 3.

12. *fly in your ointment*: Ecclesiastes x. 1.
mote in your eye: Matthew vii. 3.

13. *the one thing not needful,* cf. Luke x. 42.

14. *hail in harvest*: cf. Proverbs xxvi. 1.
the ounce of sour, &c.: contrast Spenser: 'A dram of sweet is
worth a pound of sowre', *Faerie Queene* I. iii. 30.

PAGE **10**. 12. *remainder glass*: cf. *As You Like It*, II. vii. 39, and
T. & C. II. ii. 70.

17. *tide-waiter*: Customs officer who boards ships on arrival to enforce
customs regulations.

28. *on the score of poverty*: since they are playing for money.

41. *He dare say*: a quotation of the Poor Relation's 'I dare say'.

PAGE **11**. 10. *evil under the sun*: cf. Eccles. v. 13, vi. 1; x. 5.

20. *L——s*, Lambs.

26. Aterius talked so quickly that Augustus said of him: *Aterius noster sufflaminandus est*: 'Our friend Aterius needs the drag.' Ben Jonson in his *Timber* (see note on p. 24, l. 32) applied this to Shakespeare's facility, and Dr. Johnson (*Boswell, sub anno* 1754) to Thomas Warton's walking powers.

30. *Port and Madeira*: the latter would have been more suitable for a 'female' and a poor relation.

34. *mistaken the piano for the harpsichord*: The pianoforte began to supersede the harpsichord in the early years of the nineteenth century. The harpsichord was an instrument with keys, its strings being plucked (not struck) by a quill.

36. *Richard Amlet*, in 'The Confederacy' (1705) by Sir John Vanbrugh (1664–1726).

PAGE **12**. 7. *Poor W——*. Actually Samuel Favell (1775–1812), who, as Lamb says in his 'Key to the blanks and initials used by him in *Elia*' (i. 838), left Cambridge, because he was ashamed of his father, who was a house-painter there.

18. *our tallness*: Lamb was short.

23. *Oxford*: actually Cambridge.

27. *servitor's gown*: Sizars at Cambridge (like Samuel Favell) and servitors at Oxford were very poor students who were admitted at reduced fees and granted certain allowances in return for which they had to perform some menial duties. Servitorships are now abolished. The word 'sizarship' is still applied to certain scholarships at Cambridge, to which however no menial duties attach.

27–31. Cf. *Elia*, p. 28, ll. 30–3.

28. *Nessian venom*: Herakles had avenged an insult upon the centaur Nessus, who, dying, bequeathed his blood to Deianira, wife of Herakles, as a love-charm. Later, she dipped in this blood a white shirt which her husband was to wear as a priestly garment, while he was sacrificing. The blood had been poisoned by Herakles' arrow, and the poison penetrated into his own limbs and killed him after the most excruciating agony.

29. *Latimer*, Hugh (1491–1555), Bishop of Worcester; a sizar while at Cambridge.

30. *Hooker*, Richard (*c.* 1554–1600), theologian; a servitor while at Oxford.

33. *shrunk*: we now say 'shrank'.

35. *lord of his library*: cf. *Tempest*, I. ii. 109–10.

PAGE **13**. 2. *N——, near Oxford*: fictitious, perhaps some place near Cambridge.

27. ***** *college*: Pembroke College; not Caius or Jesus, as the number of asterisks might suggest.

30. *Artist-Evangelist*: St. Luke, by tradition a painter (but not a house-painter!) as well as a physician.

35. *like Satan*: cf. Milton, *P.L.* iv. 1013–14.

39. *St Sebastian*, in Spain, on the Bay of Biscay, besieged by Welling-ton in July 1813. Actually Captain Samuel Favell ('W——') fell at Salamanca in 1812. Cf. 'Christ's Hospital', *Elia*, p. 28, l. 33.

PAGE 14. 8. *an aged gentleman*: the 'Mr. Billet' of p. 15, unidentified.

9. *sad yet comely*: cf. Canticles i. 5.

20–22. *The Mint . . . the Tower*, i.e. of London. The Mint is on Tower Hill.

38. *Young Grotiuses*: Hugo Grotius (1583–1645) founded the modern code of international law in his *De iure belli et pacis* ('Of the law of war and peace').

39. *my father had been a leading Mountaineer*: but he had left Lincoln for London at the age of seven!

PAGE 15. 18. *my aunt*, Sarah Lamb (but known as Aunt 'Hetty'), who died in February 1797. She was ten years older than Lamb's father, under whose roof she lived. She cherished an intense affection for Charles, which he has commemorated in 'Christ's Hospital' and 'My Relations' (*Elia*, pp. 17, 89), in 'The Witch Aunt' of *Mrs. Leicester's School* (ii. 393), in a poem written on the day of her funeral (ii. 542) and in a letter to Coleridge, 5 Feb. 1797.

20. *my cousin Bridget*: See note 1 on p. 159.

22. *Mr. Billet* (John): unidentified. Lamb had used the name Thomas Billet for the inn-keeper at Widford, in 'Rosamund Gray' (i. 29).

36. *escrutoire*: escritoire, writing desk.

STAGE ILLUSION (PAGE 16)

8–20. Cf. 'On Some of the Old Actors', and 'On the Artificial Comedy of the Last Century', *Elia*, pp. 177–8, and 183, l. 37 *et seq.*

26. *Jack Bannister* (1760–1836), an actor of comic parts at Drury Lane Theatre. Cf. 'On some of the old Actors' (*Elia*, pp. 175–6). '*the man was frightened*': cf. Partridge's appreciation of Garrick as *Hamlet* in Fielding's *Tom Jones*, xvi, ch. 5.

PAGE 17. 23. *the pitiable infirmities of old men*: Lamb's letter to Coleridge 2 Dec. 1796 gives a feeling account of these in his own father.

30. *Gatty*, Henry Gattie (1774–1844), a comic actor.

35. *Emery*, John (1774–1822).

36. *Tyke*, in *The School of Reform* (1805) by Thomas Morton (fl. 1792–1807): see note on p. 66, l. 25.

40–1. Cf. the end of the essay 'On some of the old Actors' (*Elia*, p. 178).

harsh and dissonant: cf. Milton, *Samson Agonistes*, l. 662.

PAGE 18. 2. *a third estate*: the lowest order or class forming part of the body politic and sharing in government. In England the Three Estates are the Lords Spiritual, the Lords Temporal, and the Commons.

19. *Macbeth*: II. i. 33.

24. *Osric*: *Hamlet*, v. ii. 81–190.

26–30. *But when the pleasant impertinent,* &c.: pp. 144–5, and more than one of Lamb's letters show how very real an infliction these intrusions on his leisure, and on his home, were to him.

PAGE 19. 6. *a very judicious actor*: probably George Bartley (?1782–1858).

8. *Wrench,* Benjamin (1778–1843). 'Easy natural Wrench', Lamb styles him elsewhere (i. 238).

9. *Free and Easy*: a musical farce by S. J. Arnold (1774–1852), produced at the English Opera 16 Sept. 1816, with Wrench and Bartley in the chief parts.

TO THE SHADE OF ELLISTON (PAGE 19)

Title. *Elliston,* Robert William (1774–1831), actor. This and the next essay were occasioned by his death in July 1831.

1–3. Cf. James Thomson's *Ode*:

> Tell me, thou soul of her I love,
> Ah ! tell me, whither art thou fled ?
> To what delightful world above,
> Appointed for the happy dead ?

4. WILD OATS, (1791) by John O'Keeffe (1747–1833) with which Elliston began his managership of Drury Lane Theatre.

5. *Avernus,* a lake close to the promontory between Cumae and Puteoli, filling the crater of an extinct volcano. Near it was the cave of the Cumæan Sibyl, through which Aeneas descended to the lower world (*Aen.* vi.).

6. ROVER, Elliston's part in 'Wild Oats'.

7. *Elysian streams*: Elysium, in Greek and Latin mythology the abode of the blessed after death. 'Bowers ever green, rich meadows *with pleasant streams,* were the most striking objects.' (Lemprière).

10. *as the vain Platonist dreams*: In the *Phaedo*, Plato imagines the evil souls wandering about 'until through the craving after the corporeal which never leaves them, they are imprisoned finally in another body. And they may be supposed to find their prisons in the same natures which they have had in their former lives'.

PAGE 20. 1. *Palace of Dainty Devices*: Lamb has 'telescoped' the titles of the poetical miscellany *The Paradise of Dainty Devices*, 1576, and the collection of stories, Painter's *Palace of Pleasure*, 1562.

Louvre: the old royal palace in Paris, afterwards (and still) an art-gallery.

White Hall: the Palace of Whitehall, between Charing Cross and Westminster.

5. *Tartarus . . . Blessed Shades*: in classical mythology, the abodes (respectively) of the damned and the blessed. See note on p. 78, l. 27.

8. *Patriarchs*: those of the Old Testament. See note on line 11. *unchrisom*, unchristened; cf. Mrs. Quickly, *Henry V*, II. iii. 12.

10. *which Milton saw*: *P.L.* iii. 445–57 and 475 of which the blank verse lines are an abridged parody.

11. *Limbo*: (Lat. limbus), the border land of Hades; (1) 'the limbo of infants, where those who die in original sin alone, and without personal mortal sin, are confined and undergo some kind of punishment.' (2) 'the limbo of the Fathers (i.e. the Patriarchs), in which the souls of the just who died before Christ awaited their admission to Heaven.' (*Catholic Encyclopædia*).

19. *the neighbouring moon*: Milton, *P.L.*, iii. 459, 726.

20. *thy Regent Planet*: the planet in the ascendant at one's birth was by the astrologers supposed to govern one's character. Lamb makes the moon to be 'regent' over Elliston's mind, with allusion to its influence on lunatics.

22. *Lessee*: i.e. of Drury Lane Theatre (1813–26).

26. *Fye on sinful Phantasy*: cf. *Merry Wives of Windsor*, v. v. 99–108.

28. *capriccios*: (Ital.) caprices; literally 'capers': gambollings as of a goat, from the Latin, *caper*, a goat.
this globe of earth: Milton, *P.R.*, i. 365.

29. *for as yet*: cf. 'She (for I know not yet her name in heaven)', Edward Young (1683–1765), *Night Thoughts* (1742) Night vi, l. 1. *thy new name in heaven*: see Rev. ii. 17; iii. 12.

32. *a poor forked shade*: cf. *Lear*, III. iv. 111. *weedy wharf*: cf. *Hamlet*, I. v. 32, 33.

Stygian wherry: the ferry over the river Styx, by which the dead are conveyed to Hades.

Footnote]—*what seem'd his tail*, &c: adapted from Milton, *P.L.*, ii. 672–3.

Yet soon he heals, &c., *P.L.*, vi. 344–50.

PAGE 21. 1. *the old boatman*: Charon, son of Erebus, who ferries the dead.

2. *raucid*: raucous, hoarse. The *O.E.D.* has no other instance of the word, but gives 'raucidity' (1703).

2–5. 'Sculls, Sculls ...'*No*: Oars': a pair of sculls would be used by one waterman; a pair of oars by two. Elliston's magnificence would engage two men rather than one.

6. *Pluto's Kingdom*: Hades, the nether world. The three brothers, Zeus (Jupiter), Poseidon, and Hades (called euphemistically Pluto, the giver of wealth), took for their respective kingdoms Heaven, the Sea, and Hades.

8. *conterminant*: terminating together.

18. *sink a navy*: *Henry VIII*, iii. ii. 384.

20. *Foppington*, see note on p. 24, ll. 30, 31.

21. *that ancient mariner* (Charon): with allusion to Coleridge's poem.

22. *the old Thracian Harper*, Orpheus, who charmed Cerberus to sleep with his lyre.

25. *pura et puta anima*: Lat. 'a pure and dear soul'.

28. *Kings and Keysars*: Spenser, *F.Q.*, ii. vii. 5.
'Keysers' = Kaisers.

34. *Rhadamanthus*: son of Zeus and Europa; one of the judges of Hell. Virgil (*Aen.* vi. 566) makes him the judge of the 'heavier', not the 'lighter', causes.

35. *his two brethren*: Minos and Aeacus.

40. *Drury*: Drury Lane Theatre.

Page 22. 3. *Medusean ringlets*: Medusa's locks were changed by Minerva into serpents.

4. '*whip the offending Adam ...*': *Henry V*, i. i. 29.

6. *the O.P. side*: the 'opposite prompter' side of a stage.

7. *Proserpine*: Lat. Proserpina: Gr. Persephone; daughter of Zeus and Demeter; wife of Pluto (see note on p. 21, l. 6).

8. Plaudito et valeto: Lat. 'applaud, and bid farewell'.
footnote: *connive at his d——n, Mr. H.* Elliston was Mr. H. in Lamb's farce of that name, played for one night only (10 Dec. 1806) at Drury Lane. 'The secret of Mr. H's real name (Hogsflesh) seemed trivial and vulgar to the audience, and in spite of Elliston's best efforts, the farce was hopelessly damned' (*D.N.B.*).

ELLISTONIANA (Page 22)

5. *Leamington Spa*: Elliston opened a circulating library there in the name of his two sons.

6–7. *whom nothing misbecame*: cf. *Henry V*, ii. iv. 118.

7. *auspicate*: 'inaugurate', both words referring to the good omens supposed to be found in the flight of birds.

19. *Lovelace ... in King Street*: in *Clarissa Harlowe* (1747–8) by Samuel Richardson (1689–1761), Letter cxxiii.

Page 23. 1. *no after repentance*, cf. Milton's sonnet to Cyriack Skinner, l. 6.

9. *Wrench*: see note on p. 19, l. 8.

12. *converse*: 'If we take the statement *All men are mortal*, its contrary is *Not all men are mortal*, its converse is *All mortal beings are men*, and its opposite is *No men are mortal*', H. W. Fowler, *Modern English Usage.*

28. *green baize carpet of tragedy*: a convention of the London stage in vogue up till the middle of the nineteenth century,—the recognized announcement that the play was a tragedy.

31. *Apelles*: the most famous of Greek painters, a contemporary of Alexander the Great. He never spent a day without practising; hence the proverb 'Nulla dies sine linea' ('No day without a line'). *G.D.*: George Dyer (1755–1841): see 'Amicus Redivivus', pp. 74–5, and notes thereto. Lamb's letters are very amusing at the expense of Dyer as a would-be poet.

37. *leaden clatter*: the curtain was weighted with lead.

PAGE 24. 9. *Ranger*: 'The Suspicious Husband' (Feb. 1747) by Benjamin Hoadly (1706–57) and his brother John (1711–76). Ranger was one of Garrick's great characters, and in his presentation 'was the most sprightly, gay, frolicksome young rake that had ever been seen on the stage' (Murphy, *Life of David Garrick*, 1801, p. 81). The character obviously lost nothing in Elliston's presentation.

10. *the general bosom*: Shakespeare, *A Lover's Complaint*, 127.

30, 31. *Cibber . . . Foppington . . . Vanbrugh.* Colley Cibber (1671–1757) played the part of Sir Novelty Fashion in his own play *Love's Last Shift*, 1695–6. The play and his performance were alike successful, and Sir John Vanbrugh (1664–1726) wrote forthwith *The Relapse*, as a sequel. In this Cibber was Lord Foppington, Sir Novelty Fashion's name in the sequel.

32. *Ben Jonson* (1573?–1637): in *Timber: or, Discoveries made upon Men and Matters*, 1641.

33–40. *Lord Bacon . . . Lord Verulam*: Francis Bacon (1561–1626) was raised to a peerage as Baron Verulam in 1618, and in 1621 he became Viscount St. Albans. It is therefore improper to call him Lord Bacon.

PAGE 25. 5. *St. Dunstan's Church*, Fleet Street. It had two gigantic figures which struck the hours. The old church was pulled down some time before the date of this essay, and Moxon records that Lamb shed tears when the giants were taken away. The 'punctual giants' are now at St. Dunstan's Home for the Blind, Regent's Park.

6. *dust and a shadow*: cf. Horace's *Pulvis et umbra*, Odes IV. viii. 16.

13. *chew upon*: *Julius Caesar*, I. ii. 170.

14. *Expressive silence . . . muse his praise*: cf. James Thomson (1700–48), 'A Hymn' (Oxf. ed. p. 249), last line: 'Come then, expressive Silence, muse his praise'.

17. *the consular exile*: Marius, in B.C. 88.

18. *a more illustrious exile*: Napoleon, banished to Elba in 1814, with the title of 'Constable'.

24. *Olympic*: Actually Elliston's tenancy of the Olympic Theatre preceded his lesseeship of Drury Lane. It was to the Surrey Theatre he retired after Drury Lane.

37. *Sir A—— C——*: Sir Anthony Carlisle (1768–1840), 'the best story-teller I ever heard' (Letter 11 Mar. 1823).

PAGE 26. 2. *Olympic Hill*: Mount Olympus, in the range separating Macedonia and Thessaly; supposed to be the residence of the gods.

2. *'highest heaven'*: Milton, *P.L.*, i. 517.

3. *'Jove in his chair* (With his nods Men and gods Keeps in awe)', *Midas* (1761) by Kane O'Hara (1714?–82). Lamb introduces the line into a letter of 11 Jan. 1825.

6. *the town, in either of its senses*: (1) fashionable society, (2) the dissolute side of town life.

15. *Vestris*, Lucia Elizabeth Bartolozzi (1797–1856), singer, dancer, actress, and manageress. Grand-daughter of Bartolozzi the engraver. Married first the Italian dancer Vestris and afterwards Charles Mathews.

that beautiful Rebel: It has been suggested that Lamb (in 1831) called her a 'beautiful Rebel' because in 1824 she played the part of Diana Vernon (a Jacobite heroine) at Drury Lane Theatre. This is unlikely.

27. *son of Peleus*: Achilles, in the *Iliad*, xxi. 97–114.

28. *Lycaon*: one of the fifty sons of Priam.

33. *an Opera pit*: superior to the usual theatre pit.

34. *Surrey Theatre*: In 1809 Elliston became manager of the Royal Circus, and renamed it the Surrey Theatre. Bankrupt in 1826, he was again lessee of this theatre 1827–31.

39. *in the Temple*: Mary and Charles Lamb lived at 16 Mitre Court Buildings from 1801–9 and in Inner Temple Lane from 1809–17.

PAGE 27. 16. *Classical was thy bringing up*: at St. Paul's School, Covent Garden, *not* the St. Paul's School founded by Colet in 1509 and now at Hammersmith. Lamb's reference to Colet is misleading.

21. *Colet*, John (1467?–1519), Dean of St. Paul's, one of the foremost humanists of the early Renaissance in England.

DETACHED THOUGHTS ON BOOKS AND READING (PAGE 27)

4. *Lord Foppington*: see note on p. 24, ll. 30, 31.

11. *I love to lose myself in*, &c.: cf. Sir Thomas Browne (1605–82): 'I love to lose myself in a mystery, to pursue my Reason to an *O altitudo!*' *Religio Medici* (1642), I. ix.

PAGE 28. 3–6. cf. motto to 'Imperfect Sympathies', *Elia*, pp. 73–4.

3. *Shaftesbury*, Anthony Ashley Cooper (1671–1713), third earl of. Author of *Characteristicks of Men, Manners, Opinions, Times* (1711). See 'The Genteel Style of writing', p. 61 below.

4. '*Jonathan Wild* the Great': a satire (1743) by Henry Fielding (1707–54) based on the life of a receiver of stolen goods and informer, hanged in 1725. The satire has scarcely any connexion with its namesake.

7. *biblia a-biblia*: Greek, the English equivalent precedes it.

10. *Statutes at Large*: The Acts of Parliament in full.

11. *Hume . . . Gibbon . . . Robertson*: ' . . . the Damned philosophical Humeian indifference, so cold, and unnatural, and inhuman . . . the damned Gibbonian fine writing, so fine and composite. . . . Mr. Robertson's periods with three members'.—Lamb (1 March 1800) so contrasts them as historians with Bishop Burnet (1643–1715). Their own dates, and histories, are: David *Hume* (1711–76), History of England (1754–61): Lamb—see last note on l. 14 below—would have liked him just as little as a philosopher.

Edward *Gibbon* (1737–94), *Decline and Fall of the Roman Empire* (1776–88); William *Robertson* (1721–93), histories of Scotland (1759), Charles V (1769), America (1777).

Beattie, James (1735–1803); poet, essayist, and moral philosopher. In a letter to Coleridge 13 Aug. 1814, Lamb speaks of Beattie's ' contributing with others to make up a prettyish system of morality and the belles-lettres'.

Soame Jenyns (1704–87). Dr. Johnson wrote a slashing review of his *Free Enquiry into the Nature and Origin of Evil* (1757) to which Jenyns replied and provoked Johnson to a rejoinder— the only known occasion on which the Great Cham of literature troubled to reply to attacks made upon him.

14. *Josephus*: (A.D. 37–c. 100), Jewish historian of *The Antiquities* and *The Wars of the Jews*.

Paley, Archdeacon William (1743–1805), author of 'Paley's Evidences', i.e. *View of the Evidences of Christianity* (1794).

Moral Philosophy, i.e. *Principles of Morals and Political Philosophy* (1785). Lamb's aversion from 'moral philosophy' and preference for 'some kind-hearted play-book' (l. 22 below) was thoroughly philosophical and is expressed in the most searching thing he ever said: 'The old play-writers are distinguished by an honest boldness of exhibition, they show every thing without being ashamed . . . we turn away from the real essences of things to hunt after their relative shadows, moral duties; whereas, if the truth of things were fairly represented, the relative duties might be safely trusted to themselves, and moral philosophy lose

the name of a science.' *Specimens of English Dramatic Poets,*
1808 (i. 61).

17. *things in books' clothing*: cf. Aesop's wolf in sheep's clothing, and
St. Matthew vii. 15.

22. *seem its leaves*: cf. Milton, *P.L.*, ii. 672, and compare p. 20,
footnote.

23. *bolt*: suddenly.

23. *Population Essay*: either the *Essay on Population* (1798) by
T. R. Malthus (1766–1834) or some other provoked by it.

24. *Steele*, Sir Richard (1672–1729), author and politician. He
started *The Tatler* (1709) and together with Addison (1672–1719)
The Spectator (1711–12), but Lamb is probably thinking of him
as a playwright, since he couples him with Farquhar. Steele's
plays were *The Conscious Lovers* (1722) and *The Tender Husband*
(1705).
Farquhar, George (1678–1707), comic dramatist, 'the most
attractive . . . of the school generally associated with Congreve'
(Sir Leslie Stephen, in *D.N.B.*). Having failed as an actor, he
commenced as a dramatist, and was given a lieutenant's commission by the Earl of Orrery. His play *The Recruiting Officer*
(1706) was suggested by a recruiting expedition in Shropshire in
1705, and is dedicated to 'all friends round the Wrekin': a phrase
that Lamb was fond of quoting in his letters. His best play was
The Beaux Stratagem (1707), and this has been recently revived.
Always in money difficulties, he died of disappointment within
two months of the appearance of his last play.
Adam Smith (1723–90): political economist, author of *The
Wealth of Nations* (1776).

25. *Encyclopaedias*: the *Encyclopaedia Metropolitana,* began to appear in 1817, professing to give 'sciences and systematic arts
entire and in their natural sequence'. Coleridge contributed to
it, and Lamb is perhaps jesting at his friend's expense. The
'Encyclopaedia Anglicana' is Lamb's invention, and is perhaps
an allusion to the *Encyclopaedia Britannica*, first published in
three volumes in 1768–71.

28. *my shivering folios*: Lamb's books were mostly old ones and
therefore second hand (cf. 'Old China', p. 96).

29. *Paracelsus*: Theophrastus Von Hohenheim (1493–1541), a
German-Swiss physician and theosophist, author of many
medical and mystical treatises. Browning's poem on him will
well repay study.

31–2. *to warm my ragged veterans in their spoils*: a line of blank verse.
Raymund Lully: Ramón Lull (*c.* 1235–1315), Catalan author,
mystic, Franciscan missionary and martyr; with an unauthentic
reputation as an alchemist. Ben Jonson, like Lamb, couples

Lully and Paracelsus in his play *Volpone, or The Fox* (1605), Act II, Sc. I.

38. *is* our *costume*: i. e. the binding of the *London Magazine*. 'The Law Robe I have ever thought as comely and as gentlemanly a garb as a Book would wish to wear'. Lamb to Wordsworth 1 Feb. 1806. Footnote 1: *Pocket Books* (*the Literary excepted*): the *Literary Pocket Book* (annually, 1819–22) edited by Leigh Hunt; contained contributions by Keats, Shelley, and others. Lamb is lending his impecunious friend Leigh Hunt a helping hand.

PAGE 29. 4. *Thomson*, James (1700–48); poet, besides *The Seasons* (1726–30) he wrote *The Castle of Indolence* (1748) and the song 'Rule, Britannia'.

10. *Tom Jones*: (1749) by Henry Fielding (1707–54).
Vicar of Wakefield: (1766) by Oliver Goldsmith (1728–74).

13. *mantua-maker*: dress-maker. Mantua = mantle, a loose gown; and has no historical connexion with the town of Mantua. Mary Lamb was a mantua-maker.

16. *Lethean cup*: 'cup of forgetfulness'. In Greek mythology Lethe was the river of oblivion in the lower world.

21. *Fielding*: see notes on pp. 28, l. 4, and 29, l. 10.
Smollett, Tobias (1721–71), novelist, historian, and miscellaneous writer. Author of *Roderick Random* (1748), *Peregrine Pickle* (1751), *Humphry Clinker* (1771). Cf. *Elia*, p. 78, ll. 11–17.
Sterne, Rev. Laurence (1713–68), author of *Tristram Shandy* (1759–67), and *A Sentimental Journey* (1768).

23. *Stereotypes*: Lamb means works of such intrinsic excellence that they must be constantly reprinted, as though from stereotype plates.

24. '*eterne*': eternal; ' . . . in them nature's copy's not eterne'— *Macbeth*, III. ii. 38.

27. *we know not*, &c.: cf. *Othello*, v. ii. 12.

30. *by his Duchess*: Margaret Cavendish, first Duchess of Newcastle (1624?–7?), authoress of voluminous works of poetry and philosophy, dramas, and an autobiography, besides the *Life*, here referred to, of her husband, who was a pillar of the royalist cause; 'Madge Newcastle' Lamb called her affectionately in a letter. Cf. *Elia*, p. 96.

34. *Sir Philip Sidney* (1554–86), poet, man of letters, and soldier; author of the pastoral romance *Arcadia* (1590). See also the essay on his sonnets, pp. 79–87.
Taylor, Jeremy (1613–67), Bishop of Down and Connor, author of *Holy Living, Holy Dying*, sermons, and other theological works.
Milton in his prose-works: *Areopagitica* (1644, a pamphlet written in favour of the liberty of the press) and other con-

troversial writings. For Lamb's appreciation of these see a letter
to Coleridge, 4 Nov. 1802.

35. *Fuller*, Thomas (1608–61), author of The *Worthies of England*
and *The Holy and Profane State*: 'the golden works of the dear,
fine, silly old angel' as Lamb called them in a letter. He wrote
also an essay on Fuller (i. 142).

37. *endenizened themselves*: made themselves denizens or citizens.

40. *First Folio of Shakespeare*: (1623) the first collective edition of
Shakespeare's plays. Separate plays had previously appeared
from time to time in quarto. A book is said to be *in folio* when
it is printed on sheets folded once, i.e. into two leaves, and *in
quarto*, *octavo*, etc. when the sheets are folded into four or eight
leaves; hence, books made of sheets so folded are described as
folios, quartos, or octavos respectively. In general use a book
of large size came to be called a folio.

PAGE **30**. 2. *Rowe and Tonson*: Jacob Tonson (1656–1736) was the
publisher and Nicholas Rowe (1674–1718) the editor of the first
octavo edition of Shakespeare (1709), in six volumes, with plates.

6. *Shakespeare gallery engravings.* John Boydell (1719–1804), an
engraver, print-seller, and Lord Mayor of London, commissioned
the best English artists to paint pictures illustrative of Shakespeare's plays, and exhibited them as the 'Shakespeare Gallery'
at the British Institution in Pall Mall. Engravings were made
of the pictures, and were issued to the public by subscription in
1802.

10. *Beaumont and Fletcher*: Francis Beaumont (1584–1616) and
John Fletcher (1579–1625), joint authors of a number of tragedies
and comedies. See pp. 123–4, for the Lambs' purchase of this
folio.

15. '*The Anatomy of Melancholy*: what it is, with all the kinds,
causes, symptoms, prognostics, and general cures of it. In three
partitions: with their several sections, members, and subsections,
philosophically, historically opened and cut up [hence *The
Anatomy*] by Democritus Junior' (1621). Democritus (5th century
B.C.) was a Greek known as 'The Laughing Philosopher' 'Democritus Junior' was the pseudonym of Robert Burton (1577–
1640). Five editions were issued during the author's life and a
final one in 1651–2. The reprint which roused Lamb's ire was
presumably that of 1821. The book was a favourite with Lamb,
and in 1800 at Coleridge's suggestion he wrote some pretended
Fragments of Burton (i. 37).

18. *modern censure*: *As You Like It*, IV. i. 8.

20. *Malone*, Edmond (1741–1812), a scholar and critic who published
an edition of Shakespeare (1790). The bust was painted white,
not whitewashed, in 1793. It had already been repainted in

colours in 1649 and 1746, and perhaps again in 1769, and Malone may well have thought the colouring had no longer any first-hand authority. But in 1861 the white-lead paint was removed and the colouring restored.

31. *trouble-tombs*: perhaps an allusion to Shakespeare's epitaph:

> Good friend, for Jesus' sake forbeare
> To dig the dust enclosed heare:
> Bleste be the man that spares these stones,
> And curst be he that moves my bones.

36. *staled*: cf. *Julius Caesar*, IV. i. 38.

footnote: *Gifford*, William (1756–1826), edited Ben Jonson in 1816. He was the first editor of the *Quarterly Review*, and an enemy of the 'Cockney School' (see note on p. 36, l. 1). Lamb wrote a sonnet in derision of Gifford (ii. 661), and in a letter of Sept. 1816 to Wordsworth he records that 'Gifford (whom God curse) has persuaded squinting Murray' not to publish his *Works*, which were thus delayed for two years. Having 'advanced true friends' in a previous footnote (see note on p. 28, footnote 1), he 'beats down baffling foes' in this one.

PAGE 31. 1. *Marlowe*: Christopher (1564–93), poet and dramatist.

2. *Drayton*, Michael (1563–1631), poet. But Lamb's taste was more robust than to be content with selections: he read the Polyolbion (about 24,000 lines, including the incidental prose) and characterizes Drayton as 'that Panegyrist of my native Earth; who has gone over her soil, in his Polyolbion, with the fidelity of a herald, and the painful love of a son; who has not left a rivulet, so narrow that it may be stept over, without honourable mention; and has animated hills and streams with life and passion beyond the dreams of old mythology' (i. 59).

Drummond, William (1585–1649), laird of Hawthornden, near Edinburgh; poet.

Cowley, see note on p. 5, l. 20.

5. *The Fairy Queen*: (1590–6) by Edmund Spenser (1552?–99).

6. *Andrewes*, Lancelot (1555–1626), successively Bishop of Chichester, Ely, and Winchester, one of the translators of the Bible.

8. *a solemn service of music*: Milton's own poem 'At a Solemn Musick' invokes music as specifically attuning us to what were the themes of *Paradise Lost* and *Paradise Regained*.

10, 11. *had need bring docile thoughts, and purged ears*: cf. this verse with Milton, *Arcades*, ll. 72–3.

12. *the world shut out*: Edward Young (1683–1765), *Night Thoughts*, ix. 1441.

13. *gentle Shakespeare*: from Ben Jonson's epithet, both in the verses under the portrait in the First Folio, 1623, and in the *Lines to the memory of Shakespeare*, l. 56.

25. *The Times*: founded in 1785 as *The London Daily Universal Register*, and first called by its present name in 1788.
The Chronicle: The *Morning Chronicle* was founded in the democratic interest in 1772.

26. *pro bono publico*: Lat. 'for the general good'.

37. *Nando's*: probably a contraction for Ferdinand's or Ferdinando's, after the hypothetical owner. It existed in 1697. It used to be identified with No. 17 Fleet Street, where is 'Prince Henry's Room' (Henry, the eldest son of James I: the room is believed to have been the office and council-chamber of the Duchy of Cornwall); but it is now suggested that it was identical with the Rainbow Tavern, No. 15 Fleet Street.
Footnote: *Diurnals*: journals.

PAGE 32. 5. *the old Town and Country Magazine* (1769–92): one of its features was a series of portraits, coupled *tête-à-tête*, of well-known men, whose names were disguised, with their reputed mistresses. Mr. Horace Bleackley has identified a large number of the characters represented, of which the following may be regarded as typical examples: 'Jemmy Twitcher and Miss R ... y' Lord Sandwich and Miss Martha Ray; 'Baron Otranto and Mrs. Heidelburg'; Horace Walpole and Mrs. Clive. See *Notes and Queries*, 23 Sept. 1905, 241 ff.

6. *Lady G——*: Lady Grosvenor (d. 1828). The Royal Lover was George III's brother, Henry Frederick, the Duke of Cumberland, and the scandal culminated in a *cause célèbre* in 1771.
Platonic: a lady who loves (as she thinks) platonically.

10. *Poor Tobin*: James Webbe Tobin, son of a merchant, and grandson of a rich sugar planter, was a friend of Lamb and Coleridge. He died at Nevis in the West Indies (1814).

16. *Candide* (February 1759), by Voltaire (1694–1778), an amusing satirical romance, passages in which verge upon the indecent. It was directed against the philosophy of Leibnitz.

19. *Primrose Hill*: in the N.W. district of London.
Cythera: an island off the coast of Greece, sacred to Aphrodite.

20. *Pamela; or Virtue Rewarded* (1741), by Samuel Richardson (1689–1761): the tale of a servant whose obstinate virtue is rewarded by marriage with her master. 'The precise strait-laced Richardson has strengthened Vice, from the mouth of Lovelace [in *Clarissa*], with entangling sophistries and abstruse pleas against her adversary Virtue' (i. 56).

32. *Snow Hill* runs from Farringdon Street to Newgate.
Skinner's-street was not: and now again is not. It was projected by Alderman Skinner in 1802 to provide a more convenient thoroughfare than Snow Hill, between Newgate St. and Holborn. The last remains of the street disappeared with the building of

Holborn Viaduct in 1867. In a letter of 26 Feb. 1808 Lamb writes: 'Godwin keeps a shop in Skinner Street, Snow Hill, he is turned children's bookseller, and sells penny, twopenny, threepenny and fourpenny books.' From this address Godwin published Lamb's *Tales from Shakespeare* (1807) and *The Adventures of Ulysses* (1808), both for children.

34. *Lardner*, Nathaniel (1684–1768), Unitarian theologian.

37. *porters' knot*: a pad used by porters when carrying weights on the head.

PAGE **33**. 2. *the five points*: the five main articles of Calvinistic doctrine: Original Sin, Predestination, Irresistible Grace, Particular Redemption, the Final Perseverance of the Saints. Here in the *L.M.* comes the following paragraph, omitted in the *Last Essays*, 1833:—'I was once amused—there is a pleasure in *affecting* affectation—at the indignation of a crowd that was justling in with me at the pit-door of Covent Garden theatre, to have a sight of Master Betty[1]—then at once in his dawn and his meridian —in Hamlet. I had been invited quite unexpectedly to join a party, whom I met near the door of the playhouse, and I happened to have in my hand a large octavo of Johnson and Steevens's[2] Shakspeare, which, the time not admitting of my carrying it home, of course went with me to the theatre. Just in the very heat and pressure of the doors opening—the *rush*, as they term it—I deliberately held the volume over my head, open at the scene in which the young Roscius[3] had been most cried up, and quietly read by the lamp-light. The clamour became universal. "The affectation of the fellow," cried one. "Look at that gentleman *reading*, papa," squeaked a young lady, who in her admiration of the novelty almost forgot her fears. I read on. "He ought to have his book knocked out of his hand," exclaimed a pursy cit,[4] whose arms were too fast pinioned to his side to suffer him to execute his kind intention. Still I read on—and, till the time came to pay my

[1] William Henry West Betty (1791–1874), known as the 'Young Roscius'. An infant prodigy, he made his first appearance on the stage at the age of 11, and appeared as a boy actor at the age of 17; acted occasionally from 1812 till 1824, and then retired; surviving his notoriety for 50 years.

[2] *Johnson and Steevens's Shakspeare*; Dr Samuel Johnson (1709–84) first published his edition of Shakespeare in 1765 in eight vols.; he issued a second edition also in eight vols. in 1768. This edition was re-edited by George Steevens (1736–1800) at Johnson's suggestion, in 1773 in ten vols.

[3] *Roscius*: the most celebrated comic actor of Rome. For 'The Young Roscius' see note 1.

[4] Slang abbreviation of 'citizen' applied contemptuously.

money, kept as unmoved, as Saint Antony[1] at his Holy Offices,[2] with the satyrs, apes, and hobgoblins, mopping, and making mouths at him, in the picture, while the good man sits undisturbed at the sight, as if he were sole tenant of the desart.[3]— The individual rabble (I recognised more than one of their ugly faces), had damned a slight piece of mine[4] but a few nights before, and I was determined the culprits should not a second time put me out of countenance.'

7. *envious*: grudging.
   thinking when: 'wondering when'.
9. *expecting ... when*: for a similar usage see *Titus Andronicus*, III. i. 97.
11. '*snatch a fearful joy*': from Gray's 'Ode on a distant prospect of Eton College', l. 40.
    Martin B——: Martin Charles Burney (1788–1853) barrister; son of Admiral Burney (see note on 770, 35), etc. Lamb dedicated his prose *Works* in 1818 to Burney in verses which evince a deep affection.
13. *Clarissa*: see note on p. 22, l. 27. The early editions were in seven volumes, duodecimo.
18. *a quaint poetess*: Lamb's sister Mary, in *Poetry for Children*, 1809. Footnote] (*To be continued*): it never was.

THE OLD MARGATE HOY (Page 34)

(A popular topic in light literature of the day. Lamb's essay is one of several.)

Title] 'The [Margate] hoy went to London every week, loaded with mackerel and herrings, and returned loaded with company'. —William Cowper, Letter of July 1779 to Rev. William Unwin.
1. *I believe ... before*: in 'Oxford in the Vacation', *Elia*, p. 12.
5. *my beloved Thames*: In the summer of 1804 Charles and Mary Lamb spent a month at Richmond 'wandering about, and comparing the views from the banks of the Thames with your moun-

[1] The first of the Christian hermits (*c.* 250–356). He had his abode among the tombs near his native village of Coma in the Fayum, where he was tormented and tempted by demons.
[2] Daily service in the Roman Catholic breviary.
[3] *Desart*, desert; an old spelling, used by Coventry Patmore as late as 1878.
[4] His farce; 'Mr. H.', produced on 10 Dec. 1806 at Drury Lane. The 'Young Roscius' had appeared in *Hamlet* at Covent Garden, in April and May 1805 and again in April 1806; and at Drury Lane on 31 Dec. 1805; but at neither theatre 'a few nights' after 'Mr. H.' Lamb is once again mystifying.

tain scenery, and tried, and wished to persuade ourselves that
it was almost as beautiful' (Mary Lamb to Dorothy Wordsworth,
13 Oct. 1804).

6. *my cousin*: 'Bridget Elia' (really his sister, Mary).

8. *dull at Worthing*: probably a fiction.

9. *duller at Brighton,* in August 1817.
   dullest at Eastbourn(e): probably a fiction.

11. *many years ago*: in 1790, since Lamb tells us that he was 15 at
    the time. In his *Rosamund Gray* (1798, i. 24) there is a possible
    reminiscence of this visit: 'Burns—you know we read him for
    the first time together at Margate'.

10, 11. 'I abused Hastings but learned its value'. Lamb to Bernard
    Barton, 10 July 1823.

20. *the modern steam-packet*: about 1815 the old sailing-boat gave
    way to a steam boat, *The Thames*.

27. *sea chimaera*: the Chimaera was a fire-breathing monster, part
    lion, part goat, and part dragon, killed by Bellerophon.

28–9. *that fire-god*: Hephaestus.
    parching up Scamander: see Iliad xx, xxi: the River Scamander
    rose to destroy Achilles, but Hephaestus was sent by Zeus to beat
    back the water with fire.

PAGE 35. 5, 6. *neat-fingered*: cf. 'neat handed', Milton, *L'Allegro*, l. 86.

7. *inland nurture*: cf. *As You Like It*, II. vii. 96–7.

8. *Eastcheap,* near the tower of London. (*See 1 Henry IV*, II. iv,
   etc.) Stow, *Survey of London*, 1598, speaks of it as famous for
   cook-shops (i.e. restaurants).

10 *Ariel*: see *Tempest* I. ii. 196–8.

11. *assist the tempest*: *Tempest*, I. i. 15, 16.

17. *officious*: either 'attentive, eager to please', as in Johnson's
    poem on Robert Levet, or 'efficacious', an Elizabethan sense.

22. *additaments*: anything added or appended: additions; a legal
    term.

22–3. *a fellow passenger*: Perhaps Lamb had read the *Life and
    Adventures of Joseph Emin, an Armenian, by himself* (1792),
    —though he nowhere mentions it by name—and is here pretend-
    ing to have met him. Maurice Hewlett wrote a very amusing
    summary of Emin's book in his *Extemporary Essays* ('An
    Armenian Knight's Entertainment'), but did not connect him
    with Charles Lamb's real or pretended fellow passenger.
    thorough-paced liar: from *The Spanish Friar* (1681), v. i, a play
    by John Dryden (1631–1700).

25. *Azores*: Portuguese Islands in the North Atlantic.

35. *shivering upon the brink*: from Isaac Watts's hymn: 'There is
    a land of pure delight' (l. 15).

38. *Not many rich,* &c.: cf. 1 Corinthians i. 26.

PAGE 36. 1. *our enemies*: *Blackwood's Magazine* attacked 'the
Cockney School', by whom they meant Leigh Hunt and his
friends, including Keats and Lamb. 'Cockneys' would be the
'worse name'.

2. *Aldermanbury*, in the City of London, near the Guildhall.
Watling-street, an old street so named runs east from St. Paul's
Churchyard to the junction of Queen Street and Queen Victoria
Street. The Roman Watling Street from Dover to Chester did
not enter the City, but crossed the Thames at Westminster.

18. *Carimania*: Karmania, now Kerman, a province of Persia.

25. *a Princess*: this would have been Elizabeth (1770–1840),
Landgravine of Hesse-Homburg, daughter of George III; but
Lamb expressly disavows exactitude here.

33. *the vulgar error*: a reminiscence of his favourite Sir Thomas
Browne's book: *Vulgar Errors*.

37. *'ignorant present'*: *Macbeth*, I. v. 58. Lamb had quoted this
phrase with deeper feeling in his letter to Coleridge 3 Oct.
1796.

38. *hardying*: becoming bold (a coinage of Lamb's own).
Footnote] *Thames or Tooley-street*: Thames Street runs parallel
with the north bank of the Thames from Blackfriars to London
Bridge and Tooley Street parallel with the south bank of the
Thames from London Bridge to the Tower Bridge.

PAGE 37. 1. *the Colossus at Rhodes*: a gigantic bronze statue of the
sun-god Helios at Rhodes, 105 feet high. The statue was thrown
down by an earthquake about the year 224 B.C. It stood in the
entrance to the harbour, but not across its mouth.
the Reculvers: the two western towers of the church of Reculver,
near Herne Bay; a landmark for sailors.

26. *with us, but not of us*: cf. 1 John ii, 19.

35. *the Infirmary there*: the Royal Sea Bathing Infirmary, opened
in 1796.

PAGE 38. 2. *pent up in populous cities*: cf. Milton, *P.L.*, ix. 445.

5. *chew upon*: see note on p. 25, l. 13.

36. *the great deep*: Isaiah, li. 10.

37. *those who go down*, &c.: cf. Psalm cvii, 23, 24.

39. *Plata . . . Orellana*: Rivers Plate and Amazon. Thomson has
'The mighty Orellana . . . The sea-like Plata' (*Seasons*,
Summer, ll. 840, 843): Lamb has transferred the epithet 'mighty'
from one river to the other. He had quoted the passage with its
context (ll. 834–59) at length in the *London Magazine* two months
previous to this article (i. 288).

PAGE 39. 1, 2. *For many a day . . . stormy Cape*: Thomson's *Seasons*,
Summer, ll. 1002–3. The Cape of Good Hope was earlier named
the Cape of Storms.

3. *the 'still-vexed Bermoothes'*: *Tempest*, I. ii. 229.

4. *sunken ships, and sumless treasures*: cf. *Henry V*, I. ii. 165.

8, 9. *Be but as buggs . . . sea's entral*: cf. Spenser, F.Q. II. xii. For 'frighten' read 'fearen'. 'Buggs': hobgoblins, bugbears.

10. *Juan Fernandez*: Robinson Crusoe's reputed island: about 400 miles off the coast of Chili.

11. *enchanted isles*: *Comus*, l. 517.

24. *vast o'er-curtaining sky*: perhaps a reminiscence of *Hamlet* II. ii. 318–20.

27. *Gebir* (1798), by Walter Savage Landor (1775–1864). The reference is to v. 129.

29. *Cinque Port*: certain ports (originally five only: Hastings, Romney, Hythe, Dover, and Sandwich) on the SE. coast, with ancient privileges.

32. *amateur*: connoisseur.

34. *I cry out . . . and pant . . .* : cf. Psalm xlii. 1.

35. *inland murmurs*: Wordsworth, *Tintern Abbey*, l. 4.

PAGE 40. 1. *chains, as of iron*: cf. Psalm cxlix. 8.

5. *Amphitrite*: wife of Poseidon (Neptune), the sea-god.

12. *to dwell with Meschek* (for Mesech): cf. Psalm cxx. 5.

24. *preventive service*: the coast-guards, who 'prevent' smuggling.

26. *run-hollands*: smuggled Hollands gin.

a foolish dace: see Walton's *Compleat Angler*, Fifth Day: 'the roach is accounted the water-sheep for his simplicity or foolishness . . . the roach and dace be much of a kind in matter of cunning . . .'

37. *a book 'to read strange matter in'*: cf. *Macbeth*, I. v. 63–4.

40–1. *All is false and hollow*: cf. Milton, *P.L.*, ii. 112.

PAGE 41. 4. *shall bring*: an archaism for 'will bring'.

11. *I could interpret*: cf. *Hamlet* III. ii. 260.

15. *Twickenham*: in Middlesex, on the Thames.

16. *emigrants*: migrants, having 'migrated' from London to Hastings.

24. '*What a sensation . . . in Lothbury*?' Perhaps with allusion to Wordsworth's 'Reverie of Poor Susan', l. 7: 'Bright volumes of vapour through Lothbury glide'. The next line: 'And a river flows on through the vale of Cheapside' may have occasioned Lamb's following reference to Cheapside.

Lothbury: a street on the north side of the Bank of England.

27. *The daughters of Cheapside, &c.*: imperfectly remembered from the Ode to Master Anthony Stafford, by Thomas Randolph (1605–35): 'The beauties of the Cheap, and wives of Lombard Street'.

35. *Thamesis*: Latin form of 'Thames'.

THE CONVALESCENT (Page 42)

5. *this month*: the *London Magazine* was a monthly, and the *Essays of Elia* appeared in it almost monthly from Aug. 1820 to Dec. 1823; twice only in 1824. In this present year (1825) Lamb was again contributing regularly.

6. *sick men's dreams*: cf. 'Aegri somnia'. Hor. *Ars Poet.* 7.

10–11. *the sun . . . the works*: cf. Ecclesiastes, i. 14.

23. *tergiversation*: a pun on the literal sense of the word.

24. *Mare Clausum*: a 'closed' sea, i.e. that part of the sea within which a particular country has sovereign rights. John Selden wrote a book on international law with this title.

28. *Two Tables of the Law*: Exod. xxxi. 18; Deut. ix. 10.

32. *A little while ago*: in 1822–3 Lamb was very active on behalf of William Godwin, who, owing largely to a flaw in the title-deed of his house, was threatened with a ruinous law-suit.

refreshing: a 'refresher' is an extra fee paid to counsel in prolonged or frequently adjourned cases.

PAGE 43. 7. *his friend is ruined*: unhistorical; Godwin's legal difficulty was a thing of the past by 1825.

17. *honing*: from Old French and Anglo-Norman; now dialectal; 'to grumble, mutter, murmur, to repine; also, to whine as a child' (Cotgrave: 1611). Lamb had already used the word in his imitation of Robert Burton (see note on p. 30, l. 15) i. 43, l. 2. He may have met with it in Mandeville's *Fable of the Bees* (1714).

18. *he yearneth . . . his bowels*: cf. Genesis xliii. 30; 1 Kings iii. 26.

29. *scull*: skull.

32. *discipline of humanity, and tender heart*: cf. Bacon, *Essays*, 'On Marriage and Single Life'.

PAGE 44. 7. *thin douceur*: probably a banknote, since Lamb in his *Specimens of English Dramatic Poets* says: 'The substitution of a thin, unsatisfying medium in the place of the good old tangible metal, has made avarice quite a Platonic affection. A banknote can no more satisfy the touch of a true sensualist in this passion, than', etc. (i. 67).

PAGE 45. 13. *coverlid*: coverlet.

17, 19. *Lernean pangs . . . Philoctetes*: after slaying the Lernean hydra, Herakles poisoned his arrows with its bile, whence the wounds inflicted by them were generally incurable. Herakles bequeathed his bow and poisoned arrows to his friend and armour-bearer Philoctetes. On his way to the siege of Troy Philoctetes was either bitten by a snake or wounded by his own poisoned arrows. He was left behind at Lemnos till the tenth year of the siege, when an oracle declared that Troy could not be taken without the arrows of Herakles. On his coming to Troy he was cured by Aesculapius.

20. *the sick man's dream*: see note on p. 42, l. 6.

23. *this man of news*, &c.: Sir Anthony Carlisle. See note on p. 25, l. 37.

30. *desart*: See note 3 on p. 179.

33. *alonely*: solely. Lamb is reviving an old word.

34–5. *a world unto himself, his own theatre*: cf. the last page of text and the notes thereto; also *Elia*, p. 45, l. 33–5.

36. *What a speck*, &c: unidentified. It would be amusing to conjecture that Lamb thought he was quoting *Lear* IV. vi 17. He said that he did once in all good faith invent a supposed quotation from Dante.

40. *In Articulo Mortis*: Lat. 'at the point of death'.

PAGE 46. 1. *quibble*: play upon words, pun: 'requesting an article. In death an article'.

9. *hypochondriac flatus*: a feeling of distension in the region of the stomach. The hypochondria are the spaces on each side of the epigastric region; when they are diseased the patient generally suffers from great depression and morbid hallucinations; hence the term hypochondriac is often used to mean 'of a melancholy disposition.' (Note by C. B. Wheeler.)

12. *Tityus*: a giant slain by Zeus and cast into Tartarus, where his body covered nine acres, while two vultures or snakes devoured his liver.

SANITY OF TRUE GENIUS (PAGE 46)

Heading] *That great Wit is allied to Madness*: 'Great wits are sure to madness near allied', Dryden, *Absalom and Achitophel*, i. 156.

2. *genius, in our modern way of speaking*: in a letter to Manning, late Feb. 1801, Lamb writes: 'genius (which is a short word now-a-days for "what-a-great-man-am-I")', i. e. he would prefer to confine the word to the sense either of 'tutelary spirit' or of the direction (rather than the quality) of a man's individuality.

10. *Cowley*: see note on p. 21, l. 21.
So strong a wit, &c.: 'On the death of Mr. William Harvey', No. 352 in *The Oxford Book of English Verse*.

14. *Tempering*: Regulating.

PAGE 47. 6, 7. *In the groves of Eden, . . . ascends the empyrean heaven*: the references are to Milton and his epic (see *P.L.*, x. 321).

9, 10. Cf. Milton, *P.L.*, i. 296, ii. 1016, i. 543.

11. *a 'human mind untuned'*: cf. *Lear*, IV. vii. 16.

17. *Kent*: *King Lear*, III, iv, vi. 'the noblest pattern of virtue which even Shakespeare has conceived' (i. 94); 'the noblest feature of the conceptions of Shakespeare's divine mind' (i. 448). 'Lovel' (Lamb's own father) in 'The Old Benchers' is identified with Kent by the quotation (*Elia*, p. 110, l. 36) from *Lear*, v. iii. 286–7.

18. *Flavius: Timon of Athens*, IV. iii. 482–545.
25. *ideal tribes*: Coleridge, *Religious Musings*, ll. 368–70.

> ... he of mortal kind
> Wisest, he first who marked the ideal tribes
> Up the fine fibres through the sentient brain.

27. *Proteus*: a prophet of the future, who tended the flocks of seals belonging to Poseidon (Neptune). At midday he rose from the sea (cf. Wordsworth's Sonnet: 'The world is too much with us'), and slept in the shade of the rocks, with the monsters of the deep lying around him. Cf. Virgil, *Georg.* iv. 394.
30. *Caliban*: in *The Tempest.*   *the Witches*: in *Macbeth.*
32. *differenced*: differentiated.
38–9. *men in sick dreams*: cf. p. 42, l. 6, and p. 45, l. 20.
PAGE 48. 4. *wantonized*: wantoned. The earlier uses in the *O.E.D.* are all of the sixteenth and seventeenth centuries.
  6. *shall more deviate*: see note on p. 41, l. 4.
  8. '*maddest fits*': George Wither (1588–1667) *The Shepherds Hunting* (1615), eclogue IV, l. 409. Swinburne, in his *Miscellanies* ('Charles Lamb and George Wither') has an interesting discussion of the context of this phrase; Lamb wrote an essay on Wither (i. 227).
  9. *Withers*: an alternative form of the surname, now obsolete.
10. *Lane's novels*: novels published, *c.* 1800, by William Lane (1738–1814) of the Minerva Press, Leadenhall Street. The name became proverbial for trashy novels.
13. *a happier genius*: Sir Walter Scott (1771–1832) in his Waverley Novels (1814–32).
15. *betossed*: *Romeo and Juliet*, v. iii. 76.
20–21. *Lord Glendamour ... Miss Rivers ... Bath and Bond Street.* Lane's novels were concerned with fashionable life.
23. *fairy grounds of Spenser*: in *The Faerie Queene* (see note on p. 31, l. 3).
28. *fantasques*: fancies, whims.
31. *prate not of their 'whereabout'*: cf. *Macbeth*, II. i. 58.
34. *the other to the wildest dreams*: cf. *M.N.D.*, v. i. 12–17.
33. *acquainted*: cf. 2 *Henry IV*, v. ii. 139.
38. *the cave of Mammon*: Spenser *F.Q.*, II. vii. The particular stanzas are noted below.
41. *Ambition*: a translation of Spenser's Greek name 'Philotime' (stanza 49).
PAGE 49. 1. *Hesperian fruit*: [stanza 54] golden apples on a tree sacred to Hera, guarded by three sisters, the Hesperides, and a dragon. It was one of the twelve labours of Herakles to obtain possession of these apples.
  2. *Tantalus*: [stanzas 57–60] See *P.O.D.*, s.v. 'tantalize'.

Pilate washing his hands: [stanza 61] Matthew xxvi, 24, &c.

3. *not impertinently, in the same stream*: Pilate is washing his hands vainly, since they will never be clean, and it is not impertinently (i.e. without meaning) that he is washing them in the stream where Tantalus is tortured, for the water mocks both the thirst of Tantalus and Pilate's desire for exculpation.

11–23. this concluding paragraph may well be compared with the last paragraph of ' Witches and other Night-Fears' (*Elia*, p. 88) and the variant form from the MS. at South Kensington (see i. 845) which includes the sentence : 'What dreams must not Spenser have had.'

21. *a monster for a god*; cf. *The Tempest*, v. i. 296.

CAPTAIN JACKSON (PAGE 49)

1. *in our obituary*: not to be found among the obituaries in the *London Magazine*.

2. *the Bath Road*: the Bayswater Road, leading through Oxford to Bath.

3. *Captain Jackson*: unidentified. The essay is a mystification, but 'Captain Jackson' may have been suggested by the character of Randal Norris (see pp. 120–2.)

8. *Westbourn Green*: now Westbourne Grove, Paddington.

PAGE 50. 12. *Althea's horn*: this should be 'Amalthea's horn' (Lamb has it right in his 'John Woodvil', ii. 714). She was a nymph who nursed the infant Zeus, and was rewarded with the horn of plenty.

16. *foregone meal*: the previous (foregoing) meal. If the family had fasted at midday to provide a dinner for guests at night, the adjective should have been 'forgone'. Cf. p. 150, l. 8.

19. *the mind, the mind, Master Shallow*: cf. *2 Henry IV*, III. ii. 281, and *V*. iii. 30–32.

22. *the widow's cruse*: 1 Kings xvii. 12.
the loaves and fishes: Matthew xiv. 19, &c.

22–3. *carving could not lessen nor helping diminish it*: cf. 'Age could not wither her, nor custom stale Her infinite variety', *A. & C.* II. ii. 243.

25. *accidents*: in metaphysics, a non-essential property; in theology. the 'outward and visible form' of the Sacramental elements.

30. *smoking boards*: table covered with steaming viands. In the *O.E.D.* the latest quotation of 'smoking' for 'steaming', with the spelling 'smoaking', is from Dryden's *Virgil*, 1697.
feast-oppressed: heaped with food (cf. 'heat oppressed'. *Macbeth*, II. i. 39).

31. *ratio*: 'ration' in the Army sense. *Single Gloucester*: cheese made in Gloucestershire, less rich than 'double Gloucester'.

33. *remanent*: remaining.
34. '*the nearer the bone* the sweeter the meat'.
38. *verè hospitibus sacra*: Lat. 'truly sacred to guests'.
PAGE 51. 2. *the remainder crust*: cf. note on p. 10, l. 12.
14. *flustered*: cf. *Othello*, II. iii. 61.
17. '*Why, Soldiers, Why*': the first line is 'How stands the glass
    around'. It is first found in the ballad-opera, *The Patron*, 1729.
    Sometimes called 'General Wolfe's song', as having been sung
    by him in camp on the eve of the assault of Quebec.
18. *British Grenadiers*: traditional, 'cannot be older than 1678,
    when the Grenadier Company was formed, nor later than 1714,
    when hand-grenades were discontinued' (*War Songs*, '*Oxford
    Miscellany*', No. 29).
27. *bunch*, i. e. of keys: Lamb couldn't resist a pun.
40. *Glover*, Richard (1712–85): poet, author of *Leonidas* (1737).
    There is no evidence that he ever lived at Westbourne Green.
PAGE 52. 27. *at a demur*: at a loss, from Lat. *demoror*, I delay, or
    hesitate.
30. *properly termed* Content: which might be defined as self-con-
    tainment.
PAGE 53. 14. *the old ballad*: 'O waly waly up the bank'. The rest of
    the ballad is curiously inappropriate to Lamb's context, but it
    was a favourite poem with him.
18. *cramasie*: cramoisy, crimson cloth.
26. '*equipage etern*': perhaps a reminiscence of Milton, *P.L.*, vii. 203.
32. *Tibbs*; Beau Tibbs in Oliver Goldsmith's *Citizen of the World*,
    Nos. 54, 55.
    Bobadil, in *Every Man in his Humour* (1598) by Ben Jonson.
35. *steeped . . . to the lips*: cf. *Othello* IV. ii. 49.

THE SUPERANNUATED MAN (PAGE 54)

First motto] '*Sera tamen . . .*' From Virgil, *Eclogues*, I. 27;
    Libertas quae sera tamen respexit . . . ('Freedom which turned
    and looked upon me, albeit late').
Second Motto] '*A Clerk I was . . .*' (Lamb had applied this verse
    to himself and to the possible amelioration of his official duties
    as early as 1815 in a letter to Wordsworth) not from the farce-
    writer John O'Keeffe (1747–1833), but from *Inkle and Yarico*
    (1787), by George Colman the younger (1762–1836). Lamb says
    (1819) of his beloved Fanny Kelly (see pp. 66–71 and notes),
    'her Yarico is the most intense piece of acting which I ever wit-
    nessed, the most heart-rending spectacle' (i. 236).
9. *my deliverance*: 'I have left the d——d India House for Ever.
    Give me great joy. C. Lamb'—to Crabb Robinson, 29 March
    1825.

10. *six and thirty years*: Lamb was in the India House from 1792–
    1825, thirty-three years; but before that he had been a clerk for
    three years, first with Joseph Paice (see 'Modern Gallantry',
    Elia, p. 101) and then in the South Sea House (see 'The South
    Sea House', *Elia*, p. 3).

11. *Mincing-lane*, near the Tower of London, is the centre of the
    tea trade.

13–14. *eight, nine, and sometimes ten hours a day*: Lamb's normal
    hours were from ten till four, but every now and again he had to
    work nine, eleven, and (once) thirteen hours a day.

21. *recreation*: Here in 1825 the following footnote is appended:—
    'Our ancestors, the noble old Puritans of Cromwell's day,
    could distinguish between a day of religious rest and a day of
    recreation; and while they exacted a rigorous abstinence from
    all amusements (even to the walking out of nursery maids with
    their little charges in the fields) upon the Sabbath; in the lieu of
    the superstitious observance of the Saint's day, which they abro-
    gated, they humanely gave to the apprentices, and poorer sort of
    people, every alternate Thursday for a day of entire sport and
    recreation. A strain of piety and policy to be commended above
    the profane mockery of the Stuarts and their Book of Sports.'[1]

PAGE 55. 13. *my native fields of Hertfordshire*: compare 'Blakesmoor'
    (p. 5) and note on p. 6, l. 37.

28–37. The letters bear testimony to the genuineness of these feelings.

29. *sense of incapacity for business*: the letters show that he had been
    feeling this for eleven years.

35. *I served once again . . . in my sleep*: cf. letter to Wordsworth
    19 Sept. 1814.

37. *I was fifty years of age* [on 10 Feb.]: this was Lamb's actual age
    at retirement. 'Still I am a young *Pensioner*, and have served
    but 33 years, very few I assure you retire before 40, 45, or 50
    years' service'. (Letter, 18 April 1825.)

38. *I had grown to my desk*: 'this dead wood of the desk instead of
    your living tree' (Letter to Manning, 28 May 1819). 'I sit like
    Philomel all day (but not singing) with my breast against this
    thorn of a desk'. (Letter to Wordsworth, 20 March 1822.)

39. *the wood had entered into my soul*: cf. Psalm cv. 18 (P.B.V.) 'the

[1] Or more properly, the Declaration of Sports (1617), an order issued
by James I to settle the conflict between the Puritans and the gentry over
Sunday amusements. Archery, leaping, vaulting, may-games, Whitsun-
ales, and morris dancing were permitted, and bear- and bull-baiting,
interludes and bowling forbidden. In 1618 the clergy were ordered to read
the declaration from the pulpit, but an effective opposition was made to
this. In 1633 Charles I insisted upon having it read by the clergy, many
of whom were punished for refusing.

iron entered into his soul'. ('The desk enters into my soul'.
Letter of 19 July 1824.)

PAGE 56. 4. *L——*: Lacy, of the fictitious firm named in p. 57, ll. 2–3.

14. *a week passed*: Lamb was actually in suspense for ten weeks after
he had himself broached the subject of his superannuation.

16. *12th of April*: At a Court of Directors of the India House held
on 29 March 1825 it was resolved that Lamb's resignation should
be accepted and that he should be allowed a pension.

24. *B——*: Boldero, of the fictitious firm named in p. 57, ll. 2–3; Lamb
has elsewhere (i. 844: in a postscript to his 'Chapter on Ears')
pretended that this was Leigh Hunt's real name.

34. *a pension for life*: '£441 a year for the remainder of my life . . .
£441, i. e. £450 with a deduction of £9 for a provision secured to
my sister, she being survivor'. Lamb to Wordsworth, 6 April 1825.

40. *I went home—for ever*: Lamb used the same phrase in his letters
to Crabb Robinson, to Wordsworth, to Bernard Barton, announc-
ing his retirement.

PAGE 57. 2. *Merryweather*: in Lamb's pretended memoir of Liston
(i. 317) he gives him for godmother a 'Maria Merryweather'.

3. *Esto Perpetua*: (Lat.) May it last for ever ! The dying prayer of
Father Paul Sarpi. In his life of him Johnson writes: 'As his end
evidently approached, the brethren of the convent came to pronounce the last prayers, with which he could only join in his
thoughts, being able to pronounce no more than these words,
"Esto perpetua", mayst thou last for ever; which was understood to be a prayer for the prosperity of his country'. Johnson's
Works, 1826, vi, p. 269.

'*Boldero, Merryweather, Bosanquet, and Lacy*': although the
motto Lamb ascribes to O'Keeffe is not his, it may be said that
this is his: it has almost exactly the metre of the long line in his
stanza:

> Amo, amas,
> I love a lass
>   As cedar tall and slender;
> Sweet cowslip's grace
> Is her nominative case,
>   And she's of the feminine gender.
> Horum quorum,
> Sunt divorum,
>   Harum, scarum, divo:
> Tag rag, merry derry, periwig and Hatband,
> Hic, hoc, harum, genitivo.

9. *a prisoner*: Dickens in 'The Holly Tree' (*Christmas Stories*) mentions an unidentified prisoner 'who was released in his old age
from the Bastille' who besought 'to be taken back again to the
five windows, the ten curtains, and the sinuous drapery'.

Bastile: Bastille, Paris prison-fortress taken and destroyed by the Revolutionaries in 1789.

11–29. *It was like the passing out of time into Eternity*: this repeats the substance of part of his letter to Wordsworth, 6 Apr. 1825.

23. *giddy raptures*: cf. 'dizzy raptures', Wordsworth, *Tintern Abbey*, l. 85.

28–9. *thirty miles a day*: compare 'Old China', p. 127, l. 25; but in a letter to Dorothy Wordsworth, 21 Nov. 1817, Mary says that fifteen miles is exactly her 'stint'.

36. '*That's born . . .*': Thomas Middleton (1570?–1627), *Mayor of Quinborough* (1661), I. i. 101–3, with 'rough' for 'green'.

39. *superannuated*: with this as a phrase of contempt, cp. p. 15, l. 28.

PAGE 58. 1–10. expanded from the letter to Wordsworth.

4–7. cf. 'Time that a man may call his own is life'. Lamb to Wordsworth, 7 April 1815.

7–10. contrast 'So of the little that is left of my life I may reckon two-thirds as dead'. Lamb to Wordsworth, 7 April 1815.

20. *a tragedy by Sir Robert Howard* (1626–98): 'The Vestal Virgin, or the Roman Ladies' (1665), v. i.

26. This paragraph is expanded from six lines in the letter to Bernard Barton, 6 April 1825.

PAGE 59. 9. *Ch*——: John Chambers, educated at Christ's Hospital.

10. *Do*——: Henry Dodwell, to whom Lamb wrote a delightful letter from Calne in Wiltshire, 'Friday, July something, Old Style, 1816. No new style here—all the styles are old, and some of the gates too for that matter'. *slow to move*: 'Dodwell is willing, but alas ! slow'. Letter, 16 Dec. 1822.

11. *Pl*——: W. D. Plumley.

13. *Gresham*, Sir Richard (1485?–1549), lord mayor of London; or Sir Thomas Gresham (1519?–79), his second son, founder of the Royal Exchange ('The Royal Exchange, Gresham's Folly, hath me body and spirit', Lamb wrote, 10 Jan. 1820, when his India House work was irksome).

Whittington, Richard (d. 1423), three times Mayor of London: the 'Dick Whittington' of the nursery tale.

14–16. 'this candle-light fog-den of Leadenhall' (—to Coleridge, 24 Dec. 1818).

19. *my 'works'*: Lamb's *Works* were published in two volumes in 1818. He makes this pun frequently in his Letters: 'I am pre-engaged for a series of dissertations on India and India-pendance, to be completed at the expense of the Company in I know not (yet) how many volumes foolscap folio. I am busy getting up my Hindoo mythology; and for the purpose I am once more enduring Southey's Curse' [*The Curse of Kehama*, 1810]. Lamb to John Collier (10 Dec. 1817); cf. also the note to p. 4, l. 9; and

i. 420: 'his true works may be found on the shelves of Leaden-hall Street, filling some hundred Folios'.

21. *Aquinas*: St. Thomas of Aquino (1224–74), the master of Catholic philosophy. Two years after the date of this essay Lamb for the first time made the acquaintance in print of St. Thomas Aquinas and promised himself great pleasure in his ' cobwebs and subtleties'.

22. *My mantle I bequeath among ye*: cf. 2 Kings ii. 8–15.

28–32. cf. p. 57, ll. 8–10.

33–7. cf. prophetic letter to Wordsworth, 9 Aug. 1815.

35. *Bond-street*: see note on p. 50, l. 21.

37. *Soho*: in the angle of Oxford Street and the Charing Cross Road.

PAGE 60. 2. *Fish-street Hill*: where the Monument stands.

Fenchurch-street: between Cornhill and Aldgate.

3, 4. *Mincing Lane*: see note on p. 55, ll. 10, 11.

5. *everlasting flints*: cf. *Romeo and Juliet*, II. vi. 17.

6. *indent*: probably a pun is intended. 'I now indent (make foot-prints) in the pavements of Pall Mall, whereas I used at the India House to indent (draw up documents in duplicate, *or* make an order upon persons for so-and-so, *or* order goods by indent)'.

7. *Elgin Marbles*: i.e. at the British Museum. Lord Elgin collected a number of bas-reliefs and statues, chiefly from the Parthenon at Athens, which were purchased from him for the nation in 1816.

20. *washed that Ethiop white*: cf. Jeremiah xiii. 23.

gone of: become of.

21. *Black Monday*; the first schoolday after a vacation.

26. *huge cantle*: cf. *1 Henry IV*, III. i. 100.

29. *insult over him*: perhaps a combination of 'exult over' and 'insult'. Cf. 'crow over him'.

30–31. *an invitation . . . this fine May morning*: cf. the opening of Walton's *Compleat Angler* (Oxf. ed. p. 19).

31. *Lucretian*, a reference to the passage in Lucretius, 'suave mari magno', &c. (ii. 1 f.) describing the pleasure we feel at seeing a ship labouring at sea from the secure vantage of the land.

33. *carking*: concerned, anxious. For over five hundred years the words 'carking' and 'caring' have been associated.

Here, in 1825, comes the passage:—'I recite those verses of Cowley,[1] which so mightily agree with my constitution.

> 'Business ! the frivolous pretence
> Of human lusts to shake off innocence:
> Business ! the grave impertinence:
> Business ! the thing which I of all things hate:
> Business ! the contradiction of my fate.

[1] 'The Complaint', ll. 43–7: but 'my' in the last line should be 'thy'; the Muse is speaking to Cowley. Lamb's misquotation was probably intentional.

'Or I repeat my own lines,[1] written in my Clerk state:—

   'Who first invented work—and bound the free
   And holiday-rejoicing spirit down
   To the ever-haunting importunity
   Of business, in the green fields, and the town—
   To plough, loom, anvil, spade—and oh ! most sad,
   To this dry drudgery of the desk's dead wood?
   Who but the Being unblest, alien from good,
   Sabbathless Satan ! he who his unglad
   Task ever plies 'mid rotatory burnings,
   That round and round incalculably reel—
   For wrath divine hath made him like a wheel—
   In that red realm from whence are no returnings;
   Where toiling, and turmoiling, ever and aye
   He, and his thoughts, keep pensive worky-day !

'O this divine Leisure ! Reader, if thou art furnished with the Old Series of the London, turn incontinently to the third volume (page 367), and you will see my present condition there touched in a "Wish",[2] by a daintier pen than I can pretend to. I subscribe to that Sonnet *toto corde* [heartily].'

37. *Nothing-to-do*: he had (in July 1819) written of 'man's original blest charter of blue skies, and vagrancy, and nothing to do' (i. 239), but four years after his own retirement he wrote to Bernard Barton: 'I pity you for overwork, but I assure you that no-work is worse. The mind preys on itself, the most unwholesome food. I brag'd formerly that I could not have too much time. I have a surfeit. With few years to come, the days are wearisome.' (3 June 1829).

PAGE 61. 1. *cotton mills*: perhaps those belonging to the East India Company (see 'Oxford in the Vacation', *Elia*, p. 10, l. 20).

4. *As low as to the fiends*: Hamlet II. ii. 527.

6. *Retired Leisure . . . trim gardens*, Milton, *Il Penseroso*, 49, 50.

8, 9. B. W. Procter noted that Lamb when at the India House 'walked with a short resolute step City-wards. He looked no one in the face for more than a moment, yet contrived to see everything as he went on'.

10. *cum dignitate*: (Lat.) with dignity. The reference is to 'otium cum dignitate': 'leisure with dignity': a phrase often used and varied upon by Lamb in connexion with his longed-for superannuation: 'Otium *cum* vel *sine* [with or without] dignitate' (to Matilda Betham, 1815).

14. *Opus operatum est*: (Lat.) the work is finished; with the punning sense here: 'my business is (now) the Opera'.

[1] *my own lines*: i. 588.
[2] *a 'Wish'*. This is Lamb's own sonnet, 'They talk of time, and of time's galling yoke' ('Leisure', i. 588).

THE GENTEEL STYLE IN WRITING (Page 61)

1. *Shaftesbury*: see note on p. 28, l. 3.
2. *Sir William Temple* (1628–99), statesman and author.
5. *inflated finical rhapsodies of Shaftesbury*: contrast p. 28, l. 3, written four years earlier.
6. *chit-chat*, cf. Lamb on Cowper's poetry: 'I would not call that man my friend who should be offended with the "divine chit-chat of Cowper".' The phrase was Coleridge's.
13. *Shene*: East Sheen, near Richmond, Surrey, whereto Temple had removed from Ireland in 1663.
14. *Nimeguen, and the Hague*, in Holland. Temple was English Ambassador at the Hague from 1668–71 and was an envoy in 1679 to the conference at Nimeguen, at which peace was signed between Louis XIV and the Dutch.

Page 62. 1–33: the references are to Temple's essay 'Of Health and Long Life'.

Don Francisco de Melo: probably Dom Francisco Manuel de Mello (1608–66), Portugal's leading lyric poet and greatest prose-writer of the seventeenth century. He was himself exiled to Brazil (1655–9) for a political offence, and was for the second time in England, not as an exile but as a secret envoy, in 1663, when it may be that Sir William Temple met him.

8. *remove*: removal, as in *Ant. and Cleop.*, I. ii. 209.
14. *not worth the candle*: 'le jeu ne vaut pas la chandelle': the winnings (at cards) will not be enough to pay for the candles we shall burn.
15. *Pompone*, Simon Arnauld (1616–99), marquis de Pomponne, Minister of Foreign Affairs to Louis XIV.
23. *Robert*, [second] *Earl of Leicester*, 1595–1677: father of Algernon Sidney (see note on p. 79, l. 19). A diary of his records the stories he had heard of the Countess.
24. *Countess of Desmond*: Katharine Fitzgerald, became the second wife of Thomas Fitzgerald, the twelfth Earl of Desmond, some-time between 1505 and 1524, and died in 1604 at the age of at least 104, although (as Temple went on to say) she 'was counted to have died some years above a hundred and forty'. The *D.N.B.* may well be consulted.
28. *morrice-dancers*, in fancy costumes, usually characters in the Robin Hood legend.

Hertfordshire: the folio of 1720 has Herefordshire.
29. *Maid Marian*, the legendary wife of the legendary Robin Hood: 'no trace of the lady has been recovered in English Literature earlier than about 1500.' (*D.N.B.*) Johnson in his *Dict.* injudiciously truncated the quotation from Temple, so that when he

O

came to define it he thought Maid Marian was 'a kind of dance'.
tabor, a small drum: cf. 'tambour' and 'tambourine'.

34, 41. the references are to Temple's essay 'Upon the Cure of the
Gout by Moxa'.

34. *Monsieur Zulichem*: Sir Constantijn Huygens (1596–1687), lord
of Zulichem, father of Christian Huygens, the physicist. He was
in England in 1618 where he became intimate with Donne,
whose poems he translated. In 1622 he was knighted by James I.
He was President of the Council of the Prince of Orange, and to
him Sir William Temple addressed the essay in question. See
the *Encyc. Brit.* article on him by Sir Edmund Gosse.

36. *Monsieur Serinchamps*, 'once envoy of the Duke of *Lorraine*'
(Temple).

37. *Maurice of Nassau* (1604–79), not the famous general of that
name who died in 1625.

41. *Count Egmont* (d. 1707), not the patriot who died in 1568.

PAGE 63. 1. *Maestricht*: besieged in July 1676 by William, Prince of
Orange, afterwards William III of England.

3. et seq. the references are to Temple's essay 'Upon the Gardens
of Epicurus, or, Of Gardening, In the year 1685'.

10. *Fontainebleau*: forty miles SSE. of Paris, where are the royal
palace and park.

15. *Frontignac*: the white wines of Frontignan, in Languedoc, are
among the best of France.
Muscat-grape: in Eastern Arabia, from whence 'muscatels.'

28. *the Bishop of Munster* 'that made so much noise in his time'
(Temple): Christopher Bernard Matthew von Galen (1606–1678),
prince-bishop of Münster. He was of noble birth, but when the
loss of his inheritance reduced him to poverty, he took Holy
Orders, and in 1650 became Bishop of Münster, in Westphalian
Prussia. He fought for the emperor Ferdinand III in the Thirty
Years' War, and crushing an insurrection which had sprung up
after he had restored some degree of peace and prosperity within
his principality, he established a large standing army, which he
used for the formation of many fickle but mutually beneficial
martial alliances against the Turk, and the Dutch, uniting in
turn with the imperial army, Charles II, Louis XIV, Leopold I,
Brandenburg and Denmark. There is in the British Museum
a poem printed in 1666, entitled *A Letter to the Bishop of Munster:
containing a Panegyrick of his heroick atchievments in heroick verse.*
Cosevelt: Kösfeld, capital of West Münster.

32. *Cowley*: see note on p. 5, l. 20. Among Cowley's essays is one on
'The Garden'.

PAGE 64. 18. *Horace* (Q. Horatius Flaccus, 65–8 B.C.) Latin poet;
the quotation is from Epistle I. xviii, 104–11.

20. *Digentian*: the Digentia (now Licenza) was a stream that flowed through the Sabine farm of Horace.

29. *On one occasion*: towards the beginning of his essay 'Of Health and Long Life'.

32. *Addison*, Joseph (1672–1719), essayist, poet, and statesman. Friend of Sir Richard Steele, with whom he was associated in the *Tatler, Spectator, Guardian*, &c.

36. *a white staff*: the official emblem of the Lord High Treasurer.

37. *blue riband*: that of the Order of the Garter.

40. *eased by wearing a crown*: cf. *2 Henry IV*, III. i. 31.

PAGE 65. 2. *controversy . . . learning*: Temple's contribution was the 'Essay on Ancient and Modern Learning' (1690). His protégé and former secretary, Swift, supported his side in 'The Battle of the Books' (1710).

 9. *Gothic*: used in the sense of 'barbarian', as distinct from 'classical'.

28. *pretend to be wise*, &c.: cf. *Mer. of Venice*, I. i. 88–94.

31–5. cf. the same play, v. i. 83–8.

41. to end. Cf. Pope, *Essay on Man*, ii. 281–4.

BARBARA S—— (PAGE 66)

 2. *Barbara S——*: Lamb's note on p. 71 shows that S—— stands for 'Street': but that note is an intentional mystification. The story is that of Fanny Kelly (see note to p. 68, l. 7).

24. *young Arthur*, in *King John*, IV. i. (see note on p. 67, l. 34). *Richard*: in *Richard III*, III. i.

27. *She would have done the elder child, . . . to the life*: an ingenious way of intimating that Miss Kelly *did* play the elder child in 1793 (Canon Ainger).
Morton, Thomas (1764–1838), author of *Children in the Wood* (1793), and the inventor of 'Mrs. Grundy' (in *Speed the Plough*, 1798).

28–9. *as yet . . . was not*: see note on p. 32, ll. 32–3.

PAGE 67. 11. *principia*: her primer, possibly 'Principia Latina'.

14. *pumice stone*: used as an ink-eraser.

20. *the quantity of real present emotion*: cf. the opening of the essay on 'Stage Illusion', p. 16.

31. *to instance in*: to take an instance from.

33. *Mrs. Porter*: Mary Porter (d. 1765) was left without a rival on the stage when Mrs. Oldfield retired in 1730. But actually it was Mrs. Siddons, in the part of Constance, who wept over Fanny Kelly, in the part of Arthur, in *King John*, 1800. According to Dr. Johnson, Mrs. Porter was so much the favourite of her time, that she was 'welcomed on the stage when she trod it by the help of a stick'.

33. *Isabella,* in Garrick's version of *The Fatal Marriage* (1694), by Thomas Southerne (1660–1746).

(*I think it was*): i. e. he knows that it was not ! cf. l. 39.

PAGE 68. 3. *kept me out of the pulpit*: but for his stammer Lamb would have been a Grecian at Christ's Hospital, and would have gone to the University (probably Cambridge) with a view to taking holy orders.

certain personal disqualifications: for these, see 'The Tombs in the Abbey', p. 71, ll. 1–3.

7. *Miss Kelly*: Frances Maria Kelly (1790–1882), actress and singer. In the Oxford 'Lamb' (i. 235–43) are four dramatic criticisms of the year 1819, all in praise of Miss Kelly. In the second of these, dated 4–5 July, he pretends that a stranger sitting beside him in the theatre said of Miss Kelly: 'What a lass that were to go a gipseying through the world with'. On 19 July he wrote to her proposing marriage, as a way of releasing her from the burdensome life of the stage; she replied the next day kindly but firmly declining; and, the same day, he wrote once more, this time 'in a lackadaisacal now-how-ish kind of a humour' accepting her decision. In the third of the dramatic criticisms, dated 1–2 August, he says of her acting: 'She is in truth not framed to tease or torment even in jest, but to utter a hearty *Yes* or *No*; to yield or refuse assent with a noble sincerity. We have not the pleasure of being acquainted with her, but we have been told that she carries the same cordial manners into private life'.

8 *Liston,* John (1775–1846): comic actor. Lamb had, three months before the present essay, written a pretended biographical memoir of him in the *London Magazine* (i. 315). 'A life more improbable for him [Liston] to have lived would not be easily invented'. Lamb to Bernard Barton, 10 Feb. 1825.

8. *Mrs. Charles Kemble*: Marie Thérèse Kemble, *née* De Camp (1774–1828), actress and playwright. She went on the stage as a child, married Charles Kemble in 1806, and retired in 1819. Fanny Kemble (1809–93) was her daughter.

10. *her accomplished husband*: Charles Kemble (1775–1854), actor; son of Roger and younger brother of John Philip Kemble.

12. *Macready,* William Charles (1793–1873), actor. See Tennyson's sonnet to him. Lamb was introduced to Macready by Charles Lloyd, but we have no record of their interview. Nine years later than this essay, in the last year of Lamb's life, he met Macready once more, who notes in his diary 'the odd saying of Lamb, that "the last breath he drew in he wished might be thro' a pipe, and exhaled in a pun"'.

13. *Mr. Matthews's*: Charles Mathews the elder (1776–1835), actor.

He collected a celebrated gallery of portraits of actors, now in the Garrick Club.

18. *Dodd*, James (1740–96). See 'On some of the old Actors' (*Elia*, pp. 172–4).
Parsons, William (1736–95), was associated with Drury Lane Theatre all his life. Known as the 'Comic Roscius', he excelled in playing old men.
Baddeley, Robert (1733–94), was at first a cook and valet and then joined the Drury Lane Company. His *forte* was the part of a foreign footman.

19. *Edwin*, John (1749–90): cf. 'On the Acting of Munden' (*Elia*, p. 187, l. 21).

22. *Diamond's*: Tressel Dimond was manager of the theatre at Bath during the later part of the eighteenth century.

27. *my own infirmity*: Lamb was easily made tipsy.

PAGE 69. 31. *poor men's smoky cabins . . . porticoes of moral philosophy*: perhaps Lamb is telescoping two lines of Wordsworth:

> Love had he found in *huts where poor men lie*;
> *His daily teachers* had been woods and rills, &c.
>
> *Song at the Feast of Brougham Castle* (1807).

32. *porticoes*: an allusion to the *stoa*, or porch, in Athens, where Zeno, the founder of the Stoic philosophy, taught his pupils.

PAGE 70. 1. *punctuality*: exactitude (cf. 'punctiliousness').

24–5. cf. the last two lines of Milton's *Comus*.

27. *a reason above reasoning*: an intuition superior to logic.

37. *brightened up the feet and the prospects*: a syllepsis; see 'Zeugma' in H. W. Fowler's *Modern English Usage*, and the cross reference there.

PAGE 71. 5. *Mrs. Crawford*: in *D.N.B.* as Ann Spranger Barry, née Street (1734–1801), actress. She married first, in early life, a Mr. Dancer, who died young. For years she acted with Spranger Barry (1719–77) and married him in 1768. After his death she married a Mr. Crawford. Both she and Barry are buried in the Cloisters of Westminster Abbey. '*Apropos*, I never saw Mrs. Crauford in my life, nevertheless 'tis all true of Somebody'.—Lamb to Bernard Barton, 6 Apr. 1825.

11. *part of Lady Randolph*, in *Douglas* (1757) by John Home (1722–1808). Sarah Siddons (1755–1831) made her last appearance (1817) in this character. In 1796 Lamb wrote a poem (ii. 530) 'to perpetuate the memory of so exquisite a pleasure as I have often received . . . when Mrs. Siddons has been the Lady Randolph'. Mrs. Siddons was the daughter of Roger and sister of John Philip Kemble (see note on p. 68, l. 10).

THE TOMBS IN THE ABBEY (PAGE 71)

After the first paragraph this essay consists of the two concluding paragraphs of an open letter to Southey, published in
the *London Magazine* for Oct. 1823, remonstrating with him for
some remarks in the *Quarterly Review* (January 1823) that
were likely to harm Lamb's reputation with narrowly religious
people, and to damage the sale of the *Essays of Elia* [First series]
then recently published in book form.

R—— S——: Robert Southey (1774–1843), Poet-Laureate and
prose-writer, educated at Westminster School.

3. *church . . . historified*, in Southey's *The Book of the Church* (1824).

8. *last Wednesday*: the letter is not dated, so the occasion cannot be
identified.

PAGE 72. 25. *in your Journal*: the *Quarterly Review*, with which
Southey was associated.

26. *Beautiful Temple*: cf. Acts iii. 2.

35. *the adjacent Park*: St. James's Park.

41. *two shillings*: J. T. Smith (1766–1833) according to his post-
humously published *Book for a Rainy Day* (1845) seems to have
obtained permission for sixpence.

PAGE 73. 5. *a respected friend of ours*: perhaps Wordsworth, who
was in London in the spring of 1823.

12, 13. *Perhaps . . . Nelson*: Southey had published the *Life of Nelson*
in 1813, and Lamb may be appealing to his feelings as an author.

20. *Sellers . . . Temple*: cf. Matthew xxi. 12, &c.

34. *André*, John (1751–80), hanged by the Americans for plotting
the betrayal of West Point to the British. A monument was
erected to his memory in Westminster Abbey, and in 1821 his
remains were transferred there. Mr. Wilfred Whitten, in his notes
to J. T. Smith's *Book for a Rainy Day*, says that the injury was
actually done to the figure of Washington in André's monument.
is it for this: cf. p. 9, l. 9; and p. 77, l. 17.

PAGE 74. 6. *Peter's Pence*: an annual tax levied by the Popes, since
the tenth century, nominally a penny from every household. It
is now a freewill offering from the faithful. Lamb alludes to the
dedication of Westminster Abbey to St. Peter.

7. *ragged*: cf. *2 Henry IV*, Induc. 35; and *Richard III*, IV. i. 101.

AMICUS REDIVIVUS (PAGE 74)

Title] *Amicus Redivivus*: 'a friend restored to life'.
The germ of this essay is to be found in Lamb's letter to Sarah
Hazlitt, Nov. 1823.

Motto] Milton, *Lycidas*, ll. 50–1.

2. *G. D.*, George Dyer (1755–1841), author; educated at Christ's Hospital and Emmanuel College, Cambridge; a convert to Unitarianism; and supposed by himself to be a poet. In 1800 and 1801 Lamb played with the idea of making Dyer the hero of a novel, if he 'could but calculate the date of his death'. 'I can scarcely conceive a more amusing novel'.

4. *at Islington*, the Lambs lived at 19 Colebrooke Row (now Duncan Terrace), from 1823 to 1827.

20. *who bore Anchises*: Aeneas, *Aeneid*, II. 707–23; cf. *Julius Caesar*, I. ii. 114.

PAGE 75. 10. *as if an Angel had spoken*: cf. E. Young, *Night Thoughts* (Night the First), l. 56.

14. *Monoculus*, 'the one-eyed'. Lamb describes him in a letter as 'a one-eyed fellow, dirty and drunk, fetched from the Public House at the end, where it seems he lives, for the sake of picking up water-practice [cf. ll. 26–31], having formerly had a medal from the Humane Society' [see p. 76, l. 3]. In the Essay Lamb runs no risk of prosecution for libel !

17. *truckled to the pedantry of a diploma*: i.e. he was not a properly qualified doctor.

20. *the vital spark*: Pope, 'The Dying Christian to his soul', l. 1.

25. *Cannabis*: hemp. The 'wilful application outwardly' would of course be suicide by hanging.

28. *the grand repository*: the reservoir (now covered in with gardens).

30. *The Middleton's Head*, a public house called after Sir Hugh Myddelton, or Middleton (1560?–1631), the projector of the New River.

PAGE 76. 5. *been dinged*, become dingy.

26. *absentee*: used here humorously for an absent-minded man.

33. *Colebrooke*, see note on p. 74, l. 14.

34–40. the construction of this passage seems to be imitated from 1 Cor. xi. 26–8.

37. *Trumpington*, two miles south of Cambridge.

38. *Pembroke*, i.e. Pembroke College, Cambridge. Dyer was of Emmanuel College, Cambridge, and wrote a *History of the University of Cambridge* (1814).

PAGE 77. 4. *tremor cordis*: palpitation of the heart. Cf. *Winter's Tale*, I. ii. 110.

8, 9. *in the latter crisis . . . good Sir Hugh*: i. e. 'a case of impending danger' when Sir Hugh Evans has a duel pending with Dr. Caius, *M.W.W.*, III. i.

11. *Sir Hugh Middleton*: see note on p. 75, l. 22.

17. *was it for this*: cf. pp. 9, l. 9; and 73, l. 34.

18. *that Abyssinian traveller*: James Bruce (1730–94), explorer, and author of *Travels to discover the source of the Nile* (1790).

19. *Amwell*: near 'Blakesmoor', the source of the New River. There is another Amwell near 'Mackery End'.

21. *Enfield*: in Middlesex, ten miles north of London. The Lambs lived there from 1827–33.
    swans: it is a legend that the swan, when about to die, conceals itself, and sings its sweetest song. Thence the swan became an emblem of the poets (e.g. 'The Swan of Avon'=Shakespeare; 'The Swan of Lichfield'=Anne Seward).

25. *Cam*: the river at Cambridge.

28. *novity*: newness.

30. *Dyerian*, cf. Pierian, an epithet applied to the Muses. 'Drink deep, or taste not the Pierian spring'. Pope, *Essay on Criticism*, l. 16.

31–2.
> But can his spatious Virtue find a Grave
> Within the imposthum'd bubble of a Wave?

John Cleveland, in *Obsequies to the Memorie of Mr. Edward King*, 1638 (one of the obsequies was Milton's 'Lycidas').

38. *Euripus*: the strait between Euboea and Boeotia. Aristotle is said to have drowned himself in the Euripus out of vexation at being unable to solve the problem of its tides ... 'he (William Wordsworth, Junior, aged 9) put another question as to the flux and reflux, which being rather cunningly evaded by that she-Aristotle Mary, who muttered something about its getting up sooner and sooner every day ...' Lamb to Dorothy Wordsworth (25 Nov. 1819).

39. *dipper*: a believer in baptism by immersion. Dyer had written *An Inquiry into the nature of Subscription to the 39 Articles* (?1800) which provoked a reply: *On the nature, design, uses and history of the ordinance of Baptism* (1811). Actually Dyer had been a Baptist minister, but was now a Unitarian.

PAGE 78. 2. *Clarence*: *Richard III*, I. iv. 9–33.

3–4. *Christian ... Hopeful*: Bunyan, *P.P.*, I, *ad fin.*

5–6. *I sink*, &c.: cf. Psalms xlii. 7; lxix. 2.

7. *Palinurus*: a skilful pilot of Aeneas's ship. He fell into the sea in his sleep, and, making the shore, was killed by the inhabitants. *Aen.* v. 854–61.

11. *watchet*: blue (see note on p. 8, l. 18).
    constrained Lazari: compelled to return like Lazarus from the dead (Lazari = Lazaruses).

13. *Arion*: Lyric poet of Lesbos. Herodotus relates how, when he was menaced by sailors at sea, he arrayed himself in his singing garments and sang a 'swan song' from the prow. He then cast himself into the sea, and, being conveyed to land on the back of a dolphin, astounded his would-be murderers by again appearing before them in his poetic garb.

14–15. *singing garments . . . votive garland*: cf. Milton, *Reason of Church Government*, ɪɪ . . . 'a Poet soaring in the high region of his fancies with his garland and singing robes about him . . .'
votive garland: offered in fulfilment of a vow.
Machaon (son of Aesculapius) (see note on p. 79, l. 2), himself a physician.
Hawes, William (1736–1808), physician: founded Royal Humane Society in 1774.

16. *to the stern God of Sea*: last line of Milton's translation of Horace, *Odes*, ɪ. 5.

19. *wharfs*: cf. 'Lethe wharf', *Hamlet*, ɪ. v. 33. See also p. 20, l. 32.

20. *muddy death*: Hamlet, ɪᴠ. vii. 184.

25. *the grim Feature*: Death. Milton, *P.L.*, x. 279.

27. *Tantalus*: see note on p. 49, l. 2.

28. *A pulse . . . was felt along the line*: cf. Pope, *Essay on Man*, i. 217.
Elysian shades: the shades here are spirits of the blessed; in p. 20, l. 5, the 'Blessed Shades' (see note) are shady places.

34. *scholiast*: annotator, commentator. Dyer contributed 'all that was original' to A. J. Valpy's 'Delphin' edition of the Classics in 141 volumes, 1819–30.
Markland, Jeremiah (1693–1776), Fellow of St. Peter's College, Cambridge; a classical scholar. Like Dyer and Lamb he was a Bluecoat boy.
Tyrwhitt, Thomas (1730–84), fellow of Merton College, Oxford, and clerk to the House of Commons. A classical scholar, and editor of Chaucer. But the reference may be to his brother Robert (1735–1817), a Cambridge man and a Unitarian.
the sweet lyrist of Peter House: Thomas Gray (1716–71), 'admitted pensioner (age 18) at Peterhouse, July 4, 1734 . . . Migrated to Pembroke [College], March 6, 1756'. Lamb's own style (especially in his letters) is very like that of the earlier among Gray's letters.

37. *Christ's*: Christ's Hospital, the Bluecoat School.

Footnote] *Graium tantum vidit*: 'Gray he only just saw' (and perhaps not even that, since Gray died in 1771 and Dyer went to Cambridge in 1774) adapted from Ovid's regret in his *Tristia* ɪᴠ. x. 5: *Virgilium vidi tantum*: 'I had but a glimpse of Virgil'.

PAGE 79. 1. *Askew*, Anthony (1722–74), M.D. of Emmanuel College, Cambridge, physician to Christ's Hospital; an early patron of Dyer.

  2. *Æsculapian chair*: Aesculapius, son of Apollo, was the god of medicine.

SOME SONNETS OF SIR PHILIP SYDNEY (PAGE 79)

Title and throughout: the usual spelling is Sidney. For Sir
Philip Sidney, see note to p. 29, l. 34.

4 *Milton*, John (1608–74). In *Eikonoklastes* (1649), ch. i, he censures
Charles I for having included in his *Eikon Basilike* (1648–9) 'a
prayer stolen word for word from the mouth of a heathen woman
praying to a heathen god; and that in no serious book, but the
vain amatorious poem of Sir Philip Sidney's' *Arcadia*; a book in
that kind full of worth and wit, but among religious thoughts and
duties not to be named; nor to be read at any time without good
caution, much less in time of trouble and affliction to be a Christian's prayerbook'.

6. *the Arcadia* (1590) written for the amusement of the Countess of
Pembroke, Sidney's sister. It is a medley of prose romance, and
pastoral eclogues.

7. *application*: Lamb seems to use the word in the sense of 'supplement', but the *O.E.D.* does not illustrate the word in this
sense.

12. *the Masque at Ludlow Castle*: *Comus* (1643), which was first
'presented at Ludlow Castle, 1634, before the Earl of Bridge-
water, then President of Wales'.

13. *Arcades*: 'Part of an entertainment presented to the Countess
Dowager of Derby at Harefield, by some noble persons of her
family', 1633.

16. *the Revolution*: of 1688.

19. *a later Sydney*: Algernon Sidney (1622–83), great-nephew of
Sir Philip. A republican tried, condemned, and beheaded for
treason against Charles II.

20. *the French match*: the proposed marriage (1580) of Queen Elizabeth with François Duc d'Anjou (1552–84): Queen Elizabeth
entered into negotiations for a marriage with him, but broke
them off, saying that their marriage would be neither to his
happiness nor to hers. 'You don't know the English people: a
prince who is both a Catholic and Frenchman could never
reckon on their obedience' she is reported to have said.

24, 25. *Those of Sydney*: in *Astrophel and Stella* (1591).

27. *hey-day of his blood*: cf. *Hamlet*, III. iv. 69.

PAGE 80. 5. *circum praecordia frigus*: 'the cold [blood] around my
heart'. Cf. Virgil, *Georgics* II, 484.

12. *Tibullus*: Roman elegiac poet (*c.* B.C. 54–A.D. 19).

13. *the Schoolmistress* (1742), by William Shenstone (1714–63). 'The
true rustic style, the Arcadian English, I think is to be found in
Shenstone. Would his Schoolmistress, the prettiest of his poems,

have been better if he had used quite the Goody's own language?'
Lamb to J. Clare, 31 Aug. 1822.

creep and whine: cf. Pope, *Essay on Criticism*, ii. 144.

15. *ad Leonoram*: to Leonora. Cowper, who translated the rest of
Milton's Latin poems, omitted this one, perhaps from the same
scruple as Lamb's. Leigh Hunt has translated it as follows:

> To every one (so have ye faith) is given
> A winged guardian from the ranks of heaven.
> A greater, Leonora, visits thee:
> Thy voice proclaims the present deity.
> Either the present deity we hear,
> Or he of the third heaven hath left his sphere,
> And through the bosom's pure and warbling wells,
> Breathes tenderly his smoothed oracles;
> Breathes tenderly, and so with easy rounds
> Teaches our mortal hearts to bear immortal sounds.
> If god is all, and in all nature dwells,
> In thee alone he speaks, mute ruler in all else.

36. *the pale Dian*: The moon. Diana was the moon-goddess.
41. *That busy Archer*: Cupid.

PAGE 81. 19. *prease*: the press (of the crowd).
28. *Stella*: Lady Penelope Devereux (1562–1607), daughter of the
second Earl of Essex. In 1581 she married Robert, Lord Rich,
afterwards Earl of Warwick, who divorced her some time after
1601. In 1605 she was illegally married to Charles Blount, Earl
of Devonshire. It is not certain that there was any love between
her and Sidney.
34. *how my spring I did address*: how I devoted my youth (to study).
35. *plies*: bends.
36. *the Prince*: Queen Elizabeth, as the sovereign prince or ruler.

PAGE 82. 3. *seems most alone*, &c.: contrast *Nunquam minus solus,
quam cum solus esset*, 'Never less alone than when alone'.
(Cicero, *De Repub.* I. xvii, 27).
17. *this day* (and cf. l. 29): On Whit-Monday and Whit-Tuesday,
15 and 16 May 1581 Sidney distinguished himself in an elaborate
tournament held at Whitehall in honour of an embassy from
France.
20. *that sweet enemy*: England was at peace with France, but their
policies were at variance. In a letter to Wordsworth, Sept. 1805,
Lamb uses this phrase for tobacco: the temptation that so easily
beset him.
25. *of both sides . . . my blood*: his father was Sir Henry Sidney, of
Penshurst, Kent; his mother was Lady Mary Dudley, daughter
of John, Duke of Northumberland.

PAGE 83. 18. *his mother*: Venus, the mother of Cupid.

21. STAR, 'Stella'. Lat. a star.

27. *those scarlet judges*: Stella's lips, with reference to a judge's scarlet robes.

32. *Aganippe*: a fountain in Boeotia sacred to the Muses.

33. *Tempe*: a valley in Thessaly between Olympus and Oeta.

36. *Poets' fury*: the ecstasy of inspiration: cf. 'sacred rage'.

38. *the blackest brook of Hell*: Acheron.

43, 44. '*what is it thus*' ... '*Or so?*' these are the imagined interlocutor's guesses, which the poet rejects.

PAGE 84. 5. *imp*: to graft a wing with fresh feathers: cf. *Richard II*, II. i. 292.

7. *His sire's revenge*: Edward IV became king after the retreat of the Lancastrians at Towton (1461), which avenged his father's defeat at Wakefield (1460).

9. *Balance ... Sword*: Diplomacy and war.

10. *Floure-de-Luce*: France as symbolized by her emblem, the fleur-de-lys. The reference is to Edward's invasion of France in 1475.

12. *witty Lewis*: Louis XI. By the treaty of Picquigny (1475) Louis was to pay Edward an annual tribute of 75,000 crowns during the joint lives of the two kings. 'Witty' here means 'astute', not verbally funny.

14–15. In 1464 Edward IV avowed his secret marriage with Elizabeth Woodville, Lady Grey, thus offending Warwick (the 'kingmaker') and other barons.

25. *those Aeol's youth*: the children of Aeolus, lord of the winds.

34. *tempers*: adapts, perhaps with reference to 'tempo'.

PAGE 85. 5. *Spenser*: Edmund. See note on p. 31, l. 5. He dedicated his '*Shepheardes Calendar*' (1579) 'to the noble and vertuous gentleman most worthy of all the titles both of learning and chevalrie M. Philip Sidney' and bids his book present itself:

> 'To him that is the president
> Of noblesse and of chevalrie.'

26. ' ... *diet of dainty words.*' Here in the *L.M.* the following footnote is appended:—'A profusion of verbal dainties, with a disproportionate lack of matter and circumstance, is I think one reason of the coldness with which the public has received the poetry of a nobleman now living; which, upon the score of exquisite diction alone, is entitled to something better than neglect. I will venture to copy one of his Sonnets in this place, which for quiet sweetness, and unaffected morality, has scarcely its parallel in our language.

'TO A BIRD THAT HAUNTED THE WATERS OF
LACKEN IN THE WINTER

'*By Lord Thurlow*[1]

' O melancholy Bird, a winter's day,
Thou standest by the margin of the pool,
And, taught by God, dost thy whole being school
To Patience, which all evil can allay.
God has appointed thee the Fish thy prey;
And given thyself a lesson to the Fool
Unthrifty, to submit to moral rule,
And his unthinking course by thee to weigh.
There need not schools, nor the Professor's chair,
Though these be good, true wisdom to impart.
He who has not enough, for these, to spare
Of time, or gold, may yet amend his heart,
And teach his soul, by brooks, and rivers fair:
Nature is always wise in every part.'

29. *an historical thread*: not, of course, the references to Edward IV,
but to the events of Sidney's own love and life: he 'looked into
his life and wrote' what he found there.

35. *W. H.*: William Hazlitt (1772–1830). Essayist and critic.
takes every occasion: e.g. in his *Table Talk* (1821–2), Essay xviii,
on Milton's Sonnets, and in his *Lectures on the Literature of the
Age of Elizabeth* (1820).

PAGE 86. 10. *a foolish nobleman*: Edward de Vere, seventeenth Earl
of Oxford, quarrelled with Sidney in 1579, and called him a
puppy.

11. *the epitaph*, see 'Oxford Poets' *Spenser*, pp. 558–9.

13. *the beautiful lines*, by Matthew Roydon ('Oxford Poets' *Spenser*,
p. 556).

14. *Astrophel*: Gr. 'lover of a star', i.e. of 'Stella'.

22. *Arcady*: Arcadia, is an inland country of Peloponessus. 'The
inhabitants were for the most part shepherds, who lived upon
acorns, were skilful warriors, and able musicians. They thought
themselves more ancient than the moon. Pan, the god of
shepherds, chiefly lived among them.' Lemprière.

24. *Partheny*: Mount Parthenius in Arcadia.

28–9. cf. Exodus xxxiv, 29, 30.

31. *eyne*: eyes.

Footnote] *Lord Brooke*: Fulke Greville, Lord Brooke (1554–1628),
schoolfellow, lifelong friend, and biographer of Sidney. ('Lamb
then named Sir Thomas Browne and Fulke Greville, the friend

[1] Edward Thurlow, second Baron (1781–1829); author of *Poems*,
1813, and other volumes of verse. He had a special devotion to Sir
Philip Sidney.

of Sir Philip Sidney, as the two worthies whom he should feel the greatest pleasure to encounter on the floor of his apartment in their nightgown and slippers, and to exchange friendly greeting with them'. Hazlitt 'Of Persons one would wish to have seen'.)

PAGE 87. 2. *approved*: proved.

14–17. *the Poem . . . beginning 'Silence augmenteth grief'*, in 'Oxford Poets' *Spenser*, p. 559. 'I will be crucified if it be not Lord Brooke's. Hang you, and all meddling researchers, hereafter, that by raking into learned dust may find me out wrong in my conjecture!' Lamb to John Collier 16 May 1821. It was attributed by Malone (see note on p. 30, l. 20) to Sir Edward Dyer (d. 1607) and by John Hannah (1818–88) to Sir Walter Raleigh (1552–1618).

NEWSPAPERS THIRTY-FIVE YEARS AGO (PAGE 87)

1. *Stuart*, Daniel (1766–1846), became proprietor of the *Morning Post* in 1795 and of the *Courier* in 1796. Lamb wrote for him from 1802–4. Writing in the *Gentleman's Magazine* for June 1838 Daniel Stuart said: 'But as for good Charles Lamb, I never could make anything of his writings' [i.e. journalistically]. 'Coleridge often and repeatedly pressed me to settle on him a salary, and often and repeatedly did I try; but it would not do. Of politics he knew nothing; they were out of his line of reading and thought; and his drollery was vapid, when given in short paragraphs fit for a newspaper: yet he has produced some agreeable books . . . in a quaint style, which it is amusing to read, and cheering to remember.'

   us: Lamb uses the newspaper-editor's 'we' and 'us' throughout this essay.

2. *Somerset House*: in the Strand. The Royal Academy exhibitions were held there from 1780 to 1837.

10. *the same abstinence with Daniel*, i.e. with Dan Stuart, but with a punning reference to the prophet Daniel's vegetarianism (for a similar identification of the two Daniels see p. 91, l. 29).

13. *Perry*, James (1756–1821).

PAGE 88. 3. *We have worked for both these gentlemen*: for Perry and the *Morning Chronicle* in 1801: for Stuart and the *Morning Post* intermittently in 1802–4.

6, 7. *with holy reverence*, &c.: John Armstrong (1709–79), *Art of Preserving Health* (1744), ii. 358.

8. *the Abyssinian Pilgrim*: James Bruce. See note on p. 77, l. 18.

10, 11. *a 'whole day's leave'*, . . . *not very well provisioned*; cf. 'Christ's Hospital' (*Elia*, pp. 17–18).

14. *Middletonian Stream*: cf. p. 75, l. 22 (and note) and p. 77. . 11. *scaturient*, flowing out, or gushing forth. Lamb may have found the word 'scaturiency' in the *Divine Dialogues* (1668) of Henry More (1614–87), a favourite writer with Coleridge.

15. *Amwell*: cf. p. 77, l. 19 and note.

19. *Hornsey*: now a northern suburb of London.
Hope trained us on: cf. *1 Henry IV*, v. ii. 21.

24. *Bowes Farm*: Bowes Park is also now a northern suburb of London.

33. *The Gnat*: a poem of doubtful authenticity ascribed to the youthful Virgil.
the Duck which Samuel Johnson trod on: the 'poem' referred to is said to have been composed by Johnson, who disowned it, at the age of three. Boswell's version is:

> Here lies good master duck,
> Whom Samuel Johnson trod on;
> If it had lived, it had been good luck,
> For then we'd had an odd one.

Footnote] line 2. *Managers*: the reference is to the two essays on Elliston, pp. 19–27 *supra*.
R.A.'s: *Recollections of a late Royal Academician* (George Dawe), i. 429.

PAGE 89. 14. *Cytherea*: Aphrodite; her flower was the rose.

14, 15. *flaming costume . . . 'many waters'*; see Revelation xvii. 1–4.

20. *posture-master*: an acrobat or professional contortionist, or a teacher of deportment, like Mr. Turveydrop in *Bleak House*.

23. *'both seem either'*: cf. Milton *P.L.*, ii. 670.

24. *Autolycus-like*: see *Winter's Tale*, IV. iv. 199–200.
tickles our midriff: makes us laugh.

28. *Astrea ultima . . . reliquit*: Ovid, *Metam*. i. 150. Astrea, the goddess of justice, was 'last of the heavenly ones to leave the earth'. She became the constellation Virgo. (During the golden age, the divinities lived on earth.)

39. *their whiteness*: it would seem that women usually wore white stockings then.

PAGE 90. 2. *more than single meanings*: 'doubles ententes'.

8. *Man goeth forth*, &c.: Psalm civ. 23.

10. *our main occupation*: at the India House, see note on p. 54, ll. 13, 14, 'eight till five' would normally include his walk there and back.

17. *No Man's Land*: There was in the fourteenth century a 'none-manneslonde' outside the city wall used as a place where criminals were burnt or executed. The phrase is also used for a 'common'; and during the late War it meant the space between the trenches of the opposed armies.

22. *preposterously*: see note on p. 9, 'Poor Relations', l. 3.

26–8. *go-to-beds . . . rising*: cf. 'Popular Fallacies', Nos. xiv, xv, pp. 149–153.

30. *Aquarius,* the Water-carrier, a sign in the Zodiac.

31. *incapable of Bacchus* (the god of wine); unable to drink wine.

32. *Basilian water-sponges*: Lamb's friend Basil Montagu was a teetotaller, and Lamb's 'Confessions of a Drunkard' (1813) was reprinted in Montagu's *Some Enquiries into the Effects of fermented Liquors,* 1814.

33. *Mount Ague*: a pun, signifying both Basil Montagu's household and the 'ague' which would come from too watery a climate.

34. *toping Capulets*: i. e. opposed to the Montagues, as in *Romeo and Juliet.*

37. *Bohea*: originally the best kind of black tea; in later times degraded to the lowest quality; contrast 'Hyson', p. 123, l. 14.

PAGE 91. 4–7. *'Facil' . . . 'descending' . . . revocare,* &c.: cf. Virgil, Aeneid, vi. 126–9: 'It is easy to go down into Avernus (see note on p. 19, l. 22); night and day the gate of black Dis stands open; but to retrace one's steps and to escape to the upper air, this is the work, this is the labour.'

8, 9. *malice prepended*: 'malice prepense', i.e. aforethought.

10. *Egyptian taskmaster*: see Exodus i. 11.

11. *operants*: 'operatives', workpeople.

turned out: struck work.

17. *when the mountain must go to Mahomet*: 'Mahomet made the people believe that he would call a hill to him, and from the top of it offer up his prayers for the observers of his land. The people assembled: Mahomet called the hill to come to him again and again; and when the hill stood still, he was never a whit abashed, but said, If the hill will not come to Mahomet, Mahomet will go to the hill.' Bacon's *Essays* ('Of Boldness').

25. *distillation*: cf. Deut. viii. 15.

25–7. *tale of brickmaking,* &c.: Exodus, v. 18.

28. *Bel's temple . . . Daniel*: see *Bel and the Dragon* in the *Apocrypha.* See note on p. 87, l. 10.

33. *'easy writing'*: contrast

> 'You write with ease to show your breeding,
> But easy writing's cursed hard reading.'
>
> R. B. Sheridan, *Memoirs,* by Moore, i. 155.

Bob Allen: (1772–1805) see 'Christ's Hospital', *Elia,* p. 28; went to Oxford as an exhibitioner from Christ's Hospital, 1792. B.A., 1796; M.A., M.B., M.D., 1803. Deputy-Surgeon to the 2nd Royal Dragoons in Portugal, 1797. Journalist.

35. *the 'Oracle'*: a newspaper started by Peter (an elder brother of Daniel) Stuart, about 1788.

Footnote] *'taking pitch,* &c.': *Bel and the Dragon,* 27.

PAGE 92. 4. *Snow Hill*: see note on p. 32, l. 32.

who: should be 'whom'.

Mr. Deputy Humphreys: not in the *D.N.B.*

19. *Common Council Man*: a representative on the governing body of the City of London.

27. *The 'True Briton'* (1793–1806) started under the editorship of John Heriot (1760–1833), in support of Pitt.

28. *the 'Star'*: the first regular London evening paper, also (like the 'Oracle') started by Peter Stuart, in 1788; the leading evening paper on the Whig side.

the 'Traveller', an evening paper, edited by Edward Quin (d. 1823), the organ of the commercial traveller.

33. *Blue Balls*: *brass* balls in actual use.

37. *College of Heralds*: in Queen Victoria Street, on the site of 'Derby House' acquired from Queen Mary Tudor. The powers vested by the Crown in the Earl Marshal with regard to all state cere-monial, and the granting and use of armorial bearings, are exercised by this College.

40. *Este* (or D'Este), Charles (1753–1829): a political-minded clergy-man who wrote for the *World*, and with whom Thomas Holcroft (1745–1809) used to discuss the news of the day at Debrett's in Piccadilly.

41. *Topham*, Edward (1751–1820), founder of *The World* newspaper in 1787.

PAGE 93. 1. *Boaden*, James (1762–1839), edited the *Oracle* in 1789, and wrote the life of Mrs. Siddons, 1827.

5. *Mrs. Siddons*: see note to p. 71, l. 11.

8. *Astræan allusion*: see p. 89, l. 28 and note.

12–13. *transferred to the Albion Newspaper*: actually the other way round. *The Albion* came to an end in Aug. 1801, and after a little while with the *Morning Chronicle* Lamb wrote for the *Morning Post* from Sept. 1803 to Feb. 1804.

14. *Rackstrow* (d. 1772). His museum was at 197 Fleet Street, the third door from Chancery Lane; it contained natural curiosities and anatomical figures.

23. *the 'Bigod' of Elia*: see 'The Two Races of Men', *Elia*, pp. 30–2 (and note), and 'The Praise of Chimney-Sweepers', p. 142.

24. *John Fenwick* (d. 1820): the typical borrower in the essay on 'The Two Races of Men'. He wrote a political pamphlet in 1798 on the Rev. James O'Coigley, executed in that year.

30. *Lovell*: there was a Daniel Lovell (d. 1818), who owned and edited *The Statesman*, an anti-ministerial journal (1806–18), and who was in 1811 sentenced to twelve months' imprisonment for a criticism on the conduct of the military; in 1812 he was sentenced to eighteen months' imprisonment and a fine of £500 for a libel

on the transport commissioners; unable to pay his fine or to find securities, he remained in prison until 1815. In 1817 he was again heavily fined for a political criticism. He does not seem actually to have stood in the pillory, nor to have owned the 'Albion', nor to have sold it to Fenwick. He did, however, sell the 'Statesman' to Sampson Perry (1747–1823). Lamb is perhaps attacking the policy of the Prince Regent and his Government towards newspaper criticism with a fictitious example.

38. *Seven-shilling pieces*: in the British Museum collection of coins are two George III third-guinea, or seven-shilling, gold pieces, dated 1797 and 1804, about the size of a sixpence.

39. *the Stamp Office*: A stamp duty on newspapers of one halfpenny on every half-sheet was imposed by Bolingbroke (and opposed by Swift) in 1712, ostensibly for revenue but really for the repression of opinion; enforced by Walpole; increased to a penny in 1757; to three halfpence in 1776; to twopence (by Pitt) in 1789; to threepence in 1797, to threepence-halfpenny in 1804, and to fourpence in 1815. In 1837 it was reduced to one penny, and abolished in 1854. If one may judge from the chart at the end of Crane and Kaye's *Eng. Periodicals* (1927) the stamp duty had little or no effect on the production and sale of newspapers; there were many complaints, however. The stamp was not adhesive but was impressed on the newspaper.

PAGE 94. 3. *now*: the historic present; i.e. then.

6. *some who are accounted very good men now*: i.e. Wordsworth, Coleridge, and Southey.

12. *flowers*: 'flowers of speech'.

13. *Mr. Bayes*: the pompous and incapable playwright, meant for Dryden, in George Villiers, Duke of Buckingham's (1628–87), *Rehearsal* (1671). The reference is to Act I, Sc. i (middle).

15. *the lurking snake*: in allusion to Virgil's proverbial phrase; 'latet anguis in herba' (*Eclogue* iii. 93).

20. *a gentleman at the Treasury*: unidentified.

24. *Sir J[ame]s M[ackintos]h*: (1765–1832), barrister, historian, and philosopher, appointed recorder of Bombay in 1804. His *Vindiciæ Gallicæ* (1791) had been written in defence of the French Revolution against Burke, but like those others 'who are accounted very good men now' his views had changed. Lamb's epigram (in the *Albion*, Aug. 1801) was as follows:

'Though thou'rt like Judas, an apostate black,
In the resemblance one thing thou dost lack:
When he had gotten his ill-purchased pelf,
He went away, and wisely hanged himself:
This thou may'st do at last; yet much I doubt,
If thou hast any *bowels* to gush out !'

28. *Citizen Stanhope*: Charles, third Earl of Stanhope (1753–1811), nicknamed 'Citizen' Stanhope from his sympathy with the French Revolution.

BARRENNESS OF THE IMAGINATIVE FACULTY IN THE PRODUCTIONS OF MODERN ART (PAGE 95)

1. *Hogarth*, William (1697–1764): painter and engraver. Lamb wrote an essay on him (i. 99–112).
any one painter: it seems curious that Lamb should thus exclude his friend B. R. Haydon (1786–1846) and Sir David Wilkie (1785–1841). Actually he had, three years previously, complimented Haydon on the 'true broad Hogarthian fun' of his 'Chairing the Member'; and only the previous year he had written an article (i. 423) to accompany a reproduction of Wilkie's 'Saturday Night'.
2. *humour of exhibiting*: cf. note on preceding Essay, lines 2 and 3.
18. *Titian* (1477?–1576): shares with Tintoretto the leadership of the Italian School of Painting.
19. '*Ariadne*': the 'Bacchus and Ariadne' in the Venetian School at the National Gallery. In a subsequent letter to Wordsworth, Lamb confesses '*Inter nos*, the Ariadne is not a darling with me, several incongruous things are in it, but in the composition it served me as illustrative'.
23. *born in fire*: Bacchus was the son of Zeus and Semele. At her prayer Zeus appeared to her in visible form, and she was consumed by the fire of his presence.
the Cretan: Ariadne, daughter of Minos, King of Crete.
PAGE 96. 1. *Guido*: (1575–1642), a prime master of the Bolognese School of Painting. His 'Ariadne' was one of his latest works and used to be in the Gallery of the Capitol at Rome.
8. *Theseus*: one of the seven Athenian youths sent as tribute to Minos to be devoured by the Minotaur. He slew the monster and was saved from the labyrinth by Ariadne. He basely deserted her at Naxos, where she was afterwards married to Bacchus.
25. *a fine rough print*: from the series in the *Loggie* of the Vatican; reproduced in Mr. E. V. Lucas's 1903 edition, ii. 449.
26. *Raphael* (1483–1520), one of the greatest painters of the Italian Renaissance.
the Vatican: the Papal palace in Rome, with a well-furnished art-gallery.
31. *tolerably modern*: a colloquialism not easy to define or defend.
PAGE 97. 2 *Somerset House*: see note on p. 87, l. 2.
16. *neoteric*: modern. If 'this justly admired neoteric' was J. M. W. Turner, then Lamb has in both his epithets anticipated Ruskin,

the chief of whose 'Modern Painters'— whose superiority over the 'ancients' he asserted—was Turner. Turner's 'Garden of the Hesperides' was exhibited at the British Institution in 1806 and is now in the Tate Gallery, No. 477.

18. *Hesperides*: see note on p. 49, l. 1.

20. *Polypheme*: a Cyclops, 'a monster of strength, and of a tall stature, with one eye in the middle of the forehead'. He seized Ulysses and his companions, confined them in a cave and daily devoured two of them. Ulysses escaped, and one of Turner's best-known pictures in the National Gallery, is of 'Ulysses deriding Polyphemus'.

Poussin, Nicholas (1594–1665): a great French painter; his 'Polypheme' is in the Hermitage, Petrograd.

22. '*still-climbing Hercules*': cf. *Love's Labour's Lost*, IV. iii. 340–1.

25. *custos*: (Lat.) 'guard, custodian'.

'*lidless eyes*': 'Lidless dragon-eyes', Coleridge: *Ode on the Departing Year*, l. 145.

27. *Hercules aut Diabolus*: (Lat.) Hercules or the Devil.

37. *Watteauish*: after Antoine Watteau (1684–1721), a French painter of fashionable conventional pastoral pictures.

39. *Daughters three* . . . Milton, *Comus*, ll. 982–3.

PAGE 98. 4. *a modern artist*: John Martin (1787–1854).

7. *the material sublime*: 'this expression . . . like a hundred others which have slipped into general use, came originally from Mr. Coleridge, and was by him in the first instance applied to Schiller's *Robbers*'—Note by H. N. Coleridge in the *Table Talk* of S.T.C., 1835.

9. *Assyrian ruins old*: the inversion suggests that this is a quotation, but it has not been identified.

14. *Belshazzar's Feast*: exhibited at the British Institution in 1821.

16. *at the first dinner*: this incident is apocryphal and was developed into this particularity from the mere generalization in Lamb's letter of 11 June 1827 to Bernard Barton, criticizing this same picture. 'Then the *letters* are nothing more than a transparency lighted up, such as a lord might order to be lit up on a sudden at a Xmas gambol to scare the ladies.'

17. *the late King*: George IV (1762–1830), Prince Regent 1811–20.

18. *Pavilion*: at Brighton, begun by the Prince Regent in 1784. 'a costly absurdity, decorated in the oriental, especially the Chinese style' (*D.N.B.*).

23. *the Tower* of London, where the Crown jewels are kept.

24. *the Rev.* ****: unidentified.

33. *Mrs. Fitz-what's-her-name*: Mrs. Fitzherbert (d. 1837), the morganatic wife of George IV, still living at the date of this essay.

34. *the Countess of* ****: perhaps a disguise for the Marchioness Conyngham, who had great influence over George IV, and who survived till 1861.

37. *a pantomime hoax*: characteristic, if Lamb is himself hoaxing us in this anecdote of George IV.

PAGE 99. **1.** *Farley*, Charles (?1771–1859), manager of the Covent Garden pantomimes.

15. *Belus*: the mythological founder of Babylon.

19, 20. *such as we have witnessed*, &c.: there is no record in the letters of Lamb having witnessed a fire in a theatre.

27. *Eliphaz . . . the Temanite*: Job iv. 13–15.

32. *the words of Daniel*: Daniel v.

PAGE 100. **7.** *The queen herself*: in verses 10–12.

13. *as Joseph did . . .*: Genesis xli. 25–32.

32–3. this combats the theory of 'Pre-Raphaelitism' and leads on to 'Impressionism'.

34. *Veronese*, Paul, properly Paolo Cagliari (1528–88), one of the great Venetian painters. His 'Marriage of Cana' is in the Louvre (see note on p. 20, l. 1) in Paris.

35. *Titian*: see note on p. 95, l. 12.

39. *'day of lesser horrors, yet divine'*: this quotation has not been identified.

40. *impious feast*: from the heading in the English Bible to Daniel v.

PAGE 101. **7.** *Michael Angelo* Buonarroti (1474–1564). The reference is to his fresco of the Last Judgement, in the Sistine Chapel of the Vatican.

15. *the swallowing up of Pompeii*: by the eruption of Vesuvius in A.D. 79.

24. Systematic excavations of Pompeii were begun in 1763, and the work received additional stimulus during the period of French government (1806–14).

28. *Sun, stand thou . . . Ajalon*: cf. Joshua x. 12.

31. *the greater and lesser light*: Genesis i. 16.

36. *synchronic*: synchronous. The present is the earliest instance of the word in the *O.E.D.*, which, however, gives three seventeenth-century instances of 'synchronical'.

37. *the picture of this subject*: by John Martin. It was exhibited at the British Institution in 1816.

PAGE 102. **3.** *'dart through rank and file traverse'*: cf. Milton, *P.L.*, I. 567–9.

8. *the world has nothing to show*, &c.: here again (as on p. 95, ll. 1–3) Lamb seems rather strangely to ignore Haydon's *Lazarus* (exhibited eight years before the date of this essay), which was painted in emulation of Sebastian del Piombo.

10. *Lazarus*: St. John xi. 44.

10. *the great picture*: by Sebastian del Piombo (1485–1577) among the Venetian School in the National Gallery.

Angerstein's: John Julius Angerstein (1735–1823), merchant and philanthropist, acquired a collection of pictures which, at his death, formed the nucleus of the National Gallery.

31. *presential*: present. Lamb may have found this word in Jeremy Taylor's *Liberty of Prophesying*, xiv. 204 (1646).

39. *Julio Romano*: Giulio Pippi (1492–1546), one of Raphael's pupils. In the *Winter's Tale*, v. ii. 109, Shakespeare erroneously made him a sculptor.

PAGE 103. 3. *her connatural tree*: the tree whose nature she shared; the epithet is in Coleridge's 'Religious Musings', l. 173.

4. *till both seemed either*: see note on p. 89, l. 23.

9. *Ovidian transformations*: the Metamorphoses of Ovid (see note on p. 5, ll. 32–6).

14. *Raphael*, see note on p. 95, l. 26.

16. '*Building of the Ark*': reproduced in E. V. Lucas's edition, ii. 456.

20. *the cartoons*: these may be seen in the Victoria and Albert Museum at South Kensington.

22. *Coleridge's friend*: 'When I was at Rome, among many other visits to the tomb of Julius II, I went thither once with a Prussian artist, a man of genius and great vivacity of feeling. As we were gazing on Michael Angelo's Moses, our conversation turned on the horns and beard of that stupendous statue. . . . We called to mind the horns of the rising sun, and I repeated the noble passage from Taylor's Holy Dying . . . when, lo ! two French officers of distinction and rank entered the church ! "Mark you," whispered the Prussian, " the first thing which those scoundrels will notice . . . will be the horns and the beard. And the associations which they will immediately connect with them will be those of a *he-goat* and a *cuckold*." Never did man guess more luckily . . . for even as he had said, so it came to pass'. *Biographia Literaria* (1817), ch. xxi.

24. *the Moses of Michael Angelo*: a statue which forms part of the unfinished tomb of Pope Julius II in the church of St. Peter-in-Chains in Rome.

25. *Cornuto*: a horned man; with the secondary meaning, a cuckold.

28. *Woolwich*: on the south side of the Thames, 9½ miles from London Bridge.

29. *the depôt at Chatham*: the Naval Dockyard.

30. *the mote and the beam*: cf. Matthew vii. 3, &c.

31. *Civita Vecchia*: the seaport at the mouth of the Tiber.

38. *solitary but sufficient Three*: Shem, Ham, and Japhet, sufficient to repopulate the earth.

40. *Demiurgus*: in Gnostic philosophy, the creator of the world and of man, subordinate to the supreme God.

PAGE **104.** 3. *Mongibello*: the Sicilian name for Etna: used in Dante's *Inferno*, xiv. 53 and Spenser, *F.Q.*, II. ix. 29.

Brontes, Steropes and Pyracmon: the two former were Cyclopes. Pyracmon worked at Vulcan's forge under Etna.

plump Jack: see *1 Henry IV*, II. iv. 534.

20. *Sancho*: Sancho Panza, Don Quixote's squire, who accompanied him on his expeditions.

32. '*strange bedfellows*, &c.': *Tempest*, II. ii. 42.

33. *Cervantes*: (1547–1616).

34. *in thy Second Part*: Don Quixote, Part II, chap. 58.

39. *Actæon*: see note on p. 5, l. 32.

PAGE **105.** 14. '*fine frenzies*': *Midsummer Night's Dream*, v. i. 12.

17. *monstered*: cf. *Coriolanus*, II. ii. 82.

24, 25. *Goneril ... Regan*: neither of them, in *King Lear*, 'make fun' of their father; there is nothing frivolous in their hatred.

27. *in Duchesses' halls*: Don Quixote, Part II, chapter XXX.

28. *that unworthy nobleman.* In a letter to Southey 10 Aug. 1825—six years before this essay—Lamb calls her husband and herself 'that unworthy duke and most contemptible duchess'.

Footnote] *waiting-women with beards*: Part II, chapters XXXVI to XLI.

PAGE **106.** 5. *in the present day*: it is not so now, and perhaps the change dates from this passage of Lamb's.

  6. *Anticipating, what did actually happen*: the first part of *Don Quixote* appeared in 1605, the second part not till 1615. Cervantes 'might have delayed still longer had not an apocryphal sequel been issued ... in 1614 by Alonso Fernandez de Avellaneda'. (J. Fitzmaurice-Kelly).

  8. *the Author of '*Guzman de Alfarache*'* (1599): Mateo Aleman (1547–1609 ?). In 1623 was published 'that excellent old translation' of 'that good old book "The Spanish Rogue"' by James Mabbe, of which Lamb speaks, and from which he quotes at length, in his *Specimens of English Dramatic Authors* (1808) (i. 67, 819).

  10. *judging, that it would be easier*, &c.: in his letter to Southey (10 Aug. 1825) he says that in this Second Part 'Cervantes sacrificed his instinct to his understanding'.

  18. *two for a pair*: a score in cribbage.

  19. *a downright Knave*: as though Sam Weller should despise and practise against Mr. Pickwick.

  21. *at one time*: Part II, chapter LX.

REJOICINGS UPON THE NEW YEAR'S COMING OF AGE
(PAGE 106)

Title] Note that Lamb has elsewhere done much to individualize the days of the year: see 'New Year's Eve', 'All Fools' Day', 'Valentine's Day' (*Elia*, pp. 34, 53, 70 respectively) and 'Remarkable Correspondent' [The Twenty-Ninth of February], 'Dog Days', 'Twelfth of August' (i. 376, 378, 383, respectively): these last, appropriately, in Hone's *Every-Day Book*: also a 'Fable for Twelfth Day' (i. 44). The first traces of this train of fancy are in a letter to Southey, 28 July 1798, when Southey was engaged upon a 'Calendar'.

PAGE 107. 7. *Domine*: schoolmaster ('dominie').

20. *Moveables*: moveable feasts and fasts whose dates depend upon Easter.

24. *Lady Day*: 25 March, the feast of the Annunciation of Our Lady; but Lamb used Lady Day as if it were a title.

25. *Twelfth Day*: old Christmas Day, twelve days after 25 Dec., and now the feast of the Epiphany.

27. *a frost-cake*: Lamb's 'Fable for Twelfth Day' (i. 44) narrates the (apocryphal) genesis of Twelfth Day's 'frost-cake'.

27. *Epiphanous*: from Epiphany (the Manifestation of Christ to the Gentiles), with the punning meaning, manifest, notable.

37. *Erra Pater*: who published '*The Pronostycacion For ever of Erra Pater*: A Jew borne in Jewery, a Doctour in Astronomye and Physycke. Profytable to kepe the bodye in helth. And also Ptholomeus sayth the same. This Pronostycacion serveth for all the worlde over' [1535?]. He seems to have enjoyed the same sort of reputation as 'Old Moore'.

41. *Twenty First of June . . . Twenty Second of December*: the longest and shortest days of the year.

PAGE 108. 9. *dried ling*: a fish course. Ash Wednesday's menu had not gone beyond this.

12. *the great custard*: a traditional feature of the Lord Mayor's banquet on November 9.

17. *Second of September*: partridge shooting begins on the first of September. Pheasant shooting begins on the first of October. Perhaps Lamb was confusing them.
cock broth: the sport of cock-fighting was particularly connected with Shrove Tuesday.

23. *Thirtieth of January*: execution of Charles I (1648-9). Up till 1859 the Book of Common Prayer contained 'a form of Prayer with fasting to be used yearly on the Thirtieth of January, Being the Day of the Martyrdom of the Blessed King Charles the First'.

26. *a calf's head*: the Roundheads were said to celebrate the 30 Jan.

by dining off a calf's head. For the Calf's Head Club see Leigh Hunt's *The Town* (1848), chap. ix.

31. *Herodias' daughter*: St. Matthew xiv. 6–11.

34. *Restorative . . . Oak Apple*: with reference to Oak-apple Day (29 May) and the Restoration of Charles II.

38. *Twelfth of August*: the actual birthday of King George IV, but St. George's Day was the official celebration. In Aug. 1825, two and a half years later than this essay, Lamb sent to Hone, the editor of *The Every-Day Book*, a letter headed 'The Humble Petition of an Unfortunate Day', signed 'Twelfth Day of August': 'I am the *Day*, Sir, upon which it pleased the course of nature that your gracious Sovereign should be born. As such, before his Accession, I was always observed and honoured. But since that happy event, in which naturally none had a greater interest than myself, a flaw has been discovered in my title. My lustre has been eclipsed, and—to use the words of one of your own poets,—

I fade into the light of common *day*.

It seems, that about that time, an Impostor crept into Court, who has the effrontery to usurp my honours, and to style herself the *King's-birth-Day*, upon some shallow pretence that, being *St. George's-Day*, she must needs be *King George's Day* also. *All-Saints-Day* we have heard of, and *All-Souls-Day* we are willing to admit; but does it follow that this foolish *Twenty-third of April* must be all *All-George's Day*, and enjoy a monopoly of the whole name from George of Cappadocia to George of Leyden, and from George-a-Green down to George Dyer?' (i. 383).

12. *rounded*: whispered. Cf. *King John*, ii. i. 566.

14. *bi-geny*: as bigamy is the crime of double marriage, so Lamb pretends that there must be a crime of being born twice, if the King is to have two birthdays.

15. *Candlemas*: 2 February, when, in Roman Catholic churches, candles are blessed.

17. *burning daylight*: cf. *R. & J.*, i. iv. 43.

19. *Washing*: Candlemas is the Feast of the Purification of the Blessed Virgin.

39. *boutefeu*: a firebrand, either literally or figuratively.

PAGE 110. 4. *Twenty Ninth of February*: Leap Year's Day, which comes every fourth year.

5. *mumchance*: silent.

12. *Greek Calends*: The Roman Calends fell on the first day of the month. The Greeks, however, had no Calends, hence the expression means *never*.

Latter Lammas: Lammas ('Loaf Mass'), August 1. There is no 'Latter Lammas', as there are no Greek Calends.

17. *Miserere*: Psalm li.
18. *mumping*: begging.
19. *Old Mortification*: Ash Wednesday.
25. *Which is the properest day to drink?*: from *Favourite Catches and Glees sung at Ranelagh*, 1766.
36. *Dog Days*: The period of summer commencing with the rising of Sirius, the Dog Star, during which the greatest heat prevails; at this time dogs are popularly supposed to be specially liable to madness. On 14 July 1825, Lamb sent to Hone's *Every-Day Book* a letter signed 'Pompey' protesting (in the person of a dog) against this superstition (i. 378–9).

PAGE 111. 2. *Ember Days*: the three fast days in each quarter (A. S. *ymbryne*, a circuit). Lamb pretends that 'ember' here means a live coal.

4. *Septuagesima*: the seventieth day before Easter.
boasts herself the mother of the days: since all the movable feasts follow at definite intervals from Septuagesima, whereas Septuagesima does not follow at a definite interval after Epiphany: the number of the Sundays after Epiphany varying.

7. *Rogation Day(s)*: the three days before Ascension Day. Lamb intends a pun on 'interrogation'.
15. *Lord Mayor's Day*: 9 November.
18. *Two* Vigils: perhaps Christmas Eve and the Vigil of St. Thomas (20 Dec.).
20. *patrole*: patrol.
21. *Eve of St. Christopher*: 24 July. St. Christopher carried travellers on his shoulders across a river. Once it was a child who grew heavier and heavier all the time, and when at last St. Christopher put him down on the further side it proved to be Christ himself: whence Christopher got his name (Christo-phóros, Christ-bearer).
25. *'On the bat's back do I fly'*: *The Tempest*, v. i. 91. Lamb himself was twice carried home in this way from a dinner party, and after each occasion quoted this song of Ariel's. (See letters to Crabb Robinson, May 1809, and an undated letter to J. V. Asbury, No. 512 in Mr. E. V. Lucas's edition.)
27. *Penitentiaries*: the Penitential Psalms.

THE WEDDING (PAGE 111)

First nine lines] Canon Ainger noted that 'in matter, language, and cadence, this might have been taken bodily from the *Spectator*'.
2. *last week*: the wedding was in April 1821, Lamb's 'last week' was four years ago!

PAGE 112. 1. *a friend's daughter*: 'the "wedding" you of course found out to be Sally [Sarah Harriet] Burney's',—Lamb to Miss Rickman (23 May 1833).

2. *us old people*: Lamb was 46 at the time of the wedding.

4–5. *our own youthful disappointment*: Lamb is probably thinking of his own youthful passion for Ann Simmons (see note on p. 8, l. 19).

25, 26. *abated . . . ardours*: cf. *Tempest*, IV. i. 56.

28. *his wife*, who was at least partly the model for 'Mrs. Battle' (*Elia*, pp. 41–8). See note on p. 5, l. 38.

30. *the growing infirmities of the old gentleman*: he died seven months after the wedding, 17 Nov. 1821.

35. *Admiral ——*: Rear-Admiral James Burney (1750–1821), brother of Fanny Burney: 'a merry *natural* captain who pleases himself vastly with once having made a pun at Otaheite in the O. language' (he had sailed with Captain Cook) ''Tis the same man who said Shakespeare he liked, because he was *so much of the Gentleman*'.—Lamb to Thomas Manning, 19 Feb. 1803.

37. *John Thomas Payne*, a bookseller.

PAGE 113. 12. *experimentally*: by experience.

16. *unparallel subjects*: 'subjects' perhaps in the sense of subjects to a monarch; 'unparallel' in that their relations to her are dissimilar.

35. *preposterously*: see note on p. 9, l. 3.

PAGE 114. 4. *déjeuné*: current in Lamb's time for 'déjeûner', the 'wedding breakfast'.

13. *candid*: from Latin *candidus*, 'shining white'; with the metaphorical meaning, 'frank, ingenuous'.

15. *Diana's nymphs—Foresters indeed*: cf. *1 Henry IV*, I. ii. 29.

23. *Iphigenia*: daughter of Agamemnon king of Mycenae and Argos. She was to be sacrificed in order that the ships might sail for Troy, but Artemis substituted a hind at the last moment.

25–6. Cf. 'I was at Hazlitt's marriage, and had like to have been turned out several times during the ceremony. Any thing awful makes me laugh. I misbehaved once at a funeral'. Lamb to Southey, 9 Aug. 1815.

36. *St. Mildred's in the Poultry*: 'The Poultry' (once a poultry-market) is the eastern end of Cheapside. St. Mildred's was one of Wren's churches, but it no longer exists.

PAGE 115. 5. *black has been my ordinary apparel so long*: see note below on p. 123, l. 36.

14. *Pilpay*: The fables of Bidpai (or Pilpay) (from Sanskrit *Vidyapati*, chief scholar), the name given in the Middle Ages to a famous collection of Hindu stories.

16. *the raven*: see note on p. 124, l. 16.

26. *wig and buckle*: cf. Pope, *Epistle to Bathurst*, ll. 296–7: 'That livelong wig . . . Eternal buckle'.

33–5: cf. 'Grace before Meat', *Elia*, pp. 117–19.

34. *botargoes*: sausages made of the roe of mullet or tunny.

PAGE 116. 1. *As when a*, &c.: cf. *Richard II*, v. ii. 23–5.

29 *et seq.*: cf. the description of Lamb's own 'Thursday evenings' in Hazlitt's Essay 'On the conversation of Authors' which preceded Lamb's own essay by five years in the *London Magazine*. *whist—the Admiral's favourite game*: he published 'An Essay, by way of lecture, on the game of whist', 1821.

PAGE 117. 2. *concordia discors*: a harmony that arises from seemingly discordant elements, used by Horace (*Epist.* I. xii. 19) and by Ovid (*Metam.* i. 433) of the system of nature.

5. *Miss Emily*: actually Miss Sarah; see note on p. 112, l. 1.
The instrument: Jane Austen nearly always refers to the piano by the same term. Keats usually speaks of it as 'the music'. *Pianoforte*, afterwards shortened to *Piano*, was slow to naturalize itself.

8. *Marvell*, Andrew. See note on p. 6, l. 26.
'*to make his destiny*, &c.' '*Upon Appleton House*', l. 744 (the poem already quoted on p. 6).

THE CHILD ANGEL (PAGE 117)

3. *the 'Loves of the Angels'*: by Thomas Moore (1779–1852), published just before Lamb's essay. The idea is taken (as was that of Byron's contemporary *Heaven and Earth*, in *The Liberal*, No. II, 1822), from Genesis vi. 4.

16. *gossiping*: christening-feast. Gossips are god-parents (god-sibs: 'sib' = kin).

PAGE 118. 6. *winged orders*: the nine orders, viz. angels, archangels, virtues, powers, principalities, dominations, thrones, cherubim, seraphim.

12. *an inextinguishable titter*: the 'inextinguishable laughter' of Homer's gods (*Iliad*, i. 599) at the lame Hephaestus (Vulcan) ministering nectar, brought down to the level of this occasion.

16. *which mortals* caudle *call below*: perhaps a reminiscence of Pope's *Rape of the Lock*, i. 78: 'Though Honour is the word with men below'.
caudle: warm spiced gruel, given to the sick and especially to women in childbed.

23. *the spheres*: 'This is Plato's system. Fate, or Necessity, holds a spindle of adamant: and, with her three daughters, Lachesis, Clotho, and Atropos, who handle the vital web wound about the spindle, she conducts or turns the heavenly bodies. Nine Muses,

or Syrens, sit on the summit of the spheres; which, in their revolutions, produce the most ravishing musical harmony. To this harmony the three daughters of Necessity perpetually sing in correspondent tones. In the mean time, the adamantine spindle, which is placed in the lap or on the knees of Necessity, and on which *the fate of men and gods is wound*, is also revolved. This music of the spheres, proceeding from the rapid motion of the heavens, is so loud, various, and sweet, as to exceed all aptitude or proportion of the human ear, and therefore is not heard by men. Moreover, this spherical music consists of eight unisonous melodies: the ninth is a concentration of all the rest, or a diapason of all those eight melodies; which diapason, or concentus, the nine Sirens sing or address to the supreme being'. THOMAS WARTON, *Poems . . . by John Milton, with Notes critical and explanatory.* 1785.

38. *Ge-Urania*: (Gr.) Earth-Heaven.

39, 40. cf. Wordsworth's *Ode on the Intimations of Immortality*, section v.

40. *taste of death*: cf. Matthew xvi. 28.

PAGE 119. 2. *reliance*: dependence on others, the opposite of self-reliance.

6. *the immortal lame one*: Lamb seems to be continuing (from p. 118, l. 12) the image of the lame Hephaestus, but the 'inextinguishable laughter of the blessed gods' has now become pity.

7. *Intuitive Essences*: the angels, whose nature is to know immediately, by intuition, not by reasoning; cf. *P.L.*, v. 485–90.

17. *Amphibium*: a creature capable of two modes of life, in this instance the earthly and the heavenly.

19–20. cf. Mark x. 15.

24, 25. *this green earth*: Wordsworth, *Tintern Abbey*, l. 105.

32. *the river Pison*: Genesis ii. 10, 11.

33. *Adah*: so in 1833 but Mirzah in 1823. 'Adah' is the name of one of Adam's daughters in Byron's *Cain: a Mystery* (1821).
the angel Nadir: the nadir is the point in the heavens diametrically opposite the zenith, and Lamb may have intended the name to signify the utmost degree of earthly as distinguished from heavenly passion.

36. *a correspondency*: cf. St. Matthew xviii. 10.

A DEATH-BED (PAGE 120)

In a letter, &c: an actual letter, dated 20 Jan. 1827, to Henry Crabb Robinson. Printed with some disguises, to help the dead man's family. It was included in the first edition of *The Last Essays of Elia* (1833), but, at the instance of Randall Norris's

family was omitted in the second edition, where it was replaced
by the 'Confessions of a Drunkard' (i. 168).

R.H.: Henry Crabb Robinson (1775–1867), whose Diary is a
record of his many friendships.

B——: Bury St. Edmunds. Crabb Robinson actually came
from Bury, but B—— is Lamb's disguise for the Inner Temple.
H. C. R. was a member of the Middle Temple.

3. *N. R.*: =R.N.; Randal Norris (1751–1827), for whom see
'Christ's Hospital' (*Elia*, p. 16, ll. 15, 16) and note on 'Captain
Jackson', p. 49, l. 3. He was Librarian and sub-Treasurer of
the Inner Temple, and had lived there nearly all his life.

14, 15. In his 'Letter to Southey', 1823 (i. 289) Lamb speaks of
'N., mine and my father's friend for nearly half a century', and
in a letter to Wordsworth 22 Jan. 1830, he speaks of 'old Norris
of the Temple, 60 years ours and our father's friend'.

PAGE 121. 2. *Old as I am getting*: Lamb was 52 in 1827.

8. *Lettered he was not . . . the dead, if you can*. The letter of 1827
differs, as follows:

'Letters he knew nothing of, nor did his reading extend beyond
the pages of the *Gentleman's Magazine*. Yet there was a pride of
literature about him from being amongst books (he was librarian)
and from some scraps of doubtful Latin which he had picked up
in his office of entering students, that gave him very diverting airs
of pedantry. Can I forget the erudite look with which, when he
had been in vain trying to make out a black-letter text of
Chaucer in the Temple Library, he laid it down and told me that
—'in those old books, Charley, there is sometimes a deal of very
indifferent spelling'; and seemed to console himself in the reflection ! His jokes, for he had his jokes, are now ended; but they
were old trusty perennials, staples that pleased after *decies repe-
tita*,[1] and were always as good as new. One song he had, which was
reserved for the night of Christmas Day, which we always spent
in the Temple. It was an old thing, and spoke of the flat bottoms
of our foes, and the possibility of their coming over in darkness,
and alluded to threats of an invasion many years blown over;
and when he came to the part—

> We'll still make 'em run, and we'll still make 'em sweat,
>   In spite of the Devil and Brussels Gazette,

his eyes would sparkle as with the freshness of an impending
event. And what is the *Brussels Gazette* now ? I cry while I enu-
merate these trifles. "How shall we tell them in a stranger's
ear ?"[2] His poor good girls will now have to receive their afflicted

---

[1] 'ten times repeated', Horace, *Ars Poetica*, l. 365.

[2] From one of his own poems (ii. 545).

mother in an unsuccessful hovel in an obscure village in Herts, where they have been long struggling to make a school without effect; and poor deaf Richard, and the more helpless for being so, is thrown on the wide world.

'My first motive in writing, and indeed in calling on you, was to ask if you were enough acquainted with any of the Benchers to lay a plain statement before them of the circumstances of the family. I almost fear not, for you are of another hall [1]. But if you can oblige me and my poor friend, who is now insensible to any favours, pray exert yourself. You cannot say too much good of poor Norris and his poor wife. Yours ever, CHARLES LAMB.'

9. *the old Gentleman's Magazine*: (the first periodical to be called a magazine) founded in 1731 by Edward Cave (1691–1754). Johnson began to contribute to it in 1738, a few years later wrote the Parliamentary Debates from notes supplied by others or entirely out of his own head, and for some time acted in a semi-editorial capacity. The Magazine survived until 1907.

12. *archive-keeper to your ancient city*: actually sub-treasurer and librarian of the Inner Temple.

17. *Black-lettered Chaucer*: folio, 1602. The actual copy is still in the Library of the Inner Temple.

24. *one Song*: 'Hearts of Oak', by David Garrick (1717–79) in *Harlequin's Invasion* (1759). This, Lamb tells us, in his 'My First Play' (*Elia*, p. 125) was his second play.

25. *a threatened Invasion* in 1759, during the Seven Years' War (1756–63). It was planned by Louis XV's Ministers, but abandoned when the French Fleet was defeated by Admiral Hawke in Quiberon Bay.

35. *a petty village in* ——*shire,*—Widford (in which parish was 'Blakesmoor': see pp. 4–9) in Hertfordshire.

OLD CHINA (PAGE 122)

7. *the first play*: See 'My First Play' (*Elia*, p. 122).
the first exhibition: unidentified.

12, 13. *uncircumscribed by any element*: i.e. they seem to have no connexion with earth, air, or water; they are neither walking, nor flying, nor swimming.

13, 14. Lamb to Manning, 31 August 1801: 'I heard that you were going to China with a commission from the Wedgwoods to collect hints for their pottery, and teach the Chinese *perspective*'.

PAGE 123. 5. *a right angle of incidence*: not a '*right* angle' (90 degrees), but a *correct* 'angle of incidence'; this is, in physics, the angle in which a moving body or ray of light strikes a surface.

9. *the hays*: an old country dance.

[1] i.e. of the Middle, not the Inner, Temple.

10. *couchant*: lying with his head resting on his forepaws: a term of heraldry.

12. *Cathay*: the name given by Marco Polo (*c.* 1254–1324) to a country in Eastern Asia, and now applied poetically to China; used here in a punning sense for porcelain.

14. *Hyson*: A Chinese green tea, generally used only for flavouring other kinds. In Jan. 1808 his friend Manning had sent to Lamb, for himself and Holcroft, from Canton, two cases of tea marked S & H for Souchong and Hyson; Lamb is either to use it or to sell it. 'I can only say that the tea is choise [*sic*], but so much the better for those that buy it, tho I have no doubt but that the rogues of shopkeepers will mix it'. In a contemporary letter to his father, Manning calls it 'supernaculum tea'. 'Supernaculum': 'a liquor to be drunk to the last drop' (*O.E.D.*).

15. *speciosa miracula*: Horace, *Ars Poetica*, 144, of the stories of the *Odyssey*: 'beautiful marvels'.

18. *how favourable circumstances had been to us of late years*: it is worth noting that this was written two years before Lamb retired from the India House.

36. *the brown suit*: up to a certain date Lamb habitually wore a brown suit, and after that habitually a black one (cf. p. 115, ll. 1–9 and note on 124, 13). Hazlitt, in his essay 'On the Conversation of Authors' (1820) makes out the change to be symbolical of a general change for the worse in his little circle: 'Lamb does not live where he did. By shifting his abode, his notions seem less fixed. He does not wear his old snuff-coloured coat and breeches. It looks like an alteration in his style. An author and a wit should have a separate costume, a particular cloth; he should present something positive and singular to the mind, like Mr. Douce of the Museum. Our faith in the religion of letters will not bear to be taken to pieces, and put together again by caprice or accident'. He seems to accuse Lamb of being a turncoat.

39. *Beaumont and Fletcher*: see note on p. 30, l. 10. The folio was that of 1679. Lamb bought it in 1799. It is now in the British Museum, and contains marginal notes by Lamb and Coleridge, and passages marked for Lamb's *Specimens of English Dramatic Poets* (1808).

40. *Barker's in Covent Garden*: at 19 Great Russell (now Russell) Street. Lamb lived next door, from Nov. 1817 to Aug. 1823.

PAGE 124. 3. *Islington*: the Lambs lived at 36 Chapel Street, Pentonville, from 1796 to 1800, and at Colebrooke Cottage, Islington, from 1823 to 1827.

7. *wishing it were twice as cumbersome*: cf. his purchase of 'The whole theologic works of—THOMAS AQUINAS ! [See note on p. 59, l. 21.] My arms aked with lugging it a mile to the stage,

but the burden was a pleasure, such as old Anchises was to the shoulders of Aeneas—' (Lamb to B. Barton, 25 Mar., 1829).

9. *collating*: a bookbinder 'collates' (collects in proper order) the printed sheets of a book, and the bibliographer in his turn has to check this part of the binder's work.

13. *neat black clothes*: 'His "bran" new *suit* of black cloth (in which he affected several times during the day to take great pride, and to cherish as a novelty that he had long looked for and wanted) was drolly contrasted with his very rusty silk stockings, shown from his knees, and his much too large *thick* shoes, without polish.' Mrs. Mathews in her *Memoirs* of her husband (Charles Mathews, 1776–1835), 1839.

16. *corbeau*: (Fr. = raven) dark green to black like the raven's plumage. See note on p. 115, l. 16.

18. *the mighty sum*: 'Beaumont and Fletcher in folio, not now to be met with: the octavos are about £3.' Lamb to Wordsworth (13 Oct. 1804) for whom he was buying the dramatists.

24. *Lionardo*, or Leonardo da Vinci (1452–1519), Italian painter, architect, sculptor, and engineer. 'Mr. Lamb is a good judge of prints and pictures. His admiration of Hogarth does credit to both, particularly when it is considered that Leonardo da Vinci is his next greatest favourite, and that his love of the *actual* does not proceed from want of taste for the *ideal*'. William Hazlitt in *The Spirit of the Age* (1825).

25. *'Lady Blanch'*: 'a print of two females . . . called Prudence and Beauty [or 'Modesty and Vanity'], which hangs up in our room' (2 June 1804) and for which Mary wrote two poems.

29. *Colnaghi's*: Paul Colnaghi (1751–1833), print dealer, was a Milanese by birth. The premises of the firm were in Pall Mall, East, then and up till 1910; they are now in Bond Street.

30. *a wilderness of Lionardos*: cf. *Merchant of Venice*, III. i. 128; *Titus Andronicus*, III. i. 34; and *P.L.*, v. 294.

31. *Enfield*: see note on p. 77, l. 21.

32. *Potter's Bar*, in Hertfordshire, thirteen miles from London on the Great North Road.
Waltham in Essex, thirteen miles from London.

PAGE 125. 1. *Izaak Walton* (1593–1683), author of the *Compleat Angler*: for his hostess, see Part I, Chapter ii.

2. *The Lea*: rises in Bedfordshire, flows through Hertfordshire, and joins the Thames near Blackwall.

6. *Piscator*: 'a fisher' (Lat.). A character in the *Compleat Angler*. *Trout Hall*: see *Compleat Angler*, Part I, ch. ii. Trout Hall, an inn, is supposed to have been near Edmonton.

15. *the Battle of Hexham and the Surrender of Calais*, comedies by George Colman the younger (1762–1836).

16. *Bannister*: see note on p. 16, l. 26.
17. *Mrs. Bland*: Maria Theresa Bland (1768–1838), a Jewess who
    acted and sang at Drury Lane from 1789 to 1824.
    the Children in the Wood: see p. 66, l. 28.
24. *Rosalind . . . Viola*: in *As You Like It* and *Twelfth Night* re-
    spectively. Lamb's essay on 'Some of the Old Actors' (*Elia*,
    p. 166) was occasioned by an old playbill (*c.* 1790) of *Twelfth
    Night*.
PAGE 126. 37. '*lusty brimmers*': from Cotton's lines *To the New Year*,
    quoted in 'New Year's Eve' (*Elia*, p. 40).

> Then let us welcome the new guest,
> With lusty brimmers of the best.

38. *Cotton*, Charles (1630–87) poet ('a first rate', Lamb describes him
    to Wordsworth 5 March 1803); he translated Montaigne's *Essays*
    and wrote a second part (on fly-fishing) to Walton's *Compleat
    Angler*.
39. '*coming guest*': Pope, *Imitations of Horace*, Sat. ii. l. 159; his
    Homer's *Odyssey*, xv. 84.
PAGE 127. 7. *poor—hundred pounds a year*: Lamb's India House
    salary at his retirement, two years after this essay, was £675.
10. *shake the superflux*: *King Lear*, III. iii. 37. See note on p. 132, l. 7.
25. *our thirty miles a day*: cf. p. 57, l. 29.
37. *fathom line*: *1 Henry IV*, I. iii. 203–4.
39. *Crœsus*: King of Lydia from B.C. 557–546, whose wealth was
    proverbial.
    the great Jew R——: Nathan Meyer Rothschild (1777–1836) the
    founder of the great banking-house.

POPULAR FALLACIES (PAGE 128)

Title] 'I poke out a monthly crudity for Colburn in his magazine,
which I call "Popular Fallacies", and periodically crush a proverb
or two, setting up my folly against the wisdom of nations'.
Charles Lamb to Bernard Barton, Feb. 7, 1826.

  'If not too late, I think the proverbs had better have L.
signed to them and reserve *Elia* for Essays *more Eliacal*'.
Charles Lamb to Charles Ollier [Dec. 1825].

  'I want you in the popular fallacies to like the "Home that is
no home" and "rising with the lark"' Lamb to Wordsworth 'end
of May nearly', 1833.

  Laman Blanchard (1804–45), particularly delighted with these,
added a series in the same magazine.

I. THAT A BULLY IS ALWAYS A COWARD.
  6. *The comic writers*: perhaps specially Ben Jonson, in *Every Man
    in his Humour* (1598).

20. *Hickman*: Tom Hickman, nicknamed 'the gas man', was a prizefighter whose fight with Bill Neate was described by Hazlitt in his essay *The Fight*.

21. *Clarissa* (*Harlowe*): by Samuel Richardson (see note on p. 33, l. 13).

25. *Harapha*: the Philistine giant in Milton's *Samson Agonistes*. ll. 1061–1243.

28. *Almanzor*: the hero of the double play, *Almanzor and Almahide, or, the Conquest of Granada* (1672) by John Dryden (1631–1700), poet and dramatist.

PAGE 129. 1. *Tom Brown*: (1663–1704) satirist, entered Christ Church, Oxford, 1678. Thence he became a schoolmaster at Kingston, and was afterwards a hack-writer and translator.

4. *dimidiate*: divided into halves.

5. *Bully Dawson*: Lamb had quoted Tom Brown on Bully Dawson in his essay 'On the Tragedies of Shakespeare', 1811 (i. 139).

II. THAT ILL GOTTEN GAIN NEVER PROSPERS.

15. *Church land, alienated to lay uses*: at the dissolution of the monasteries, in 1536, under Henry VIII.

III. THAT A MAN MUST NOT LAUGH AT HIS OWN JEST.

PAGE 130. 9. *Mandeville*, Bernard (1670?–1733), *Fable of the Bees* (1714).

IV. THAT SUCH A ONE SHOWS HIS BREEDING.—THAT IT IS EASY TO PERCEIVE HE IS NO GENTLEMAN.

14. *his sister, &c.*——: 'was no better than she should be' (or words to that effect).

V. THAT THE POOR COPY THE VICES OF THE RICH.

3. *sitting upon velvet*: the squire's pew would be upholstered in velvet, while the poor sat upon bare benches.

4. *the homilies*: Two books of Homilies were issued: the first in the reign of Edward the Sixth, and the second in the reign of Elizabeth. They were appointed in the 35th of the Thirty-nine Articles to be read in Churches by the Ministers.

PAGE 131. 2. *striking at the root of freewill*, &c.: see Nos. ix, x of the Thirty-nine Articles.

21. *reversionary cold meats*: the food left on their dishes, which the servants may eat. Lamb is (consciously or not) echoing Scott's 'cold meat and reversionary pasties' (*Old Mortality*, 1816, ch. xix) and Scott is varying Shakespeare's 'funeral baked-meats' which 'coldly furnish forth the marriage tables'. *Hamlet*, I.ii. 180.

PAGE 132. VI. THAT ENOUGH IS AS GOOD AS A FEAST.

1. *Guildhall*: where the Lord Mayor's banquets are held.

4. *cold-scrag-of-mutton*: see note on p. 50, l. 16.

7. *superflux*: superfluity, 'the fragments that remain'. See note on p. 127, l. 10.

16. *dirt to acres.* Cf. Shirley (1596–1666), *The Ball* (1632), II. l. 13: 'Had not you land once?' 'I had some dirty acres', and *Twelfth Night*, II. iv. 83–4. 'My love . . . Prizes not quantity of dirty lands'.

PAGE **133**. 3. *metonyme*: metonymy.

VII. OF TWO DISPUTANTS, THE WARMEST IS GENERALLY IN THE WRONG.

9. *Titubus*: from Lat. *titubare*, to stagger, and figuratively, to stammer. Lamb was himself a stammerer.
   Lincoln's Inn: one of the Inns of Court, to the north of the New Law Courts in the Strand.

PAGE **134**. VIII. THAT VERBAL ALLUSIONS ARE NOT WIT, BECAUSE THEY WILL NOT BEAR A TRANSLATION.

6. *a Terentian auditory*: an audience listening to a play by Terence (fl. *circa* 175 B.C.), the Roman playwright.

7. *Senator Urbanus*, Lamb's Latin for 'alderman'.
   Curruca, the hedge-sparrow that hatches the cuckoo's egg (from Juvenal, Satire vi); hence a cuckold.

15. *Hudibras*: c. 1663–4. A satire against the Puritans, written in couplets with two-syllabled rhymes, by Samuel Butler (1612–80).

16. *the old monkish doggerel*: Latin with two-syllabled rhymes.
   For instance, from Saint Bonaventura:

> In Passione Domini,
> Qua datur salus homini,
> Sit nostrum refrigerium
> Et cordis desiderium . . .
> Te crucifixum colimus
> Et toto corde poscimus
> Ut nos Sanctorum coetibus
> Coniungas in caelestibus.

Apart from any lack of sympathy on Lamb's part with Roman Catholicism, he would have called this verse doggerel because of its double rhymes and its other differences from classical Latin poetry.

17. *Dennis*, John (1657–1734) 'who outlived his annuity and starved at 90' (Lamb to Wordsworth, 29 March 1825), critic: the 'Appius' of Pope's *Essay on Criticism*.

18. '*a stick*' chiming to '*ecclesiastic*', *in Hudibras* (I. i. 11).

> 'When pulpit, drum ecclesiastic
> Was beat with fist, instead of a stick'.

IX. THAT THE WORST PUNS ARE THE BEST.

9. *Who has not . . . been at a party*: cf. a letter of Keats 18 Dec. 1812: 'I have seen Lamb lately—Brown and I were taken by

Hunt to Novello's—there we were devastated and excruciated with bad and repeated puns.—Brown don't want to go again'.

14. *making a poor word run the gauntlet*: perhaps a reminiscence of *Hamlet*, I. iii. 108–9: 'to crack the wind of the poor phrase, Running it thus'.

PAGE 135. 1. *ambages*: (Lat.) mazes, derived from *ambi-agere*, to lead around.

11. *a Robin Hood's shot*: cf. *Ivanhoe* (1819), chap. xiii.

12. *ulterior*: beyond, superior to.

20. *Swift*, Jonathan (1667–1745).

21. *Miscellanies*, in vol. xiv, 1779: *The Art of Punning* (Dublin, 1719) by Thomas Sheridan (1687–1738), assisted by Swift.

30. *pronunciation*: could Lamb distinguish between the *pronunciation* of 'hare' and 'hair'? !

PAGE 136. 10. *canvass*: canvas.

21. *curious felicity*: curiosa felicitas. (Petronius, 118. 5: of the style of Horace), properly means not curious felicity but ' the "careful luck" of him who tries many words, and has the wit to know when memory, or the necessity of metre or rhyme, has supplied him unexpectedly with those which are perhaps even better than he knew how to desire'. (C. Patmore.)

23. *this bi-verbal allusion*: one word with two meanings.

30. *superfœtation*: accumulation of layer upon layer. A medical term used with reference to the conception of a second child before the birth of a first.

Footnote] 'Ah! Mantua, too near neighbour to hapless Cremona'. *Eclogue*, x. 28.

PAGE 137. X. THAT HANDSOME IS AS HANDSOME DOES.

1. *Mrs Conrady*: unidentified; but she may have been Mrs. Gibbs, the landlady at Hastings, of whom Mary Lamb said (18 June 1823): 'We have exchanged a very pretty lady for an ugly one, but she is equally attractive to us'.

3. *Plotinus* (A.D. 204–270), neo-Platonic philosopher of Lycopolis in Egypt.

11. *Spenser*: see 'Oxford Poets' Spenser, p. 591, l. 127.
platonizing: following the doctrine of Plato.

15. *habit in*: inhabit.

30. *perform'd*: Spenser wrote 'deformed'.

33. *anima*: the vital principle 'animating' the soul.

PAGE 138. 11. *Apelles*: (see note on p. 23, l. 31). Lamb is confusing Apelles with Zeuxis (fl. 420–390 B.C.), who had five models for his painting of Helen, and 'Cicero (*De Invent.*, ii. l. 1) assumed that he found distributed among these five the various elements that went to make up a figure of ideal beauty'. (*Enc. Brit.*)

23. *like Stonehenge*: Lamb had seen Stonehenge while on a visit to
   Hazlitt at Winterslow in Oct. 1809.

XI. THAT WE MUST NOT LOOK A GIFT-HORSE IN THE MOUTH.

PAGE 139. 8. *Eclipse*: a famous racehorse foaled in the year of the
   great eclipse, 1764, and bred by the Duke of Cumberland. He
   won the 'Derby' on 3 May 1769: 'Eclipse first, the rest nowhere',
   the phrase had passed into a proverb and is quoted by Macaulay
   in his essay on Boswell's Johnson.

   Lightfoot: foaled in 1747, was bred by the Earl of Eglinbourne.
   In 1751 and the following years he won six important races.
   Many famous racehorses were his progeny.

16. *Mitis*: (Lat.) meek.

21. *preposterous*: see note on p. 9, 'Poor Relations', l. 3. The worst
   where the best should be.

23. *Vandyke*, Sir Anthony (1599–1641), Flemish painter. For the
   most part he painted portraits.

PAGE 140. 14. *flower*: the editorial insertion [flour] gives the sense but
   seems to convict Lamb or his printers of a misspelling; but the
   word and spelling 'flower' has this sense also in its own right.

36. '*plump corpusculum*': The quotation has not been identified.

41. *unitive*: religious perfection has three degrees, the purgative, the
   illuminative, and the unitive,—respectively, purgation, illumination, and union with the divine.

   old theologians: e.g. Henry More (1614–87), Jeremy Taylor (1613–
   67) and John Norris (1657–1711), all favourites of Lamb and
   Coleridge.

PAGE 141. 1. *certain restrictive regulations*: the Game Laws. Poaching
   was made a felony in 1817, and in 1819 the law was made still
   more severe.

5. *goût* (Fr.) taste.

XII. THAT HOME IS HOME THOUGH IT IS NEVER SO HOMELY.

Title] see note at head of first 'Fallacy'.

   'My tirade against visitors was not meant *particularly* at you
   or A. K. I scarce know what I meant, for I do not just now
   feel the grievance. I wanted to make an article'. Lamb to
   Bernard Barton (March 20, 1826).

3, 16–17. *speak to*: speak of. We 'speak to the point'.

11. *pittance*: allowance.

PAGE 143. 1. '*a babe is fed with milk and praise*': from 'The First
   Tooth' by Mary Lamb. *Poetry for Children* 1809 (ii. 431).

3. *return*: response.

PAGE 144. 8. *the position of our lodging*: Colebrooke Cottage, Islington. See note on p. 732, 'Amicus Redivivus', l. 4.

19. *knowledge nor devices*: *but* &c.: cf. Ecclesiastes ix. 10.

26. *wardrobe eaten and fretted*, &c.: cf. Psalm cii. 26, and Job xiii. 28. *concoct*: digest.

35–6. Lamb had made this same complaint in a letter to Mrs. Wordsworth in 1818 eight years before the date of the essay; and as far back as 1806 he had complained to Hazlitt of his '*nocturnal* alias *knock-eternal* visitors'.

Footnote] *Irving*, Edward (1792–1834), a famous preacher, and afterwards founder of the 'Catholic Apostolic Church'.

'He is a most amiable, sincere, modest man in a room, this Boanerges in the temple. Mrs. Montague told him the dedic^n. [of his book, to Coleridge] w^d. do him no good "That shall be a reason for doing it", was the answer. Judge now whether this man be a quack'. Lamb to Leigh Hunt,? Nov. 1824, and similarly to Bernard Barton 23 Mar. 1825 and to Wordsworth 6 April 1825.

PAGE 145. 2. *sapor*: savour.

15. *Dante's lovers*: Paolo and Francesca, in *Inferno*, v. They were reading together of Lancelot and Guinevere, and 'when of that smile we read . . . in its leaves that day we read no more'.

19. *orifice*: a gap, and hence 'a wound'.

20. *Taylor*, Jeremy (see note on p. 29, l. 35) in *A Discourse of Friendship* (1657).

PAGE 146. XIII. THAT YOU MUST LOVE ME, AND LOVE MY DOG.

35. ****: he and his tall cousin have not been and perhaps could not be identified.

38. '*Athenian Oracle*', a republication of selections from the *Athenian Mercury*, a bi-weekly periodical started by John Dunton (1659–1733) in 1691 as a sort of 'Notes and Queries'. Swift's verses were contributed in February, 1692.

39. *Pindaric Odes*: named after Pindar (about 549–435 B.C.), the famous Theban lyric poet.

40. *Sir William Temple*: see note on p. 719, 'The Genteel Style in Writing', l. 2.

PAGE 147. 6 *in the haunch of*: 2 *Henry IV*, IV. iv. 92.

10. *procerity*: tallness, loftiness, height; length. Used with this meaning by Hooker (1604), and J. Hall (1646). 'Procerity' was one of the *Brownisms* (after Sir Thomas Browne, see note on p. 27, l. 34) which convinced the historian Robertson (see note on p. 28, l. 11) that Johnson was the author of the *Memoirs of the King of Prussia*. Boswell adds that 'For the Anglo-*Latin* word *procerity* Johnson had, however, the authority of Addison'.

13–14. *Sempronia . . . Sulpicia*: Lamb is imitating the eighteenth century fashion of using classical names for imaginary people. Cf. Addison's *Spectator*, Johnson's *Rambler*, and Pope's *Rape of the Lock*.

18. *W. S.*: unidentified.
22. *a superflux*: see note on p. 132, 'That enough, &c.', l. 7.
    F. H.: unidentified.
23. *Honorius . . . his vapid wife*: 'I talk'd about somebody's *insipid
    wife*, without a correspondent object in my head, and a good
    lady, a friend's wife, whom I really *love* (don't startle, I mean in
    a licit way) has looked shyly on me ever since. The blunders of
    personal application are ludicrous. I send out a character every
    now and then, on purpose to exercise the ingenuity of my friends.'
    Charles Lamb to Bernard Barton (March 20, 1826). Nevertheless
    in Lamb's letters the references to William Godwin's second wife
    tell another story.
32. *canicular probations*: canine trials.
33. *Rutilia . . . Ruspina*: see note on ll. 13, 14 above.
38. *Scylla* and her dogs: 'Circe poured the juice of some poisonous
    herbs into the waters of the fountain where Scylla bathed, and
    no sooner had the nymph touched the place, than she found every
    part of her body below the waist, changed into frightful monsters
    like dogs'. Lemprière.
41. *Merry*, Robert (1755–1798), a dilettante who joined the English
    colony in Florence in 1784, where he became a member of the
    Della Cruscan Academy. He quarrelled with the English colony
    and returned to England, where he published a poem over the
    pseudonym 'Della Crusca'. This gave rise to the Della Cruscan
    School which 'exaggerated the worst features of his style—his
    affectation, incredibly foolish misuse of epithet, metaphor, and
    alliteration, his frantic efforts at sublimity, his obscurity and
    tasteless ornament' (*D.N.B.*).

PAGE **148**. 15. '*killed the flock*, &c.: *Twelfth Night*, I. i. 36.
16. *the Star and Garter, Richmond*: a noted place of resort, which still
    exists.
22. *Monsieur de B.*: a ballet-dancer, not identified.
25. *Buffa*: comic actress in light opera (*opera bouffe*).
    Signor Sc— and Signora Ch—: ballet-dancers, not identified.
26. *Madame V—*: probably Madame Vestris (see note on p. 26, l. 15).
36. *Delpini*, Carlo Antonio (d. 1828) a pantomimist and scene
    mechanician at Drury Lane.

PAGE **149**. 2. *Brunton*, Elizabeth (1769–1808), actress.

XIV. THAT WE SHOULD RISE WITH THE LARK.

Title] see note on general title of the 'Popular Fallacies'.
7. *this Christmas solstice.*—22 December. 'The essay was probably
    written in Jan. 1826'.
20. *Persic*: Persian. The Persian Zoroastrians (like their descend-
    ants the Parsees) were fire-worshippers.

20–24. cf. 'Christ's Hospital', *Elia*, pp. 17–18.

PAGE 150. 2–7. cf. 'Witches and other Night Fears', *Elia*, p. 88, last
    paragraph.

 8. *foregone*: cf. note on p. 50, l. 16.

15. *that Imperial forgetter*: Nebuchadnezzar: Daniel ii. 5.

22. *suit to solicit*: either a petition at court, or a claim in the law-court.

31. *stuff out of which dramas*, &c.: cf. *Tempest*, IV. i. 156–7.

35. *We are* SUPERANNUATED: cf. p. 15, l. 28.

PAGE 151. XV. THAT WE SHOULD LIE DOWN WITH THE LAMB.

 5. *long sixes*: candles weighing six to the pound.

5–6. *Hail, candle-light!*: cf. 'Hail, holy light!' *Paradise Lost*, iii. 1.

18. *Hesiod*: one of the earliest Greek poets. His *Works and Days*
    provided a model for Virgil's *Georgics*.

    Ossian: James Macpherson (1736–96) published *Fragments of
    Ancient Poetry collected in the Highlands* (1760), and *Fingal*
    (1762), an epic poem, said to have been translated from the
    original of Ossian, a supposed Gaelic bard. Johnson stated
    bluntly in his *Journey to the Western Islands* (1775) that the
    poems of Ossian 'never existed in any other form than that which
    we have seen. The editor, or author, never could show the
    original; nor can it be shown by any other.'

    This made Macpherson furious and he apparently threatened
    to chastise the Doctor—they were both big men. Johnson's
    famous reply may be read in Boswell, sub anno 1775.

PAGE 152. 2. *in fresco*: Lamb means 'in the dark', and seems to be
    confusing this with 'al fresco', in the open (fresh) air.

 7. *Sherris*: Sherry.

13. *burnishes*: 'grows plump,' an obsolete sense, except in dialect.

14. Cf. 'Detached thoughts on Books', p. 32, l. 30.

23. *Phœbus*: the sun-god, and inspirer of poetry.

26. '*Things that were born*, &c.': Ben Jonson, *Poetaster* (1602),
    'Apologetical Dialogue', ll. 29, 28 from end.

30. *mine author*: Ben Jonson again.

34. *Milton's Morning Hymn*: *P.L.*, v. 153–208.

35. *Taylor*, Jeremy. See note on p. 29, l. 34.

36. *description of a sun-rise*: from *Holy Dying* (1651), ch. 1, sect. 3.

38. *Prose has her cadences*: a reminiscence of Milton's 'Peace hath
    her victories' (Sonnet to Cromwell, l. 10).

40. '*blessing the doors*': Milton, *Il Penseroso*, ll. 83–4.
    wild sweep of winds at midnight: perhaps suggested by the
    opening lines of Coleridge's 'Ode on the Departing Year', a
    favourite passage with Lamb, who quotes it in his 'New Year's
    Eve', *Elia*, p. 35.

PAGE 153. XVI. THAT A SULKY TEMPER IS A MISFORTUNE.

4. *speak a little to it*: see note on p. 142, ll. 3, 16–17.

14. *Our old acquaintance N——*: unidentified. This essay may well
have been directed at Hazlitt, whose proneness to take offence
is well-known, and who was for long alienated even from Lamb.
And by N——, Lamb may have meant himself; cf. 'N. or M.'
in the Church Catechism.

16. *a Caius or a Titius*: see note on p. 147, ll. 13, 14.

28. *we sing not to the profane*: cf. Horace, *Odes*, III. i. 1–4.

34. *contumacies*: contumely, insulting language or treatment.

PAGE 154. 1. *that mysterious book*: Revelation x, v. 9, 10.

13. *S——*: unidentified.

PAGE 155. 15. *Arabia Stony*: Arabia was divided by Ptolemy the
astronomer (second century of Christian era) into Arabia Felix
('Araby the blest'), the cultivated part; Arabia Petraea ('Arabia
Stony'), and Arabia Deserta, the desert.

25. *benefit forgot*: cf. *As You Like It*, II. vii. 186.

39. *the noble patient in Argos* 'who', as the Latin goes on to say,
'imagined himself to hear wonderful tragedies'.

PAGE 156. 1. *Qui se credebat . . . theatro*: Horace, *Epistles*, II. ii. 129–30.

5. *Pol me . . . error*: *Ibid.*, 138–140 'you have killed me, my friends,
not helped me', he said, 'by thus snatching away my pleasure,
and forcibly robbing me of my delightful hallucination'.

PRINTED IN GREAT BRITAIN AT THE UNIVERSITY PRESS, OXFORD
BY JOHN JOHNSON, PRINTER TO THE UNIVERSITY